Leadership from an operant perspective

Komaki is the first to pinpoint the significance of monitoring and communicating, because her studies focus on leaders' ability to maintain high-quality worker output.

Psychology Today

Supervising others is the fundamental role of the manager, but so often prescriptions for what managers should do fail to acknowledge the needs of the worker. *Leadership from an Operant Perspective* provides a long awaited and innovative look at what really happens between managers and workers.

Drawing from studies conducted over the last ten years by colleagues in North America, Europe and Australia in settings as diverse as insurance company offices and racing sailboats, and with personnel ranging from police officers to film crews, Judi Komaki shows that effective managers engage in a subtle and nuanced set of interactions with workers. She has identified two key behaviors that distinguish effective managers from ineffective managers: performance monitoring and communication of consequences. Workers respond particularly to the monitoring, producing a ripple of give-and-take exchanges. Based on behavioral and interactional approaches and illustrated with transcripts of real-live conversations, this book puts forward a new model for the study of leadership: the Operant Model of Effective Supervision.

Anyone who has ever wanted to know why it is not enough to simply tell employees what to do or how to engage workers in carrying out instructions should read this book.

Judith L. Komaki is Professor of Industrial and Organizational Psychology at Baruch College at the City University of New York and has published widely in the field.

People and Organizations
Series editor: Sheldon Zedeck
Department of Psychology, University of California, Berkeley

The study of organizations has increased significantly in recent years. In recognition of the growing importance of behavioral science research to our understanding of organizations, *People and Organizations* is a new series devoted to advanced research in industrial and organizational psychology, and organizational behavior.

The books in the series are derived from empirical programmatic research on topics related to organizations and the ways in which people interact, respond to, and cope with the organization. Topics of special interest include: organizational culture, work and family, high technology, organizational commitment, careers, and studies of organizations in international markets. Books in the series are theoretically grounded and include specific guidelines for future research.

Already available:
Leadership and Information Processing
Linking Perceptions and Performance
Robert G. Lord and Karen J. Maher

Role Motivation Theories
John B. Miner

Volunteers
The Organizational Behaviour of Unpaid Workers
Jone L. Pearce

A Cognitive Approach to Performance Appraisal
A Program of Research
Angelo S. DeNisi

Leadership from an operant perspective

Judith L. Komaki

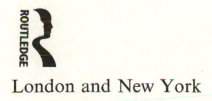

London and New York

First published 1998
by Routledge
11 New Fetter Lane, London EC4P 4EE

Simultaneously published in the USA and Canada
by Routledge
29 West 35th Street, New York, NY 10001

© 1998 Judith L. Komaki

Typeset in Times by Pure Tech India Ltd, Pondicherry
Printed and bound in Great Britain by
MPG Books Ltd, Bodmin, Cornwall

British Library Cataloguing in Publication Data
A catalogue record for this book is available from the British
Library

Library of Congress Cataloging in Publication Data
A catalogue record for this book has been requested

ISBN 0–415–09873–4

JK

To those who heard the sounds and the silences

TRIAGE

Bertolt Brecht lamented that he lived in an age when it was almost a crime to talk about trees, because that meant being silent about so much evil. Walking past a stand of tall, still healthy elms along Chicago's lakefront, I think of what Brecht said. I want to celebrate these elms which have been spared by the plague, these survivors of a once flourishing tribe commemorated by all the Elm Streets in America. But to celebrate them is to be silent about the people who sit and sleep underneath them, the homeless poor who are hauled away by the city like trash, except it has no place to dump them. To speak of one thing is to suppress another. When I talk about myself, I cannot talk about you. You know this as you listen to me, disappointment settling in your face.

Lisel Mueller (1989),
Waving from shore

Contents

Figures

Tables

Preface

As Morton Feldman speaks about composing, he moves across the room to the piano. He sits down and begins to softly play chords while he explains to a visitor, "One of the reasons I work at the piano is because it slows me down.... You can hear the *time* element much...more" (Zimmerman, 1976, p. 6). He then recalls how important it was when he and fellow composers, Christian Wolff, Earle Brown, and John Cage, got together for a week, when "we began to listen, we began to listen...for the first time" (p. 6). He learned that silence was as important as sound.

> One of the big problems in my work was that...as everything started to go into motion, I always felt that the performer in a sense didn't. They were sensitive as to how to play the sounds, but they were not listening. And they were not sensitive to the pauses I give. (p. 7)

They were not hearing, he says, the "time intervals...the time between" (p. 6). And hearing, he says, is everything. When it comes to sounds and spaces, Feldman says, he is "subservient....I do what *they* tell me, not what I tell them. Because I owe my *life* to these sounds" (pp. 12–13).

We, as researchers, also learned as we sat, not at the piano, but in darkened theaters, listening to directors talking to technical crew and lighting designers. We heard what orders they gave, when they gave them, when they asked about progress, how they tried to get the lights and sound synchronized with an actor's entrance, how they recognized others, how they reacted to blow-outs. We saw, too, when they sat silently, watching, just being there. We saw how people often approached them, making casual (and not-so-casual) comments about what they had done. We saw them, pausing in disbelief, pausing to listen.

We sat in front of video screens, seeing skippers struggle to raise sails. Eventually, amid what seemed to be sheer confusion, we began to make some sense out of all of the sounds and spaces.

But that's getting ahead of the story. To discover what effective managers should do, we developed a model: the Operant Model of Effective Supervision. As its name implies, the model owes its inspiration to the theory of operant conditioning and to the writings of its founder, B. F. Skinner.

Using the theory of operant conditioning as our guide, my colleagues, students, and I embarked upon a series of eighteen research studies that took place in North America, Europe, and Australia. Our findings represent more than a decade of work. Our most recent research explores the interaction that flows between people, like music, in a two-way motion between leaders and subordinates.

SYNOPSIS

Chapter 1 begins by reviewing the context of our operant-conditioning-based model, and our reasons for finding this to be an important path to pursue. We compare it with previous work.

In Chapter 2, we briefly outline our model and explain its four components: leaders' behaviors and sequences, the interaction process, supervisory effectiveness, and the moderators. We show how the model has grown from its modest beginnings to approach its aim of improving the workplace for both followers and leaders. We explain how certain supervisory behaviors can be predicted to distinguish effective from lackluster executives.

Chapter 3 details how we defined and measured leaders. We describe the OSTI observational instrument – the Operant Supervisory Taxonomy and Index – that we developed to study what managers actually do. We also identify time-based measures for the pacing and, eventually, the placement of behaviors.

Chapter 4 presents our program of research. We detail the initial studies, concerned with measuring leader behavior and assessing leadership success or effectiveness. We describe both the field and laboratory studies documenting the quantity, quality, and timing of effective leaders. These studies point as well to the actions of leaders lacking in effectiveness, the lackluster managers.

Chapter 5 takes these studies, documenting the impact of leaders' behaviors on subordinates, and raises a natural question: why is this so? The chapter discusses studies that shed light on these relationships. We sketch the reasons for the model's favorable predictions, many of which go beyond operant conditioning theory to point to explanations from the group process, interactional, and information processing literatures.

Chapter 6 talks about the boundaries of the model: when the model will work and when it will not. This chapter also discusses the extent to which the model's findings can be generalized across other settings, cultures, and populations.

Chapter 7 summarizes the model's findings. We draw a series of "musical" scores, showing the intricate sequences of behaviors that effective and lackluster leaders, respectively, exhibit. To illustrate, we draw upon actual transcripts, showing a strikingly symphonic interaction between the behaviors of managers and the responses of their subordinates.

Finally, Chapter 8 brings us full circle back to the crucial importance of day-to-day tasks. We suggest new directions for theory and research that may further our understanding of the motivational and supervisory process. Lastly, we make recommendations for using the model to help improve the supervisory effectiveness of leaders and thus ultimately enrich our places of work. The many, many questions raised by our research will, no doubt, occupy us well into the new millennium.

ACKNOWLEDGMENTS

Without the help and encouragement of many people, this book, and the model itself, would not have been possible. Thanks in particular to Warren Steinman, my still-idealistic dissertation advisor at the University of Illinois, who first sparked my curiosity about operant conditioning and to Milton Blood, my generous post-graduate mentor, who inspired me to enter the field of industrial/organizational (I/O) psychology.

I owe a special debt of gratitude to Mitzi Desselles, my collaborator at Purdue University, who originally planned to co-author this book with me, but then left this field to fulfill her own aspirations. The two of us spent many enriching hours exploring questions of effective leadership and followership. I miss her and wish her well.

My sincere thanks as well to a number of students: at Purdue University, Stacey Zlotnick, Marjane Jensen, and Maryalice Citera; at Baruch College, Michelle Reynard, Asli Gevgilili, Jennifer Wallace, Maria Carrera, Tom Redding, and Jennifer Scharer; and at Stuyvesant High School, Sandy Chu and Cha Lee. Thanks as well to my colleagues Sonia Goltz at Notre Dame (now at Michigan Technological University), Jim Larsen at the University of Illinois, Chicago Circle; Brian Niehoff at Kansas State University; Stina Immonen, Marita Hyttinen, and Markku Mattila in Finland; and Neil Brewer in Australia. I also wish to acknowledge the generous support of the Army Research Institute,[1] as well as the critical behind-the-scenes efforts of Dan Bollinger, Bruce Jacobs, Brendan O'Flaherty, Luis Colon, Ewa Marecka, and Shelly Zedeck. Last, but certainly not least, I thank the leaders who graciously allowed us to trail them in the course of our research. Without all of you, this book would not have come to be.

NOTE

1 This research was partially supported by the US Army Research Institute contract MDA903–91–K–0136. The views, opinions, and findings contained in this book are those of the author and should not be construed as the official position of the US Army Research Institute or as an official Department of the Army position.

1 Background

Isak Dinesen (1938) writes in *Out of Africa* of her immense responsibilities in running a farm near Nairobi, Kenya:

> Coffee-growing...does not all come out as you imagine, when, yourself young and hopeful, in the streaming rain, you carry the boxes of your shining young coffee-plants from the nurseries, and, with the whole number of farm-hands in the field, watch the plants set in the regular rows of holes in the wet ground where they are to grow...It is four or five years till the trees come into bearing, and in the meantime you will get drought on the land...diseases.... But a coffee-plantation is a thing that gets hold of you and does not let you go. (p. 7)

A coffee plantation, says Dinesen, creates a sometimes romantic world of its own: shimmering fields of fledgling plants, bittersweet scent of coffee blossoms, rich aroma of drying beans, fat sacks sewn with a saddler's needle and stacked high on wagons, the long, bumpy trip to the Nairobi rail station. People in this part of Kenya, she says, think and talk of coffee constantly, and at night they lie in their beds and meditate upon improvements in their respective plantations.

But all of this means steady work. There are many jobs to be done – not just once, but day after day and from season to season. After the planting, there are pruning the plants, picking the coffee beans, carting beans to the factory, drying them in the big rotating wheel of the coffee-dryer, and then hulling, grading, and sorting the coffee and packing it into carefully sewn sacks. Then, with the coffee safely on its way to market, it all begins again with the planting and the pruning of a new crop.

Many leaders today face the very situation described by Dinesen. They must ensure that workers perform their duties well, that they gently set the coffee plants without bending the tap roots, that they take every pain to do the job right. Furthermore, these managers must see that workers repeat their tasks, again and again: setting the plants in regular rows of holes while enduring the black-jack weeds that constantly cling to clothes and stockings, carefully tending the plants, pruning them, watching the coffee tumble until just dry, even in the middle of the night. These tasks are not unimportant. They must be done, in just the right way, week after week. If leaders can ensure the consistency and quality of the performance of workers, coffee farms like Isak Dinesen's and, by extension, today's organizations, can thrive.

But how can supervisors be most effective? Much of management itself is a sort of perpetual housekeeping: maintaining order in an environment "where faucets almost always drip and dust reappears as soon as it's wiped away" (Sayles, 1979, p. 13). A large portion of any manager's day is spent cajoling others to carry out continuously necessary tasks. Trees always need to be pruned, customers constantly await help, equipment requires ongoing maintenance. Like washing dishes, these tasks are never finished. Executives cannot spur their staffs to action by using as an incentive the completion of the mission.

In trying to bring about this kind of never-ending motivation, managers often find the situation to be more difficult than they thought. Not only must leaders expend considerable energy, much of it fragmented, on this problem, but they also discover that some subordinates are "obtuse and recalcitrant" (Sayles, 1979, p. iv) in their response. Managers typically assume that all they have to do is make decisions and issue directives. They are often perplexed when the need emerges for "skills involving extraordinary patience, endurance, continuous interaction, spontaneous compromises, and negotiation" (Sayles, 1979, p. 13).

Sayles (1979) gives the striking example of the management problems encountered by President Carter after he spotted mice in the Oval Office. First, the President made a call to the General Services Administration (GSA), who purportedly took care of the problem. Later, however, Carter heard more mice. Eventually, a mouse died in the wall, emanating a stench noticed by numerous high officials attending formal meetings in Carter's office. Upon calling the GSA again, Carter was succinctly informed that the problem had previously been solved. *All* mice from the original call had been exterminated, the representative told the President, and hence, any remaining mice had to be outdoor mice who were therefore under the purview of another administrative unit. Only after the convening of a "joint task force" – met by initial resistance from the GSA – was the problem solved.

But how can supervisors be most effective? How can they motivate followers to do quality work, not just part of the time, but steadily? We posed the very questions pondered by junior and seasoned executives alike. We wanted to learn what managers should do to ensure the sustained cooperation of workers when it is crucial that those workers do their jobs well, day after day. We wanted to know how employers and employees could work together with the utmost in ongoing synergy.

These questions form the heart of this book.

To find out what well regarded managers actually do, we developed and tested an innovative model – the Operant Model of Effective Supervision –

inspired by the established concepts of operant conditioning theory and sparked by the expressed needs of leaders and followers.

To put our model into historical perspective, let's look first at the sizable body of leadership research and see our reasons for finding this to be an important path to pursue.

LOOKING AT THE LEADERSHIP LITERATURE

What's a leader to do? Unfortunately, that remains a difficult question. In reviewing the extensive literature on the subject even in 1959, Bennis concluded that "less [is] known about leadership than about any other topic in the behavioral sciences" (p. 59), despite an abundance of published scholarship. After examining four decades of research, Stogdill (1974) characterized it as "a bewildering mass of findings" (p. vii). Subsequent descriptions have been no more encouraging, ranging from "fragmentary, trivial, unrealistic, or dull" (Lombardo & McCall, 1978, p. 3) to fraught with "blind alleys" (Salancik, Calder, Rowland, Leblebici, & Conway, 1975, p. 81). In 1994, Yukl, surveying a veritable landscape of paper in the field of leadership, complained of the difficulties of seeing "the forest for the trees" (p. 439): some 5,000 articles and growing.

Despite their overall disenchantment, however, each of these critics could point to new strides. Bass (1990) in the *Handbook of Leadership*, praised theoretical advances that tied together general and specific theories. In particular, he singled out what he referred to as "contingent reinforcement leadership" (p. 913) and the more general theory of reinforcement or operant conditioning. The key advantage of this approach, he observed, was that the specific theory profited from being grounded in a more universal and proven theory, thus strengthening the ideas and predictions.

Other directions highlighted in the literature include "implicit leadership, substitutes for leadership, prototypicality effects, transformational leadership, impression management, self-management, and upward influence" (Bass, 1990, p. 913). Baldwin and Padgett (1993) also pointed to transformational leadership and self-leadership or self-management as promising areas for management development.

Both transformational leadership and self-leadership make the same assumption: that leaders have within themselves the capacity, ideas, or visions to become more effective if they will only allow themselves to reach out for these discoveries. The self-leadership area, while not directly related to housekeeping-style tasks, calls upon leaders to use their own resources and to figure out for themselves how to advance their effectiveness to the point of becoming super-leaders (Manz & Sims, 1991). The transformational leadership area (to be discussed shortly in more detail) exhorts leaders to generate visions for the future of the organization. Both areas are very popular, perhaps because they are optimistic and inner-directed.

They never tell you how[1]

While the ideas of transformational leadership and self-leadership are ennobling, a stubborn problem remains: leaders still do not know what to do when it comes to motivating others to perform unremitting tasks. Rarely do the popular media, or even scientific literature, provide evidence to show what truly effective leaders actually do. Even today, studies in scholarly journals focus more upon the actions and attitudes of on-line workers such as telephone operators and manufacturing workers rather than on the behavior of their bosses. The role of leaders in day-to-day interchange is left a mystery.

Unsuccessfully seeking the middle ground

"More damning" than this omission, contends Sayles (1979), is that even when leaders are the subjects of research, the prescriptions for improvement are limited to what the leaders "should think and what they should achieve. Ignored is the real pay dirt *how do you do it?*" (Sayles, 1979, p. 4).

Much management advice stresses what managers should think, how they should see what is around them, and how they should view themselves. Thus, executives are told that true leaders believe in shared authority (Coch & French, 1948) or that they recognize the expressed and unexpressed wants among potential followers (Burns, 1984). Manz and Sims (1989) emphasize the importance of what leaders should think; they explicitly encourage "focusing your thinking on the naturally rewarding features of your work" and "establishing constructive...patterns in your thinking...by managing your beliefs and assumptions, mental imagery, and internal self-talk" (p. 45). In a classic leadership model referred to as "Theory X, Theory Y", McGregor (1957) also stresses the thoughts and assumptions of an excellent manager, the so-called Theory Y manager. This manager assumes that people can accomplish their own goals best by channeling their efforts toward the goals of the organization. The result, according to McGregor, is workers following their own instincts and assuming responsibility in the service of the organization. While this emphasis on thought and belief may be noteworthy, it still leaves out what the executive actually does. *How* should the Theory Y manager ensure that people work personally toward overall group goals?

Other recommendations, on the other hand, simply state what managers are supposed to achieve. Supervisors are told they should make exemplary decisions, serve as stellar examples to their followers, and accomplish noteworthy results. Bobby Bowden, the football coach at Florida State University, is an example of a manager who stresses end results. As one of his assistant coaches describes him, " 'He leaves the coaching to his assistants. He doesn't care what we do as long as we get the ball in the end zone' " (Jordan, 1995).

Just because managers know the desired result, however, does not mean that they know how to attain it. In the stock market, investors know they should buy low and sell high. The concept is surely sound, and the outcome desirable. But both neophytes and experts have trouble realizing the end result. How can investors predict market fluctuations? What is "low" enough or "high" enough to buy or sell? These critical interim steps are rarely, if ever, explained. What is needed is what Sayles (1979) refers to as the "middle ground between motive and results" (p. 7). Once leaders find this connective territory, buying low and selling high can come within their grasp.

Beyond what managers do to what they *should* do

A brief but specific look at the literature on leadership reveals why finding this essential middle ground has been so difficult. For a long time, it was not even known what managers do every day. Lewis and Dahl (1976) quipped that we know more about the peoples of Papua New Guinea than the denizens of executive suites.

In trying to learn more about managerial and executive tasks, some researchers developed job descriptive questionnaires (e.g., Hemphill, 1959; Prien, 1963; Tornow & Pinto, 1976; Dowell & Wexley, 1978), some examined diaries kept by managers (e.g., Burns, 1957; Hinrichs, 1976; Stewart, 1976), while others actually observed leaders in action (Luthans & Lockwood, 1984; Stewart, 1982). In a seminal observational study, Mintzberg (1973) watched five managers for one week each. Data on day-to-day actions were painstakingly collected, analyzed, and re-analyzed, and Mintzberg examined written communication as well as solitary activities and personal contacts. In the end, the data broke down into time spent in fairly mundane acts: desk work, phone calls, scheduled meetings, tours, and so on (McCall, Morrison, & Hannan, 1978).

All of these acts were things that managers did. Knowing what managers do, however, is not the same as knowing what they *should* do (Yukl, 1994). Knowing that leaders spend a given percentage of their time on the phone, for example, does not mean that this activity is essential to effectiveness. Nor does knowing that leaders spend only a small amount of time planning mean that the activity is unimportant. While the findings of such investigators as Mintzberg were illuminating, they again missed what lies at the heart of leadership: what these leaders should do and say during those meetings and telephone calls that will make them more effective.

In attempting to address this, some interviewers have singled out certain leaders who are recognized as effective (Kanter, 1982; Kotter, 1982; Kotter and Lawrence, 1974), or leaders employed by companies that are seen as effective organizations (Peters & Austin, 1985; Peters & Waterman, 1982). Some promising policies for leadership, such as a "creating in *all* employees the awareness that their best efforts are essential and that they will share in the rewards of the company's success" (Peters & Waterman, 1982, p. i), have been suggested.

These guidelines for effective leaders, however, leave much yet unknown. Yukl calls them "still speculative" (1994, p. 42–43), and recommends a comparison between effective and ineffective leaders at the same level of authority and within the same industry. Only with this type of comparison can researchers begin to draw hard conclusions about the actions or qualities that make certain leaders effective. But such data are regrettably rare. After reviewing the literature, Yukl (1994) concludes that "few descriptive studies using observation, diaries, interview, or job description questionnaires have taken this approach" (p. 43).

Indeed, the lack of proper empirical evidence is a common complaint, even in the extensive and relatively well evaluated training literature (Burke & Day, 1986; Campbell, 1971; Goldstein, 1980; Latham, 1988; Wexley, 1984). Campbell, Dunnette, Lawler, and Weick (1970), in their book on managerial effectiveness, lament the inundation of the field with armchair speculations. "It may appear that we are laboring the point at too great length, but we firmly believe we cannot overemphasize the essential inadequacy of opinions, hunches, speculations, and expertise as a basis for prescriptions concerning the prediction of effective executive job behavior" (p. 10).

Even when such data are collected, however, the number of comparisons and controls is sparse. Some raise issue with the way in which key terms such as "leadership effectiveness" are defined (Campbell, Dunnette, Lawler, and Weick, 1970; Schmitt & Klimoski, 1991). In a review of studies of organizational development (OD) interventions, Terpstra (1981) found a "positive bias." The OD programs showing "positive" outcomes were more likely to be less rigorously evaluated and to use research designs with fewer controls and data collection points, hence the "bias." Terpstra also found the opposite to be true. The more rigorously designed studies, in which persons had been randomly assigned to treatment and control groups and data had been collected both before and after the program, were more likely to reveal negative findings. Let the reader beware.

Leadership theories fall short

Ohio State and Michigan studies

Even prominent leadership theories leave much to be desired. The classic studies of leadership, completed at Ohio State University (Fleishman, 1953; Halpin & Winer, 1957; Hemphill & Coons, 1957) and the University of Michigan (Likert, 1967) in the 1940s, 1950s, and 1960s, attempted to identify effective managerial behaviors. The Ohio State researchers, for example, wanted to know: "What are the patterns that these people actually engage in? Which ones turn out to be effective in influencing others?" (Fleishman, 1973, p. 5). They found, using a relatively new (at that time) factor analytic technique, that a wide array of behaviors could be defined according to the presence or absence of two tendencies of leaders. The first tendency, initiating the structure of the work group, involves "establish[ing] well defined patterns and channels of communication and ways of getting the job done" (p. 8). Such a leader might emphasize deadlines, insist on standard operating procedures, and assign specific tasks. The other tendency, consideration of the work group, involves establishing "two-way communication" (p. 8) patterns with employees.

Some of the early results of this study looked promising (Fleishman, 1973). Leaders who were high in both consideration and structure were in charge of well administered university departments (Hemphill, 1959), or had highly-rated bomber crews (Halpin, 1957). Complications quickly surfaced, however. Managers at International Harvester who provided more structure than their counterparts, for example, were found to have higher proficiency *and* higher grievances (Fleishman, Harris, & Burtt, 1955).

Literally hundreds of studies followed. Researchers, armed with questionnaires designed by the Ohio State researchers to measure initiating structure and consideration, fanned out across the globe, translating into languages ranging from Norwegian to Turkish. But despite the raw mass of research, findings remained obstinately mixed. The sole consistent finding was that a leader's consideration was associated with positive worker attitudes. Findings about performance shifted from one study to another. Some workers performed better and were happier with a leader who provided more structure. Some reacted in the opposite manner. Some revealed no pattern at all.

The inconsistency drew constant complaint from reviewers. Even when results were "slightly more consistent" with one questionnaire than with another, Korman (1966) still found a "great deal of inconsistency" in the studies he reviewed. Eight years later, Kerr and Schriesheim (1974) found a more consistent pattern of results with subordinate morale and satisfaction, though with performance to "a lesser degree" (p. 564).

In the intervening years, Fisher and Edwards (1988) did a meta-analysis, combining studies on structure that included as many as 1,953 respondents. Inconsistencies persisted, but could now be traced to differences in the definition of structure. Different questionnaires yielded different results. Performance and structure were not associated, for instance, when a questionnaire included punitive, autocratic items such as whether the manager "needles subordinates for greater effort." But with another questionnaire, containing more benign items such as "letting members know what is expected of them," a positive relationship surfaced between structure and performance. Clearly, the fact that measurement could so obtrusively govern results is a sign of major definitional problems with the research. Does providing structure mean constantly prodding subordinates? Or simply clarifying expectations at the beginning? Executives still do not know.

Charismatic or transformational leadership

Another approach receiving much attention lately is charismatic or transformational leadership. This looks to heroic, charismatic leaders who purportedly transcend their own personal interests, thereby transforming passive followers into ardent ones. When the followers are sufficiently motivated, they then become leaders themselves and, in turn, convert others, creating an ever-widening spiral of influence.

To accomplish this, leaders are encouraged "to have their goals clearly and firmly in mind, to fashion new institutions relevant to those goals, to stand back from immediate events and day to day routines and understand the potential and consequences of change" (Burns, 1984, p. 103). Bass (1985) identifies transformational leaders as those who induce "respondents to work ridiculous hours and to do more than they ever expected to do" (p. 31).

Problems exist, however, with these recommendations. Many of them fail to identify the aforementioned middle ground, focusing instead on the thinking of the manager ("understand the potential and consequences of change") or on the desired outcome ("respondents work ridiculous hours"). What is lacking is what leaders can do to ensure that respondents will work those ridiculous hours.

While questions remain about the specificity of the recommendations, the results of the charismatic and transformational leadership approach have been consistently positive. Using a questionnaire, investigators have found charisma to be highly and positively related to ratings of effectiveness and performance (refer to Bass's summary (1990)). While most of these studies have obtained their ratings of effectiveness and of the leaders from the same source, several recent studies have included independent criteria. One found a substantial correlation between the charisma of Methodist ministers as assessed via a questionnaire and two independent measures of effectiveness, the parishioners' church attendance and the growth in church membership (Onnen, 1987 in Bass (1990)).

In an innovative use of archival data, House, Spangler, and Woycke (1991) used as their sample all US presidents from Washington to Reagan. They examined biographies written by cabinet members, looking for descriptions of what the presidents said or, better yet, quotations. They then coded passages for evidence of charisma, identified as "self-confidence, strong ideological conviction, high expectations of followers, showing confidence in subordinates, and consideration" (p. 377). Charisma was found to be highly and positively related to a variety of criteria including presidential direct action, an overall "subjective greatness" index, and performance related to economic and social issues. The findings supported the potency of charisma, but all of the criteria used were primarily concerned with the leader's role as a visionary and decision-maker for the nation, rather than as a motivator of people whose influence maintained their performance.

A look at the origins of this model reveals why it stresses innovation over the daily maintaining of productive performance. The transformational approach was a direct response to the threat of increasing national and international competition in the 1980s. Hence, it focuses on change, sometimes of a revolutionary nature. US companies realized that they had to transform the way they ran their businesses if they were to survive. Cosmetic touch-ups would not do. Sometimes this meant altering the entire culture of the organization. Executives were encouraged to take three steps: first, to "develop a vision of what the organization can be," then "to mobilize the organization to accept and work toward achieving the new vision," and lastly "to institutionalize the changes that must last over time" (Tichy & Ulrich, 1984, p.59).

As companies developed their visions and impelled their organizations to accept them, however, attention shifted to the third and last step, the institutionalization of the changes. As Trice and Beyer (1991) point out, there is a difference between innovation and maintenance.

Unfortunately, even proponents are finding the maintenance side of the equation more difficult than it appears. One reason is that maintaining changes is much less dramatic than innovating them, and it thus tends to be downplayed. Tichy and Ulrich (1984) refer to the "shaping and reinforcement" (p. 64), for instance, that is necessary to institutionalize change. Another reason is that leaders often hope, somewhat naively, that change will somehow sustain itself. As seasoned observers know, however, great visions can and do fall by the wayside over time. A third reason is that leaders need different qualities to maintain changes from those they needed to be innovators. They must make substantial shifts in how they behave. Exactly how is, regrettably, vague.

To institutionalize change, leadership theories encourage managers to modify their "communication, decision making, and problem-solving systems" (Tichy & Ulrich, 1984). But no discussion is forthcoming as to how these alterations should be made. Tichy and Ulrich (1984) also mention that the "human resource systems of selection, development, appraisal, and reward are major levers for institutionalizing change" (p. 64), but again, they do not identify the basis upon which leaders should be chosen, trained, evaluated, or reinforced. Trice and Beyer (1991) are more explicit: to make changes last, leaders should become less dramatic and more persuasive. They must stop being evangelists and become catalysts. Precisely what it means to be a catalyst or to be persuasive, however, is not specified. A manager who wants to act as an effective catalyst might quite correctly ask what she is supposed to do.

Even if this middle ground were specified, however, the fiercest proponents of the transformational and charismatic approach readily recognize that there would still be problems. Bass (1985) admits outright that "there are situations in which the transformational approach may not be appropriate" (p. 40). House, Spangler, and Woycke (1991) speculate that charismatic leaders are probably most effective in situations requiring "emotional commitment and extraordinary effort by both leader and followers in pursuit of ideological goals" (p. 391). But, they continue, in situations "requiring routine but reliable performance in the pursuit of pragmatic goals" (p. 391) – settings that sound very much like the coffee plantation of Isak Dinesen – "charismatic leadership ... may even be dysfunctional" (p. 391). The transformational and charismatic approaches may excel at helping leaders to create visions and to mobilize organizations to embrace these visions. But they are probably not as well suited to identifying what leaders should do to maintain these changes, or, in the case of such leaders as Isak Dinesen, the everyday performance of farm hands.

Challenges of maintaining performance

For the Isak Dinesens of the world, the question is how to motivate people to do what needs to be done conscientiously and consistently, day after day and season after season. Few doubt that sustaining these never-ending tasks is important. Finding a way to do so, however, is no easy job.

For the same reasons that it is difficult to maintain changes, it is also difficult to maintain performance. Part of this, as mentioned earlier, has to do with theatrics: maintaining performance is much less dramatic than initiating a new thrust. Not surprisingly, much less time and effort are expended on the less exciting activity. In addition to this, leaders often hope that people will simply form new performance habits, eliminating the need for leaders to do much to sustain change. And the skills needed for maintaining performance, just as those for maintaining change, are very different from those needed to visualize better ways of doing things.

But the cost of resistance to change, even in performing routine tasks, can be high. Managers of a processing company, for example, complained that "sloppy habits" were costing "tens of millions of dollars per year – a high price to pay for sloppy habits" (Gellerman, 1976, p. 89). At a wholesale bakery, injuries had jumped sharply; management was perplexed about how to get employees to be more careful (Komaki, Barwick, & Scott, 1978).

Proven solutions are elusive. Among the suggestions that have been made is for leaders to focus on the "people" aspect of the mission, and to rally employees around the task (Bass, 1990; Campbell, Dunnette, Lawler, & Weick, 1970; Yukl, 1994). In this sense, leadership is an "influence" process in which leaders intentionally and directly address the behavior of face-to-face situations (Campbell, 1977). Conceptualizing leadership as an influence process places it squarely in the realm of motivation, the major area of concern for performance in organizations today (Daniels, 1989).

In both the basic (Cofer & Appley, 1968) and the applied (Steers and Porter, 1990) motivation literature, distinctions have been made among three stages of motivation: (a) initiating or energizing behavior, (b) directing or channeling behavior, and (c) maintaining or sustaining behavior. Regrettably, even the brightest beacons in the leadership literature are not very illuminating for maintaining the habit of desired performance. With their calls for transmitting a sense of mission, the transformational and charismatic approaches are probably better suited to initiating and innovating rather than maintaining performance. Similarly, the Ohio State studies, with their emphasis on initiating the structure of the task, might be more effective with neophytes in training than with seasoned employees. While it is critical to make sure that newcomers have solid, structured ideas about what to do, once they are regularly doing the job the challenge becomes to ensure that the actions they have learned will be sustained. As Sayles (1979) succinctly phrases it: "The tough job is getting it accepted and keeping it working" (p. 20).

Agreement on the importance of leadership

There is little dispute of the critical role that leaders play in motivating workers (cf. Pfeffer, 1977). In the words of a director of production for a large defense subcontractor, "I know in my gut that the real key to productivity...and to better labor relations...is my supervisors. Any investment in them ... gets one of the best returns in this company" (Sasser, & Leonard, 1980).

Today, the benefits of effective leadership – organizational efficiency, high productivity, profit maximization – are proclaimed daily (e.g., Farkas & Wetlaufer, 1996), while the search continues for leaders who have demonstrated prowess in these areas. Sayles (1979) begins his leadership book by reiterating the crying need for managers who can deliver. "Even in periods of recession, most organizations keep looking for 'better' managers; universities, corporations, hospitals, and government agencies constantly complain about...the difficulty of obtaining truly effective managers" (p. 1). Once organizations find promising candidates, they spend, collectively, billions of dollars training managers (Baldwin & Padgett, 1993). Among large companies, leadership development has been a "high priority" and gaining in importance (as reported in a recent *Training & Development Journal* (1995, p. 13)). Between three-quarters and nine-tenths of these companies have sponsored leadership development programs (Baldwin & Padgett, 1993). Furthermore, a 1985 Bureau of Labor Statistics survey showed that one-third of executives, administrators and managers reported that they received training from their employers to improve their skills (Carey, 1985).

Books dealing with what managers should do, such as *The One Minute Manager* (Blanchard & Johnson, 1982) and *In Search of Excellence* (Peters & Waterman, 1982), regularly make the best-seller list. Covey's (1989) book, *The Seven Habits of Highly Effective People*, has been a best-seller for more than six years. In spite of the lack of proof that these approaches actually work, such books are eagerly sought out. Their popularity demonstrates, if nothing else, the dire need for guidelines.

It is sobering to consider that these same concerns have existed for centuries. In 350 BC, Aristotle wondered what qualifications were necessary for candidates for the highest offices in the land. In the end, he identified three: loyalty, administrative capacity, and virtue. Even today, we would find it hard to define such qualities. In one of the most highly requested articles of the *Harvard Business Review*, Herzberg (1968) still asked: "One more time: How do you motivate employees?"

THE IDENTIFICATION OF THE OPERANT MODEL OF EFFECTIVE SUPERVISION

Identifying performance consequences

Sparked by watching truly effective leaders

To try to answer the question of motivation, we observed leaders who were responsible for maintaining performance on a day-to-day basis. One characteristic that struck us immediately was the manner in which the most effective leaders interacted with their followers. Rather than remaining aloof, closed in their offices, they let each person know that they were aware of how they were performing their jobs. Occasionally, they would explicitly point out what they liked or did not like about what workers were doing. More often, however, they would communicate this in a variety of subtle and often casual ways throughout the day.

One supervisor stands out as an excellent example. He was a Marine Corps warrant officer (WO) known throughout the base for being a "crackerjack WO" (Komaki & Collins, 1982). One day as he dashed out for a meeting, he checked with his chief mechanic only to find him stymied by a stubborn problem with an engine. As soon as the WO returned from his meeting, he sought out the mechanic. Together they hunched over the engine, sharing an easy exchange. The officer asked what the mechanic had already tried, and the mechanic explained as best he could. Sometimes the officer just nodded. At other times he simply said "okay" or "hmm." Occasionally, the officer described what the mechanic had done: "So you've already tried that." All of these off-the-cuff comments occurred *after* the mechanic had tried to work on the engine; they concerned what the mechanic had done, and showed that the officer was aware of the mechanic's efforts. These verbal ("okay") and nonverbal (a nod) responses we classified as performance consequences.

Inspired by operant conditioning theory

This emphasis on consequences is in keeping with the theory of operant conditioning, sometimes referred to as reinforcement theory, behavior modification, or applied behavior analysis (Skinner, 1974; Stolz, Wienckowski,

& Brown, 1975). In this theory, the consequences of performance – the feedback we receive, the comments we hear – are believed to have a powerful impact on what we do from day to day. The major principles of operant conditioning – positive reinforcement, negative reinforcement, extinction, and punishment – all deal with what happens *after* the behavior. The principle of positive reinforcement, for example, predicts that if something positive (a positive consequence) happens after a particular behavior, the behavior is more likely to occur. In essence, these consequences are *the* major motivating factor behind our behavior.

Operant conditioning theory is unique in the social sciences because its two major categories – antecedents and consequences – are defined according to the time when they occur, either before or after the behavior of interest. A distinction is made between consequences, which occur *after* the behavior, and antecedents, which occur *before* the behavior. Let us say that the behavior in this case is the treatment of each employee with respect, without regard to race, religion, sex, national origin, disability or position. When companies establish antidiscrimination policies defining standards of corporate conduct or produce booklets proclaiming its commitment to diversity, these policies and booklets are generally categorized as antecedents. How companies act *after* employees do something, these are considered consequences. When managers follow through on their concerns for employees who have complained of discrimination – by offering them new duties and hence removing them from situations that they find disciminatory or dismissing them for contending they were victims of discrimination (Eichenwald, 1996) – these are considered consequences.

Evidenced by sustained improvements

A host of evidence supports the potency of consequences in motivating and, in particular, maintaining performance. In experiment after experiment, when consequences have been rearranged to be frequent and contingent on performance, dramatic improvements have resulted. This has been demonstrated in thousands of experiments at all levels of the phylogenetic scale (Honig, 1966; Ulrich, Stachnik, & Mabry, 1966; 1970; 1974).

A recent review of operant conditioning in work settings shows that at least fifty-one well controlled studies have addressed whether or not positive reinforcement improves performance on the job (Komaki, Coombs, & Schepman, 1991). Of the fifty-one studies, forty-seven revealed substantial improvements in performance, for a success rate of 92.2 percent.

Further evidence of this efficacy is in how long-lasting the effects are. Most of the studies were not cross-sectional, with data collected at only one point in time. Instead, the median length of time of the interventions was a full eight weeks. One study demonstrated success in reducing accidents for eleven years in a mine in Arizona, and for twelve years in another mine in Wyoming (Fox, Hopkins, & Anger, 1987). Similar results have been reported in other reviews of studies in work settings (Andrasik, 1979; Babb & Kopp, 1978; Hopkins & Sears, 1982; Merwin, Thomason, & Sanford, 1989; O'Hara, Johnson, Beehr, 1985; Schneier, 1974).

Not the exclusive domain of operant conditioners

Psychologists of the operant persuasion, such as Scott and Podsakoff (1985) in their book, *Behavioral Principles in the Practice of Management,* and Luthans and Kreitner (1975) in their book, *Organizational Behavior Modification*, have long posited that the link between behavior and its consequences should hold true for managers in organizations. But consequences have been recognized as being vital by non-operant theorists as well. The importance of consequences has been singled out by industrial/organizational (I/O) psychologists (e.g., Ilgen, Fisher, & Taylor, 1979), as well as by other applied psychologists (e.g., Arnett, 1969). These researchers, however, do not use the term "consequences," but instead refer to "rewards" or "incentives" (which the operant model would identify as positive consequences), "praise" and "criticism" (positive and negative social consequences), and "feedback" (positive, negative, or neutral informational consequences).

I/O psychologists have found the effectiveness of leaders to vary with different types of consequences. The strategies of "personally rewarding" and "designing feedback systems" were highly and positively related to two independent ratings of effectiveness criteria for a sample of civilian middle managers (Oldham, 1976). Similar results were found with a sample of Naval officers (Klemp, Munger, & Spencer, 1977); the more effective officers followed up on their actions and communicated the results against performance standards.

Related to worker satisfaction

I/O psychologists have also looked at how followers react to being positively reinforced by leaders. Podsakoff and Schriesheim (1985) reviewed both laboratory and field studies. They consistently found that employees' attitudes about their supervision were positive when employees described their bosses as personally complimenting them when they performed outstanding work, a classic example of providing positive and contingent consequences.

Further, growing evidence from the operant conditioning literature suggests that employees prefer systems in which they receive consequences for their performance. For example, two-thirds of the employees in a recent study, when anonymously polled, stated that they preferred a feedback system to one that provided only antecedents, such as rules and reminders (Komaki, Collins, & Penn, 1982).

For all of these demonstrated empirical and theoretical reasons, the role of performance consequences has assumed great importance in the development of our model of supervision.

The need to monitor performance

Instigated by contingent consequences

It is not enough, however, for leaders to supply consequences. They must make certain that their evaluations of performance are directly related to, i.e., contingent upon, what their followers have actually done. When the vice president tells her Human Resources Director that his recruiting efforts have been superb, she needs to be certain that the results were actually related to his performance (as opposed to, for example, its being a lucky coincidence or a misreading of the situation). At the same time, the officer who blames his troops for the high proportion of equipment out of commission or "deadlined" should ensure that maintenance practices were indeed faulty.

Scholars widely accept the significance of contingent consequences. Their importance has been emphasized by I/O psychologists as well (Arvey & Jones,1985; Campbell, 1977; House & Mitchell,1974; Ilgen, Fisher, & Taylor, 1979; Podsakoff, Todor, & Skov, 1982; Scott & Podsakoff, 1985). Bass (1990), in his *Handbook of Leadership*, talks not just of reinforcement but of contingent reinforcement, devoting three chapters to the topic.

The reality of noncontingent consequences

Despite the exhortations of managers, the appraisals they actually deliver on the job are not always as accurate as we might like to believe. In fact, Longenecker, Sims, and Gioia (1987) refer outright to the myth that accuracy is the primary concern of executives when evaluating workers.

Workers' reactions attest to this, as illustrated in Podsakoff and Schriesheim's (1985) research on contingent and noncontingent consequences. Workers filled out questionnaires identifying their reactions when their supervisors provided positive contingent (complimenting them when they did outstanding work), positive noncontingent (praising them when they did poorly *and* when they did well), negative contingent (reprimanding them when their work was below standard), and negative noncontingent consequences (holding them accountable for things over which they had no control). Few workers had trouble relating to the questions about noncontingent positive and negative consequences; clearly, this experience was not foreign to them.

Not surprisingly, workers were much more satisfied with their supervision when they felt that their superiors delivered contingent consequences. Noncontingent consequences, on the other hand, bore little relation to workers' attitudes about their supervision – except for cases in which workers felt that criticism bore little correlation to what they actually did. Workers found this (i.e., consequences that were both negative and noncontingent) to be particularly galling. Bass (1990), understanding this dynamic, contended that "this condition [of noncontingent punishment] is likely to promote learned helplessness" (p. 321).

From a single follower's perspective

A memorable account is given by a training director (as reported in Daniels (1989, p. 75)). He describes how his boss's volatile and harsh evaluation of his judgment, followed by seemingly unjustified praise for routine work, "had a cumulative effect [that] diluted the effectiveness of his use of consequences for as long as I worked for him." What happened, as the director saw it, was this: the boss sat down with the director to screen a training film that the director believed the company should purchase. In the middle of the screening, with a third person also present, the boss stood up, exclaimed angrily to the director, "I wouldn't pay $500.00 for that piece of crap!" and stormed out of the room, slamming the door. Shaken and embarrassed, the director went home. When he returned the next morning, the boss walked into his office, shoved a piece of paper across his desk, and hurried away with virtually no comment. The document was a routine memo written by the director weeks before; across the top, the boss had scribbled, "EXCELLENT WORK." Instead of feeling complimented, the director felt betrayed. He was convinced that his boss had made this perfunctory gesture only out of guilt; the boss was trying to atone for the way he had behaved the day before. Even the scribbling across the top of the memo looked hurriedly done. The director doubted that the boss had even carefully read it. Eventually, said the director, "I began to see everything he did as a result of his mood that day, or whatever, rather than contingent on my performance" (p. 75).

Note that the director was upset not only because the consequence was negative, but because it seemed entirely unrelated to his performance.

When accuracy is not the primary concern

A candid set of interviews with 60 upper-level executives vividly confirms what workers, such as the director described above, say about the seemingly nonsensical way in which they are sometimes evaluated (Longenecker, Sims, & Gioia, 1987). Many of the executives readily admitted that "Political considerations *nearly always* were part of their evaluation process" (p. 184).

When asked if and why they ever gave what were termed "deflating" appraisals, the executives gave some eye-opening answers, many of which appeared in the article as verbatim quotes. One reason given was to shock an employee, "to get him back on track" (p. 189). Another was to show followers, in one executive's words, "who the boss is" (p. 189). Yet another was the executives' "fear that discussing and documenting any positives [positive aspects] of the employee's performance might be used against them" (p. 189), in lawsuits, for instance.

On the other hand, the executives also said that they sometimes "inflated" the appraisals. Sometimes they did this in the hope of maintaining performance; they did not want to dampen the spirits of an employee who was belatedly improving. Some executives simply wanted to avoid "hanging dirty laundry out in public" (p. 188). One executive said, "I generally don't put those things down on paper...for the whole world to read, because it is generally none of their damn business...I could make all of us look bad or worse than we really are" (p. 188). Although few admitted to doing this themselves, one plant manager said: "A lot of people inflate ratings of people they can't stand, or who think they are God's gift to the department, just to get rid of them."

As we can see by the executives' own accounts, accuracy in evaluation was not their primary concern. They insisted, in fact, that they "would not allow excessively accurate ratings to cause problems for themselves" (Longenecker, Sims, & Gioia, 1987, p. 191), such as hindering a person's momentum or inciting a confrontation with a difficult subordinate. At the very least, the accounts indicate that the unspeakable does happen: leaders do deliver noncontingent consequences, and they apparently do it more often than we might like to believe.

Executives may have a valid point when they contend that certain appraisals of employees may be blown out of proportion when written down or formalized. And political forces certainly exist in any organization. But the question remains: what, if anything, can and should leaders do on a day-to-day basis to galvanize employees? A search of the literature has shown that this issue was rarely addressed.

The importance of accurate information

While Daniels (1989) is to be commended for being one of the few even to touch on this knotty topic, he typically assumes that managers have all of the information they need. "Most of the problems," he argues, "are not caused because people are insincere but because they appear insincere" (p. 78). In other words, it's a question of style, not of content. In the case of the negative consequence aimed at the training director in the film screening, this is true; the same evaluation could have been transmitted much more calmly and constructively. For the so-called positive consequence, however, style seems to be only part of the problem. The director himself was upset that his boss really *did not know* how well (or how badly) the director might be performing. The director cites the fact that his memo, labeled "EXCELLENT" by the boss, was weeks old, and that it was a "routine write-up, similar to many others I had done" (p. 75). He goes on to say that his boss "probably couldn't have quoted the topic of my memo if he had been asked" (p. 75). The boss's not knowing, not having the information on which to base a sound judgment, even a positive one, was the problem.

The significance of frequent discussions about performance

Another issue is the frequency with which information is obtained and communicated by managers. The fact that the above-mentioned memo was weeks old suggests that relatively little, if anything, had been said to the director about the quality of his work over that time. In fact, annual or at best semi-annual performance appraisals are common. When bosses learn only sporadically how subordinates are doing, the consequences that they provide will probably be like that of the executive in a *New Yorker* cartoon (by Stevenson in 1988) in which a smiling boss, striding through a crowded office, claps his hand on the back of a toiling worker and proclaims, "Keep up the good work, whatever it is, whoever you are."

Even well-meaning executives (and at least one college professor) have been known to communicate vaguely positive but regrettably noncontingent consequences. To assuage their guilt at being out of touch, and to try to live up to all of the current hoopla about recognizing exemplary employees, leaders sometimes just blurt out something, anything, just to be on the record with a positive comment.

In discussing the difficulties of appraising employees, one executive acknowledged, "Many of us have trouble rating for the entire year. If one of my people has a stellar three months prior to the review ... you don't want to do anything that impedes that person's momentum and progress" (Longenecker, Sims, & Gioia, 1987, p. 188). In this case, it sounds as if performance is rated just once a year, which is not at all unusual. In fact, in a survey of about 700 employees in one manufacturing organization, about one-third reported on an anonymous questionnaire that their performance was not evaluated even once a year (Landy, Barnes, & Murphy, 1978).

The problem with such infrequent appraisal is that the ratings of employees do not necessarily reflect their performance over the entire year, much less that particular week or month. When supervisors rely on retrospective accounts and their own memory, real problems of accuracy in judging performance can arise. Some of the problems with evaluations (such as an employee feeling unfairly rated, or bad performance going uncorrected) are a result of the sheer infrequency of the appraisals.

It's not as though it is not important

The critical need for accurate, timely information in assessing performance is stressed by writers from widely divergent points of view. Decision-making researchers emphasize the quality of information upon which decisions are based (Janis & Mann, 1977; Laming, 1973; Raiffa, 1968). Cybernetics scholars cite the importance of data in the feedback loop (Beer, 1959; Rackman & Woodward, 1970). Researchers in the field of performance appraisal underscore the significance of the information used by managers to generate evaluations (Landy & Farr, 1983). Information-processing experts highlight the quality of the information upon which evaluations are based (Lord, 1985). In organizational development interventions, Argyris (1973) explicitly recognizes the role played by information in fostering overall organizational well-being. In his view, the aim is to facilitate the "free flow of valid information" within the system, enabling members of the organization to make "free and informed choices" (p. 7).

Given this agreement on the necessity for dependable, timely knowledge, we were struck that not one writer explicitly identified how leaders should obtain this information. References to methods were infrequent and sketchy at best. McElvey's (1970) thermostat analogy includes the operation of a sensor for measuring the current status of the system, along with other features such as the standard, discriminator, and affector. Few details are mentioned, however, as to where and how the sensor is supposed to function. In short, the middle ground, i.e., what managers can do to avoid noncontingent positive or, better yet, noncontingent negative consequences, is practically nowhere to be found.

Looking again at really effective leaders

Trying to establish what leaders could constructively do to avoid the backlash of noncontingent consequences, we turned again to the Warrant Officer, mentioned previously as someone known at his US Marine base for his effectiveness, and contrasted what he did with the actions of the not-so-effective WOs. What distinguished the two was the quantity and the quality of their information-gathering efforts. The crackerjack WO did not leave fact-finding to chance. Always curious, he would often go to the work site and seek out information. He would sometimes casually ask subordinates, "What's up?" or "How's it going?" More often, he would directly sample their work, strolling through the shop, for example, to see how his mechanics were doing. All of these attempts to obtain information – work sampling, self- reports – we classified as "monitoring performance."

The crackerjack WO, using what he learned from monitoring, was able to effectively acknowledge, correct, and provide feedback. Contrastingly, the lackluster WOs would only sporadically monitor, and when they did, they tended to rely on self-reports, in formal meetings. They went less often to the work site. As a result, they missed natural opportunities to provide consequences on a day-to-day basis. Seeing this, we began to home in on the importance of actively gathering information by monitoring, particularly via work sampling on the job.

An operant penchant for monitoring via work sampling

Singling out a particular type of monitoring – in this case, work sampling – is consistent with the methods of even early operant researchers. In their book on how mental health managers should motivate workers to implement a newly developed system, Ayllon and Azrin (1968) generated a series of practical rules. One, the Direct Supervision Rule, stated that the staff should "provide systematic and direct observation" (p. 146). Managers were told that they should use a standardized coding system, and then gather data by going to the work site and observing staff in action. Only in this way, said Ayllon and Azrin (1968), "can there be a true basis for rewards for appropriate performance and punishment or criticism for inappropriate performance" (p. 146). By providing this "true basis," the Direct Supervision Rule enabled consequences to be contingent.

A logical prerequisite to contingent consequences

We reasoned, therefore, that managers who take the time to find out what workers have done are more likely to have accurate and timely information. With this information in hand, leaders can then impart consequences, whether they are positive or negative, that closely correspond to their followers' performance.

Without dependable and up-to-date information, no leader, no matter how well-meaning, can provide consequences that are directly linked to performance. Hence, companies that truly wish to ensure respect for the individual, for instance, will go beyond antecedents (antidiscrimination policies, booklets, diversity training) to monitoring (regularly auditing the hiring and promotion of minority-group workers) and then making this information available to those in corporate offices who can, if necessary, change their hiring and promotion practices.

A part of the three-step intervention process used in operant motivation programs

Another indication of the role of monitoring emerged from the three-step process traditionally used by operant researchers to set up motivational programs. The first step is to specify what workers are supposed to do; the second, to monitor or measure the desired performance; and the third, to deliver consequences, based on the findings of the monitoring.

For example, in setting up a program to improve occupational safety, we used what was then viewed as a novel method (Komaki, Barwick, & Scott, 1978). Instead of the usual antecedent-based approach of posting signs and admonishing workers to be careful, we used a three-step process. First, we *specified* desired safety practices by reviewing previous accidents and identifying what workers could do to avoid recurrences. Second, we produced an observational code for *monitoring*, wherein specific practices (e.g., "When moving conveyor, at least one person must be on each end") would be identified as safe, unsafe, or not observed. The code was reviewed with both workers and management. Observers used the code to go on-site and measure workers' safety practices. Third, using this information, feedback was provided by posting the information on a graph, which allowed management to provide *consequences* based on real behavior. This three-step process resulted in sustained safety improvements in this setting, and in others as well, as reviews of the process have indicated (Andrasik, 1979; Babb & Kopp, 1978; Hopkins & Sears, 1982; Komaki, Coombs, & Schepman, 1991; Merwin, Thomason, & Sanford, 1989; O'Hara, Johnson, & Beehr, 1985; Schneier, 1974).

For these reasons, the monitoring of performance, an integral step in successful motivational programs and a logical prerequisite to providing contingent consequences, was included as a major element in our model.

In line with leadership and group literatures

Within the leadership literature, information itself is highly valued. Mintzberg (1975) describes information as "the basic input to decision-making." In their model on effective decision-making, Vroom and his colleagues (Vroom & Jago, 1978; Vroom & Yetton, 1973) have managers ask themselves if they have "sufficient information to make a high quality decision." Depending on whether they do or not, different courses of action are recommended.

Leadership theorists have also consistently noted the role of monitoring. Meredith and Mantel (1985) note that information is needed for planning and problem solving; that monitoring provides much of this information; and that is why it is so important for managerial effectiveness. Yukl (1994), in his integrating taxonomy describing leaders' managerial behavior, includes monitoring and the collection of information.

Hackman and Walton (1986) highlight monitoring as one of the two most important behaviors available to leaders in their theory of the leadership of task-performing groups. In their theory, they emphasize what is required for leaders "to help a group do its work effectively" (p. 74). Effective leaders, they propose, are those who monitor and then, based on the information they obtain from monitoring, take action. Leaders who monitor, they say, can check on the outcomes of the group; for a group responsible for delivering consulting services, for example, the leader might check to see if the clients receiving the service are pleased with the team's product. After looking at the group's indices of effectiveness, the leader might then backtrack to look at the group's process, for example, seeing whether the group is expending enough time and effort in producing the product. Depending on what is discovered here, the leader might then go back even further, to ferret out, for example, background information about the composition of the group, its education, and the availability of training. Hackman and Walton (1986) emphasize that their model is an adaptive one. If the leader discovers problems, he or she can "invent ways of behaving that may remedy a deficiency or exploit an unrealized opportunity" (p. 105). Their model does not specify "exactly which behaviors should be exhibited in which particular circumstances" (p. 105). Instead, they propose that the effective leaders will be ones who have the very idea that monitoring and taking action is important. Although Hackman and Walton's (1986) interest is in "real" groups doing "real work (ranging from making decisions to actually producing things) in purposive social systems" (p. 73), they unfortunately provide no data, choosing to call their venture an explicitly exploratory one.

Several descriptive studies have supported the practice of monitoring. Klemp, Munger, and Spencer (1977) found that "superior Naval officers were more likely to report systematic methods for monitoring and controlling activities in their environment. Average leaders, on the other hand, were less likely to measure results against performance standards" (p. 72).

More to the point, however, is a study by Landy, Barnes, and Murphy (1978). Surveying employees of a large manufacturing organization, they found three factors related to employees' attitudes about the fairness and accuracy of their evaluations. One was how often the appraisals were done. The second was whether or not a supervisor had pointed out goals that an employee should strive toward to eliminate weaknesses. The third was how well the supervisor actually knew the subordinate's level of performance and job duties.

Even interaction within families has verified the crucial role of monitoring. In one study, monitoring was found to be one of four factors distinguishing between families with and without antisocial children (Patterson, 1982). Parents with disruptive children were less likely to monitor. That is, they were less likely to take the five minutes necessary, for example, to see that the child performed chores and performed them properly, as was more often done in families without disruptive children. In a third category of families characterized as "super normal," a subtle form of monitoring was observed, in which family members expressed genuine and regular interest in the activities and well-being of other family members.

In short, for a variety of theoretical, empirical, and practical reasons, both monitoring and consequences constitute vitally important components of our model.

IN SUMMARY

Buttressed by the substantial framework of leadership research, inspired by established concepts of operant conditioning theory, and prompted by the stated needs of leaders and followers, we set out to identify what effective leaders should do. The most effective leaders, we saw, were those who gathered information about how their followers were doing, and who then, based on this monitoring, provided consequences that showed that they really knew what was going on.

Our inclusion of performance consequences as a cornerstone of our model stemmed directly from the theory of operant conditioning. Besides the familiar tenet that behavior is a function of its consequences, successful motivation programs have employed a wide variety of consequences: from feedback posted on graphs to hand-written notes. Monitoring, a relatively new idea in leadership theory, draws its strength from the fact that it shores up the accuracy of the consequences provided by leaders. Despite myths to the contrary, the feedback that subordinates sometimes receive often bears only a tenuous relationship to what they have actually done. Monitoring should not only ensure contingent consequences, but, as we shall see, facilitate the subtle and casual off-hand comments that effective leaders use to let their followers know how they are doing on an ongoing basis.

This back-and-forth exchange is what we call "the music of management": an interactive process of exchanging information, in which leaders and followers perform together in a sort of communicative symphony. Their harmony is not always peaceful or even pretty. But it is always in tune in the sense that people start to listen and hear one another.

With all of this as background to place our model into historical perspective, we move forward in the next chapter to sketch an overall view of the model as it has evolved and as it now exists. Subsequent chapters will detail discrete elements of our model, ending with what we see for leaders in the future. Our hope is to eventually be able to tell leaders, like coffee-grower Isak Dinesen, what they can and should do on a day-to-day basis to ensure that the tap roots are not bent, and that the coffee is perfectly dried, even in the middle of the night.

2 Introducing the model

Identifying what leaders like coffee-farmer Isak Dinesen should do to best
motivate their subordinates on a day-to-day basis seemed, to us, a modest
enough aim, at least at the beginning. Because it was fueled by our hope of
humanizing our experiences at work where we all spend much of our lives,
we soon realized that our sketch in general terms was not enough in order
to find the answers we sought.

THE PRO-SOCIAL AIM OF MODEL

The seed for our model was planted during the heady, idealistic time of the
late 1960s, when those in our field found fresh promise in our ability to make
real improvements in people's lives. Children once thought to be "autistic"
and destined for lifetime institutionalization began to communicate and to
help themselves when they were reinforced for successive approximations to
desired behaviors (Lovaas, 1966). First-graders in a disadvantaged neighborhood learned skills critical to further achievement (Becker, Madsen, Arnold,
& Thomas, 1967). One story on the evening news even told of a token
economy system[1] that had been successfully implemented at an Army boot
(or training) camp at Fort Ord (Datel & Legters, 1971).

The idea of helping to make the world a better place permeates the
writings of the founder of operant conditioning, B. F. Skinner. His book,
Walden Two (1948), is the quintessential illustration of an academic model
for changing the world. Rather than merely showing how operant principles
could be used with pairs, groups, or even organizations, he did so with an
entire society.

A similarly pro-social vision emerged in the very first issue of the major
journal in the field, the *Journal of Applied Behavior Analysis*. There, Baer,
Wolf, and Risley (1968) made it clear that articles were welcome advancing
"socially important behaviors, such as retardation, crime, mental illness, or
education" (p. 91). The editors hoped that publishing such findings "may
well lead to the widespread examination of these applications, their refinement, and eventually their replacement by better applications. Better appli-

cations, it is hoped, will lead to a better state of society" (Baer, Wolf, & Risley, 1968, p. 91).

Like Skinner (1948) and Baer, Wolf, and Risley (1968), we, too, dreamed of making society, particularly workplaces, better (Komaki, 1994). We were not interested in whether to call those responsible for supervision "leaders" or "managers." We were not concerned with whether one paradigm or theory was better than another (Komaki, 1981); any paradigm was worth considering if we thought it would enhance our experiences at work. Instead, we immersed ourselves in the daily routines of busy, highly-pressured leaders and the long-neglected people under their charge.

As we watched, we saw some leaders tell people what to do again and again, while others in the same circumstances quickly went through a discernible sequence of different behaviors. Hence, our model grew from being a general portrayal of supervisory behaviors into a better-crafted definition that includes the quantity and quality of the behaviors that are delivered, as well as their pacing and placement within sequences.

Similarly, as we listened to followers, we started to pick up on what they were saying, and on how they actually influenced leaders. As a result, we moved from an overall notion of the process of interactions, to a full-blown recognition of the distinctive role of the follower and the dialogues between followers and leaders.

At the same time, we discovered that the model works well in some situations but not nearly as well in others. Hence, we went from a vague idea of the limitations of the model to a detailing of at least five specific boundaries.

These changes to the original model helped to flesh out a fuller, more complete answer to the question of what leaders should do.

THE MODEL AND ITS MAJOR COMPONENTS

A current view of our model is shown in Figure 2.1. The model contains four major components: (a) the leaders' behaviors, (b) supervisory effectiveness, (c) the interaction process, and (d) moderators or the boundaries.

Leaders' behaviors

Defined in terms of quantity and quality

Briefly, our model shows that effective leaders monitor more often and provide more consequences. Furthermore, the exemplary leaders monitor in a particular way, by *sampling the work*. They actually go to the places where followers are doing the work, and see for themselves what followers are doing.

Using all they learn from monitoring, effective leaders take advantage of these natural opportunities to provide consequences, commenting casually

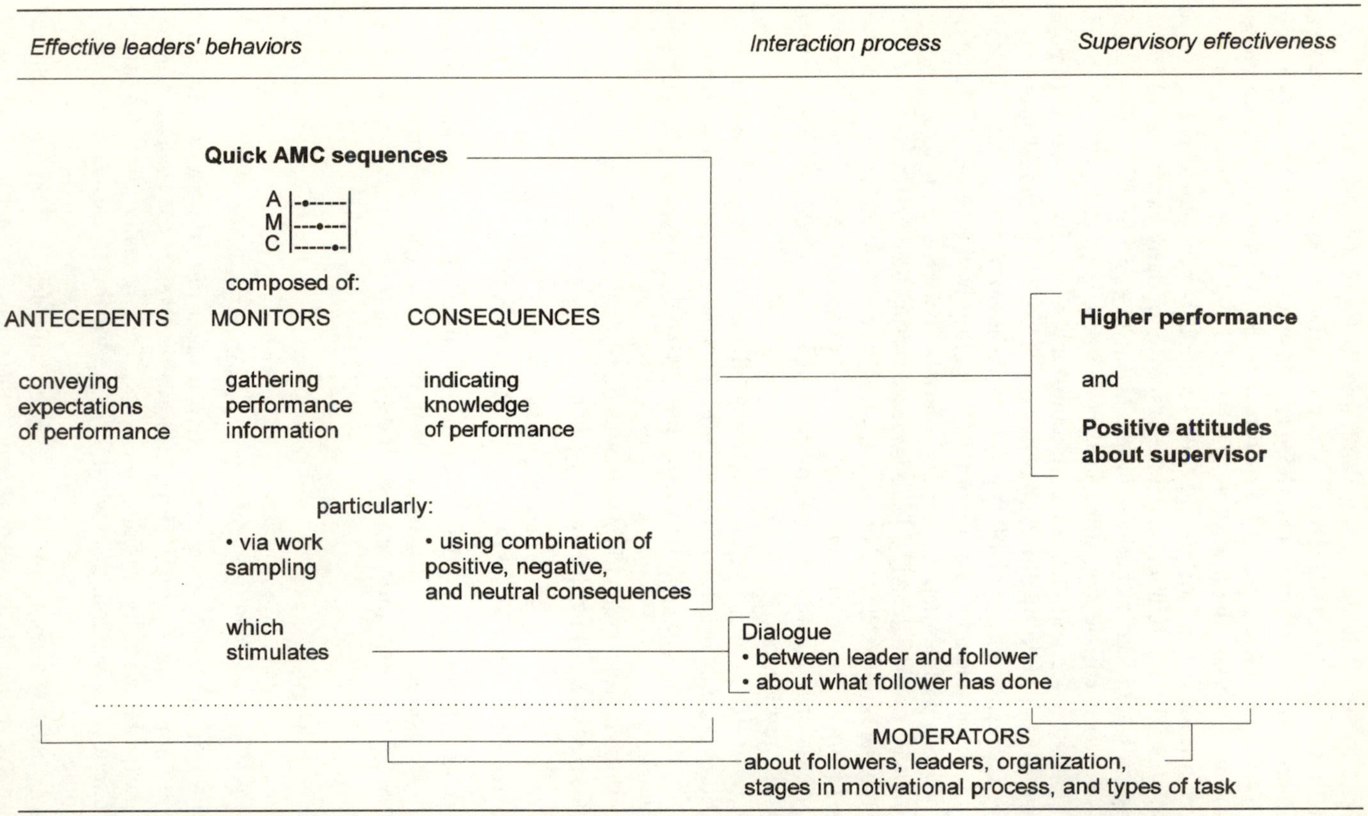

Effective leaders' behaviors | *Interaction process* | *Supervisory effectiveness*

Quick AMC sequences

A
M
C

composed of:

ANTECEDENTS   MONITORS   CONSEQUENCES

conveying expectations of performance

gathering performance information

indicating knowledge of performance

particularly:

- using combination of positive, negative, and neutral consequences

- via work sampling

which stimulates

Dialogue
- between leader and follower
- about what follower has done

Higher performance

and

Positive attitudes about supervisor

MODERATORS

about followers, leaders, organization, stages in motivational process, and types of task

Figure 2.1 Components of the operant model of effective supervision

and regularly on what followers have done. Effective leaders do not flinch from problems or shun negative consequences but look their followers in the eye and let them know what they're doing right and what they're doing wrong. And they do this regularly, distributing consequences more or less evenly among positive, negative, and neutral ones.

Defined temporally

Not only are the quantity and quality of these two supervisory behaviors critical, but their timing adds significantly to effectiveness, as we are finding in an exciting, still unfolding set of discoveries.

Effective leaders provide monitors and consequences in a particular sequence, with monitors routinely preceding consequences in what we refer to as an AMC sequence, where "A" stands for an antecedent (an order or instruction), "M" for a monitor, and "C" for a consequence. Furthermore, the exemplary leaders deliver these AMC sequences more quickly than their sluggish, less effective counterparts.

An effective leader's sequence might look like this:

```
A |-●-----|
M |----●--|
C |------●|
```

Like a musical score, the progression from left to right denotes time. The "notes" (●) are A, M, and C. On such a score, this particular leader delivered an A, then in the next interval immediately gave an M, followed in rapid succession by a C. The single vertical line represents the beginning of the AMC sequence, and the single vertical line after the C indicates the end.

In contrast, the not-so-effective leaders take considerably more time to complete an AMC sequence, as shown below:

```
A |-●--o--o--------------o-----------|
M |--------------------------●-----|
C |----------------------------------●|
```

This sluggish leader first delivers three antecedents[2] in a row, then does some other things (not yet portrayed on this score), and after considerably more time, delivers a monitor, followed by a consequence. In comparison with the first sequence, this lackluster leader takes four times as long to complete an AMC sequence.

These rapid AMC sequences clearly lead, as shown in Figure 2.1, to greater supervisory effectiveness. Although Figure 2.1, being only an initial overview, does not show the quality or timing of each of these behaviors, it does identify the salient dimensions of the supervisory behaviors, and it graphically shows that it matters *how* and *when* monitors and consequences are delivered.[3]

Supervisory effectiveness

To be considered effective in our model, leaders must have followers who perform acceptably *and* who have positive attitudes about their supervision. Both are required. The attitudes of subordinates are as important in our model as the performance itself. They are complementary components. Consider the situation in which followers produce at an optimal level, but intensely dislike their boss. Or consider the office in which employees are blissfully happy, yet are performing shoddy work. Neither situation would be acceptable, nor indicative of effective supervision.[4]

Interaction process

The interaction process, situated in Figure 2.1 between leaders' behaviors and their effectiveness, is the pattern of exchanges that occur when followers and leaders talk with one another. The patterns that augur well for effectiveness are those in which there is an easy, frequent, and lively give-and-take, a dialogue, between followers and leaders. Not just any exchange will do. The substance of the conversation makes a difference. The most fruitful exchange is one that is relevant to the task, in which both parties discuss what each will do to get the job done. We call this, in our model, a "performance-related discussion." It differs from a conversation limited to the technical details of work, referred to in our model as a "work-related discussion." A work-related discussion might focus on the designs of manhole covers rather than on the performance-related issue of whether the project team should make a bid to redesign the covers.

In another intriguing discovery, we found a link between performance-related discussions and one particular behavior of the leader: monitoring, as shown in Figure 2.1. Monitoring by the leader stimulates conversation about performance. When the leader monitors, the follower talks about his or her own performance, which, in turn, sets the stage for more discussion about performance. A reciprocal interaction occurs between the leader and the follower, with each influencing the other.[5]

Moderators

We do not assume that our model is universal, or that it will work well for all leaders and followers under all conditions. Instead, we acknowledge the influence of five *moderators*, that is, variables that change or moderate the relationship between supervisory behavior and effectiveness.

The model's moderators pertain to: (a) the characteristics of the followers, (b) the characteristics of the leaders, (c) the resources of the organization, (d) the stage of the motivational process, and (e) the type of task.

In order for the model to work, certain assumptions are made about each of the moderators. Only if the leaders and the followers possess these particular characteristics will the model operate as described in Figure 2.1. If an actor cannot remember his lines, for example, no amount of monitoring or consequences on the part of the director will result in a laudatory production. Similarly, only if the proper resources, task, and motivational stage are present will the model hold.[6]

IN SUMMARY

In this bare-bones sketch of our model, we can see its four components – leaders' behaviors, the interaction process, supervisory effectiveness, and the moderators. An observed set of supervisory behaviors, including what, how, and when the behaviors are delivered, determine effectiveness. At least one of these supervisory behaviors, monitoring, sets into motion a dialogue between the leader and the follower about performance, which in turn influences effectiveness. Moderators, on the other hand, limit what the model can and cannot do. Or, to summarize, the *sequences of antecedents, monitors and consequences*, when carried out judiciously and in a timely way, promote *supervisory effectiveness*, which is, in turn, enhanced by *the interaction process* and limited by *moderators*.

By seeing how supervisory effectiveness is limited by the moderators and enhanced by certain behaviors, sequences, and interactions, we can see that all the elements of our model interact in a complex way, challenging many of the old assumptions about how leadership works. With this bird's-eye view, we can also better glimpse what needs to be done to further our original aim: helping to make work places better places.

3 Defining and measuring what leaders do

We know more about the motives, habits, and most intimate arcana of the primitive peoples of New Guinea or elsewhere, than we do of the denizens of executive suites.

(Lewis & Stewart, 1958, p. 17)

Almost forty years later, Lewis and Stewart's description still rings true.[1] Compared with what we frequently hear or read about seemingly exotic parts of the world, we know relatively little about the occupants of corner offices. Investigators have built entire careers upon the tracking of the mammals of the Great Lakes (Burt, 1957), and even the lowly shell-breeding fish (Haussknecht & Kuenzer, 1990). Rarely, if ever, have managers been intensively and repeatedly observed in their own milieu.

ESCHEWING PAPER-AND-PENCIL MEASURES

One reason for the lack of comparable information is the very way in which data are traditionally obtained about leaders. The most common method is to have leaders and/or their followers fill out a questionnaire (e.g., Dowell & Wexley, 1978: Hemphill, 1959; Prien, 1963; Tornow & Pinto, 1976). To assess the amount of structure leaders provided in the Ohio State studies, for example, followers were asked to think about how frequently the leader engaged in certain behaviors – such as "He lets group members know what is expected of them" or "He is friendly and approachable" – and then to decide whether the described behavior happened (a) always, (b) often, (c) occasionally, (d) seldom, or (e) never (Fleishman, 1973).

Questions of accuracy

Increasingly, these questionnaires and self-report measures have been called into question (Borman, 1991; Campbell, 1977; Luthans, 1979; Rush, Thomas, & Lord, 1977; Sims & Manz, 1984). Skepticism exists about whether individuals' recollections and perceptions of what they do correspond with what they actually do (Burns, 1954; Horne & Lupton, 1965; Lewis & Dahl, 1976). Mintzberg (1973), for instance, cautions that "the interview and questionnaire methods should be recognized as useful only in the study of managers' perceptions of their own jobs" (p. 222).

Superiority of sampling behaviors

A search of the literature revealed four studies that explicitly compare self-reports and direct samples. Samplings were done in two of the studies by independent observers; in the other two studies, the managers themselves periodically recorded their own data. All four studies consistently showed differences between direct samples and self-reports. In one study, in which four naturally-occurring groups were observed, there was "never more than a 50 percent concordance between the clique structure produced by people's recall of their interaction, and that produced by their interaction" (Bernard, Killworth, & Sailer, 1979/80, p. 206). In another study, the subjects who had been observed interacting tended in their self-reports to discount interactions with persons with "whom they were relatively low- frequency co-interactants, in favor of those with whom they were reciprocally high" (Hammer, 1985).

Similar results occurred when comparisons were made between managers periodically (as often as thirty times a day over a five-week period) recording the data themselves and managers estimating what they had done (Burns, 1954; Lewis & Dahl, 1976). Substantial discrepancies were found between what managers themselves had recorded and what they estimated. Further, such disagreements were not necessarily random. One study found that managers substantially overestimated some activities (e.g., the time spent on production) and underestimated others (e.g., personnel) (Burns, 1954).

These discrepancies coincide with our own experience with the Operant Supervisory Taxonomy and Index (OSTI). When asked, managers we observed typically overestimated the amount of time they spent monitoring and providing consequences, while underestimating how much time they spent alone. Based on the lack of correspondence between observers' accounts and subjects' estimates, Hammer (1985) concluded that relying on self-reports was "sufficient to make any deductions about dyadic communication ... totally valueless" (p. 207). While managers' self-reports of their actions may shed light on their perceptions of their actions, they are not recommended as an accurate measure of what they are actually doing.

Capturing none of the silences or the sound and fury

Few disagree that problems exist with relying on self-reports. The major (and usually only) problem mentioned, however, is that of accuracy. Following a comprehensive review, Borman (1991) acknowledges the "illuminating ... ideas" about how I/O psychologists assess performance but he faults "their ability to provide accurate reports of performance" (p. 317).

While we, too, challenge the veracity of self-reports, we suggest it is not the only problem. Even if we could eliminate distortions, we would still have only dry confirmation that the behavior occurs "often" or "occasionally". A musical analogy sheds light on the point. Pianist Keith Jarrett's *The Köln Concert* was once described as "unfold(ing) at a leisurely, at times almost somnolent pace, but it burns with passion none the less, and has a clear organic logic" (Carr, 1992, p. 72). Rather than relying on a second-hand description, with all of its omissions of essence, we would recommend that you simply hear this extraordinary jazz pianist.

GETTING TO KNOW LEADERS ON THEIR OWN TERMS

Observing leaders in action

Recognizing the problems with the prevailing paper-and-pencil measures, leadership scholars have suggested alternative data collection techniques in which leaders are actually observed (McCall, Morrison, & Hannan, 1978; Martinko & Gardner, 1985; Schneier & Beatty, 1978).

Other researchers, generally viewed as qualitative rather than quantitative, also recommend direct observation (Barley, 1990; Hammer & Currall, 1989). Their reason is the nature of the information that can be obtained in this way. Patton (1980), for example, eschews second-hand techniques because he wouldn't "get close enough to the people and situation to be able to understand the depth and details of what goes on" (p. 36). Lofland (1971) also rejects knowing about someone through a second party, saying, "knowing about is not enough" (pp.1–2). Instead, he recommends that we learn what other people are about, and what their lives are like, through "direct, face-to-face association" (p. 1).

Push for direct quotations

Despite our best intentions, however, it is never possible to know every person directly. Does any reasonable substitute exist? Lofland (1971) reluctantly suggests a middle road, but at a high price. If we agree to learn about leaders through a second party, he says, there must be four stipulations. First, the observers should be close to the people they observe, watching them over an extended period of time and in a variety of circumstances, attuned to what Lofland calls "the minutiae of daily life" (p. 3). Second, the description should be "truthful," describing what the observer believes to occur, or, better yet, can actually verify. Third, the report should be rife with descriptions. Fourth, the report should contain direct quotations from the parties being observed. Declares Lofland, "No substitute for face-to-faceness can become reasonable unless it allows the participants themselves to speak – unless it allows their world to be represented precisely in its own terms. The commitment to get close, to be factual, descriptive, and quotive, constitutes a significant commitment to represent the participants *in their own terms*" (p. 4).

John Campbell (1977), an I/O psychologist, concurs with such qualitative researchers, calling for more descriptive studies after reviewing the leadership literature. He goes a step further, however, recommending that we pay equally close attention to that other party in the interaction, the follower. He concludes by suggesting

> more descriptive studies that attempt to develop reasonable taxonomies of what leaders and followers actually do when they interact, not more correlations among self-report questionnaires . . . [in spite of the fact that these strategies] will be somewhat more expensive, much more difficult, and considerably more demanding of research creativity. (p. 234)

Glimpsing the richness

Whether or not directly observing the follower and leader is more "creative" was, to us, uncertain. What we did know was that we needed, in our research, to let followers' and leaders' own words and actions convey how, what, and when they communicated. We present some of this first-hand evidence to you in this book. We also learned that when we actually did this – watching leaders and followers over an extended period of time, verifying our version of what transpired, describing and coding what the leaders and followers said and did, and quoting them verbatim – we found a deep richness and diversity in the manner in which people expressed themselves. Never could we have imagined all of the ways that a single expression can be used.

Led to confronting diversity of expression

A poignant illustration of this striking variety of expression is a problem we had while teaching others to code. Coders have to learn to classify what leaders say and do into various categories and subcategories such as positive, negative, or neutral consequences. Coders can watch leaders in action; they can also read what managers write to their workers. Particular problems occurred when coding "smiley faces". These faces or "emoticons",:-) set into type and rotated clockwise 90 degrees, were interspersed in the e-mail messages exchanged among managers in a computer center (Komaki & Newlin, 1990). At first, many of the coders made the natural error of coding each smiley face as a positive consequence. This was appropriate when it was used to express pleasure in someone's performance:

- "It will be the highlight of my otherwise drab existence :-)."

However, it was not appropriate when the smiley faces were used whimsically as in the following statements:

- "Must have been an interesting visit...:-)"
- "In our youth :-) we simply copied all the staff accounts to a new machine."

But disagreements during reliability checks forced the coders to acknowledge that any given smiley face or phrase did not always mean the same thing; the context was critical. After beating the coders gently around the head and shoulders :-), we were eventually able to help them to recognize the subtle distinctions in the ways that smiley faces were used. And their reliability scores soared.

Necessitated disclosure of meaning of each concept

Trying to get coders to code these e-mail messages reliably revealed to us the subtle complexities of a concept such as a consequence. Unlike surveyors who use questionnaires with succinctly-worded items such as "He is friendly and approachable," or laboratory experimenters who construct their world to conform to their definitions of "friendly" or "contingent consequences," we did not have the luxury of controlling input. By choosing to watch people as they lived their lives, over time, in a variety of situations, we had to take whatever they said and code it. To do this necessitated the disclosure of the meaning of each concept.

To aid in forming concept

To help clarify what we meant, we turned to concept formation scholars (Becker, 1974; Markle & Tiemann, 1970), who recommend presenting:
(a) *examples* of the concept or construct, and
(b) *non-examples*: any test case that does not possess the essential characteristics of the concept.
These examples and non-examples can be used in describing the concept, and also to test for an understanding of the concept.

Next, they tell us, rationale should be presented to help to distinguish between examples and non-examples. The rationale consist of identifying:
(c) the *critical or essential attribute(s)*: A property of every example of the concept. If it is removed, the example becomes a non-example.
(d) the *irrelevant or optional attribute(s)*: A property of any particular example which can be varied without changing the example to a non-example.

For example, to teach someone the concept of a familiar piece of furniture, a "chair", they suggest showing the trainee examples (a rocker, a swivel office chair with wheels, and a kitchen chair with three legs) and non-examples (a sofa, a kitchen stool with three legs, and an ottoman). To help the trainee make the distinction between examples and non-examples, the critical attributes – in this case, having a back and a single seat – are presented. These critical or required features of chairs are in contrast to irrelevant or optional features such as the number of legs the chair has or whether or not it rocks. While the concept of a chair is fairly straightforward, this same process is even more critical when the concept is more complex. A similar process was used to explain to coders why a smiley face should be coded as a consequence in one case and not in another.

To enhance construct validity

This same process was used to ward off "fuzzy" concepts, those ill-defined ideas noted by many observers of the research process. In their discussion of construct validity, for example, Cook and Campbell (1979), in their classic research text, specifically cite the many problems that occur because of the "inadequate preoperational explication of constructs" (p. 64). In fact, they recommend, but do not specify, that each concept (or construct) be subject to the very process that concept formation scholars have put forward.

Because the ability to recognize the many, subtle, and understated ways that leaders provide monitors and consequences is critical to a full understanding of the model, we have listed the (a) *critical* and (b) *optional* or irrelevant features of each concept, and provided numerous (c) *examples* and (d) *non-examples*. We also use written descriptions of leaders in action, along with streams of actual conversation, as practice and test cases. Our hope is that by presenting concepts in line with these recommendations, we will help leaders to discern the presence and absence of these concepts in work settings, and to incorporate them into their own ways of interacting on the job. We begin with the concept of monitoring.

DEFINING SUPERVISORY BEHAVIORS

Monitoring

Monitoring is a cornerstone of the model of effective supervision. In the leadership literature, it has not been singled out as a critical event in the life of a top-notch manager, the major exceptions being Hackman and Walton's (1986) model of task-performing groups. Instead, it is typically one of many categories used to describe what managers do (Fairhurst, Rogers, & Sarr, 1987; Mintzberg, 1975; Tornow and Pinto, 1976). Monitoring is one of eleven categories of managerial behavior in an integrating taxonomy developed by Yukl (1994), and one of twelve categories on an observational code created to describe managers by Luthans and his colleagues (1985).

Examples of different methods of monitoring

Monitoring can be carried out using at least four different methods: (a) work sampling, (b) self-report, (c) secondary source, and (d) consulting archival records.[2] We differentiated these methods, as we discuss in Chapters 4 and 8, because we believed that one of them, work sampling, would be superior to the others.

Work sampling

One vivid example of monitoring via work sampling is the behavior of observing players in action that sports managers and coaches, such as "Red" Auerbach of the Boston Celtics basketball team, do. As they stand on the sidelines observing such players as Bill Walton and Larry Bird pass and shoot in the clutch, they are monitoring by literally sampling work.

Leaders can sample in arenas beyond the basketball court. They can go to the claims processing area and watch two staff members work out an error at the computer as managers did in an insurance firm (Komaki, 1986). The same applies to a project director who attends her subordinate's staff meeting, or a wire manufacturing supervisor who oversees workers on the shop floor, or a poultry processing manager who goes to watch newly-hired employees eviscerating chickens. All would be considered to be monitoring via work sampling.

In cases in which the "work product" is vocal or verbal, the work sampling can be done by listening. Choir directors and conductors do this. A director in charge of a spring musical was coded as sampling the work when he closed his eyes and listened intently to the orchestra playing during rehearsals (Komaki, Zlotnick, and Jensen, 1986). Managers who sit in their offices with their phones programmed to hear personnel talk with clients, and airline supervisors who listen in on reservation clerks' conversations with customers, are monitoring in their own ways.

Leaders can also inspect the actual work products themselves – sorting through bundles of envelopes ready for mailing, proofreading a memo a secretary has just typed, comparing data sheets to the entries a research assistant has entered. In virtually any case that leaders obtain information by perusing what followers have done or are doing, they are considered to be monitoring via work sampling.

Self-report

Another way of gathering information about performance, referred to as monitoring via self-report, is to simply ask. The specific object of the inquiry may change, but the intention of the leader to find out what is happening does not. Leaders may ask:

- "Are we all ready for Wednesday's meeting, as far as you know?"
- "Are you ready for your count? Or did you do your count?"
- "So, did you go through some of the accounts stuff?"

- "Yes, I have a question for you. Have you put anything in the status file that's not a valid code?"

In each case, the person being asked is responsible for performing the task. The leader can direct her question:

- (To the trainee): "You know what to do?"
- (To the editor): "Did you proofread those others?"
- (To the operator): "Did you release that other batch?"
- (To the personnel assistant): "Have you finished the vacation schedule yet?"

The very act of asking counts as monitoring. But listening to the answer also counts. Hence, the construction supervisor who asks the worker: "Did you put those materials away?" (Table 3.1), and then listens to the worker's reply is considered to be monitoring.

Secondary source

Monitoring via self-report and secondary source are the same in that both involve asking about performance. When someone other than the person responsible is asked, however, it is considered monitoring via a secondary source. Sometimes the party is named:

- "Tom, what is she working on?"
- "Did he find them, Michelle?"
- "Has Anelli inputted the receipt data yet?" (Table 3.1)

At other times, the secondary source is inferred:

- "Did she just give you the codes to enter?"
- "Are they still having a problem back there?"

The same also holds true with listening to the answer. The theater director may ask the stage manager: "And the kids seem to be working out?" (Table 3.1). When the director waits and then listens to the answer, it counts as monitoring via a secondary source.

For more examples of monitoring, done by managers in four different settings, refer to Table 3.1. Refer also to Komaki (1986).

Seeing monitoring in action: food processing supervisor

An example of a supervisor actually monitoring (and providing consequences) in a natural way on an every day basis is described in a *Harvard Business Review* article by Gellerman (1976). He was asked to analyze the jobs of some of the first-line supervisors in the packaging plant of a food processing company. The excerpts in Table 3.2a are taken from his diary at the beginning of the supervisor's shift. We have inserted numbers in the text for reasons that will become apparent.

Table 3.1 Definitions and examples of categories and subcategories on the OSTI

Category/ subcategory	Definitions	Examples from Finland[a]		Examples from United States[b]	
		Construction supervisors	*Government managers*	*Theater directors*	*Sailboat skippers*
PERFORMANCE MONITORING: Collects information about a follower's performance					
Method					
a Work sampling	Direct observation of follower at work	Watching a worker lay tiles.	Standing by computer and watching while follower works.	Watching actors rehearse.	Watching crew boss adjust topping lift (topper).
b Product sampling	Inspection of subordinate's work product	Examining the quality of painting on the walls.	Scanning follower's card index of debtors.	Watching for lighting effect as filter is adjusted.	Looking toward front of boat at chute being hoisted.
c Self-report	Gathering information directly from subordinate	"Did you put those materials away?"	"How many tax rebate cards do you have?"	"You're planning to use the wood stain you showed me?"	"Is the topper up, is the topper up?"
d Secondary source	Gathering information from someone else about follower	"Did Martti tell you to put materials away yesterday?"	"Has Anelli inputted the receipt data yet?"	"And the kids seem to be working out?"	"Why does he have to trim the guy?"
PERFORMANCE CONSEQUENCES: Communicates an evaluation of or indicates knowledge of another's performance, where the indication can range from highly evaluative to neutral					
Delivery					
a Direct	Delivered to the follower	"You have done good work: no signs of errors!"	"You don't have to explain. This is quite all right."	"You've pleated so successfully the curtains don't meet."	"Come on, John, we need you to take more of a racing attitude up there."
b Indirect	Delivered to the follower about someone else.	"He has worked with care: tiles are put so straight!"	[c]	"So each guy that came in was better than the last."	"They're not gonna get their chute up either."

Evaluation

a Positive	Expresses favorable evaluation or approval of follower's work	"Great, you have done it so quickly."	"You did this well."	"Right – great – and I think that's in the lines; you accomplished that."	"Yes, yes, yes. It's a good day for Mercury."
b Negative	Conveys disapproval or doubt about a follower's work	"Oh, no! All the wrong tiles! You ought to take the blue ones to this room."	"You have made these minutes incorrectly."	"Well, I noticed that the focus was on the bedroom and I thought it was too much."	"There's too much halyard. There's no air."
c Neutral	Expresses neither approval nor disapproval of a subordinate's work	"He made a call yesterday for those materials."	"You have over 300 open cases."	"That's going along with the idea that the clothes will be real."	"Okay, you almost got it."

PERFORMANCE ANTECEDENT: Instructs, reminds, or conveys an expectation of performance

Delivery

a Direct	Delivered to the follower for him/herself	"Please go to help Liisa now!"	"Look up his balance. Do it on this pattern."	"I want rehearsal to start on time, so if you're supposed to be here, be here."	"Ready about."
b Indirect	Delivered to the follower for another	"Tell Ari to clean the room."	"Tell her that she should read those papers."	"Peter, tell John to spray that spot down a bit."	"Jim, make sure he understands (because we gotta jibe like now, guys.)"

Planning

a Current	Concerns the ongoing task	"Please put the tiles this way here."	"Go to department six and ask Maija."	"No, I mean, but we're going to let the music run some with house up and then we'll go house to half."	"Grind, grind, grind."

	Construction supervisors	Government managers	Theater directors	Sailboat skippers
b Anticipated — Concerns a future problem or task	"Come tomorrow into my office to talk about your next duties."	"This regulation comes into force some day in the future."	"Make sure you show Peter how you're arranging your homes so he can set it up for you before each performance."	"Okay guys, what's gonna happen is we're gonna put the jib up, the pole up, flip the pole."
Responsibility				
a Obvious — The person responsible for performing the task is identified	"You, Ari, please lift that sack with Pentti."	"You must get Hannu's signature here."	"Willy, will you do your magic?"	"You gotta ease the traveler down, Len."
b Not obvious — The person responsible is not specifically identified	"The railing should be put here next week."	"It would be better, if they were returned from our department."	"Listen, guys, we gotta push Wednesday night; Thursday night is okay."	"Somebody on the boom please."
OWN PERFORMANCE: Refers to leader's own performance				
Content				
a Consequence — Indicates knowledge of own performance	"I made a mistake when buying too many paint pots here."	"Do you see that, there I made a mistake."	"I did have the opportunity to tell her what it did – it's a failure of communications on my part."	"What? I did. Yeah, yeah. Well, I made 'em tack."
b Monitor — Gathers information about manager's own performance	"Did I estimate the time you need to do this correctly?"	"Do you see any mistakes in this minute?"	"Could you do this? Would you go through and check my work?"	"How am I doing on the mark there?"
c Antecedent — Conveys expectation of own performance	"I shall go to phone the customer, would he like to have those dark wallpapers also in the baby's room?"	"I have to call registry."	"Well, I have to leave now, I have to go to a reading session."	"I'm gonna go across."

WORK RELATED: Refers to work issues but not to worker performance

Type				
a Invited	Solicits a response other than yes or no	"What do you think about our new customer office building?"	"How did that swindler know to call us?"	"But who do you think we should have on headset besides you?"	"Why not? How many halyards do you have?"
b Not invited	Requires no response beyond yes or no, if any	"Are you going to look at it?"	"The bank said that the financing is okay."	"He deals with you! He deserves ten comps (complimentary tickets)!"	"We're doing a jibe set anyway."
NON-WORK-RELATED	Does not refer to work issues	"What do you think about our Prime Minister and his latest comments in the Helsingin Sanomat?"	"Have you been abroad?"	"Things like the no-no stuff will have more fat."	"He made a hundred dollars, he said it so nonchalant."
NOT COMMUNI-CATING	Interacts but does not say anything	Hearing opinions about the Prime Minister.	On the periphery of a group discussing the taxpayer's financing.	Pausing while stage manager decides about comps.	Hearing tactician talk about wind shifts during start of the race.
SOLITARY	Does not interact with others	Walking around the site from point A to point B.	Doing paperwork at desk.	Eating lunch while waiting for sound designer to cue up tape.	Sitting at tiller watching the other boats in race.

Note: OSTI = Operant Supervisory Taxonomy and Index

[a] *Source:* Komaki, Hyttinen, and Immonen (1991); Studies 5a and 5b

[b] *Source:* Komaki, Urschel, Lee, Reynard, Julien, and Fass (1993); Studies 12, and 14, respectively

[c] None were recorded

Table 3.2a Transcript of supervisor Charlie

Number	Statement/action
1	Charlie moved down the line, quickly checking each machine visually. He also paused briefly to tell each worker how the department as a whole had performed the night before. "Good running last night," he would say, "five hundred thirty-seven cases." Then he would grin and thrust out his hand for a quick congratulatory shake, and move on (p. 90).
2	Charlie patrolled continually up and down the line. He was not waiting until trouble began.... He checked moisture levels in the ingredient trays and pressure levels in the feed lines (p. 90).
3	From time to time, Charlie paused briefly at the "scope", a video display unit that could be operated from a small console near his desk.... With the scope, a supervisor can determine whether defects too subtle for the human eye have begun to develop.... "That thing is kind of spooky", he confided, "but I wouldn't want to run these high-speed babies without it."
4	Charlie was no conversationalist. His contacts were brief, almost laconic. But they were also easy, with a touch of banter. For example, he seemed to have a standing joke with one operator.... She "wouldn't permit him" to inspect more than one pack at a time; otherwise she threatened to "slap his hand." Naturally, he pretended to grab at a second pack and she pretended to slap. Then they both giggled and he said that he was really only making sure that "she... [was] still on the ball", (pp. 90–91).
5	Gellerman summarizes Charlie's behavior by noting his "frequent checking, and his repeated demonstrations that he expects his people to follow correct procedures" (p. 92).

Note: The events have been separated and numbered to indicate the order in which they happened.
Source: Gellerman (1976, pp. 90–92). Copyright © 1976 by the President and Fellows of Harvard College. Reproduced by permission of *Harvard Business Review*.

An example

In the terminology of the model, Charlie *monitored* when he inspected the packs of the operator, grabbing one and taking a quick look at it (4 in Table 3.2a). This action met the two critical attributes of performance monitoring. First, Charlie was in an *inquiry* mode. He did not know if the pack would be prepared correctly; he was looking to find out. Second, the focus of his inquiry was to find out about the *performance* of the *operator*. Preparing the packs correctly met the definition of "performance" because the operator could be held *responsible*. Moreover, there would be adverse organizational consequences for performance deficiencies or excesses. Supervisor Charlie would say or do something when the packs were not prepared in the right way.

A non-example

Was Charlie monitoring performance when he looked at the "scope" (3)? Probably not. He was gathering information, but about the machines, *not about the operators.* Furthermore, he as supervisor was responsible for checking the scope to see if defects occurred in "these high-speed babies" (3).

Was Charlie monitoring when he "checked moisture levels in the ingredient trays and pressure levels in the feed lines" (2)? Again, probably not. Only when he gathered information about performance, in this case, the operators', was he considered to be monitoring performance. Hence, when Gellerman (1976) describes Charlie's "frequent checking" (5), the checking does not always refer to monitoring performance. Charlie sometimes checked on pressure levels in the feed lines. Distinguishing between examples and non-examples of performance is among the most difficult discriminations to make in our model, but it is critical to a full understanding of supervisory effectiveness. Hence, we will continue to provide such cases as these to help clarify this important distinction.

Critical attributes

The rationale behind these examples of monitoring is that they include two essential characteristics:

Seeking to obtain information. One of the critical attributes of leaders' monitoring is the gathering of information. The leader does not yet know, so she probes, she inquires, she gathers information about followers, groups, or the organization.

Only information concerned with performance. The second critical attribute of monitoring is that the information being sought must be of a particular variety. It must be about "performance", that is, something the person is responsible for and for which there would be adverse consequences from the boss if it were not done properly.

Irrelevant attributes of monitoring

Monitoring has four characteristics that are considered to be nonessential. In other words, changing them does not alter the fact that the behavior is a monitor.

Monitoring can be verbal or nonverbal. Leaders can ask or they can monitor without saying a word. Work sampling, for instance, is typically nonverbal. Supervisor Charlie would sometimes inspect the packs of the operators without saying much at all. A comptroller can look silently at budget sheets. A Marine Corps Warrant Officer can glance at the mechanics as he leaves for a meeting without saying anything, or the Officer can ask: "How's it going?" It does not matter whether monitoring takes place verbally or nonverbally.

Followers do not necessarily have to be present or aware of the occurrence of monitoring. Monitoring in person has distinct advantages (in that it enables interaction between leader and follower which we will discuss later), but is not necessary in order for monitoring to take place. When "Red" Auerbach watches from the sidelines, the players know he is there. But he could also monitor without followers knowing their work is being inspected, perhaps by looking over the team's statistics. Supervisor Charlie can tally the success of a shift before or after the workers have gone home. The follower's awareness, or lack thereof, is irrelevant to whether or not monitoring has occurred.[3]

Subordinates need not have an opportunity to interact while monitoring takes place. Another irrelevant characteristic of monitoring is whether or not followers have an opportunity to interact. Supervisor Charlie, for example, could track down a human error through an operator's statement or by studying daily performance logs. The crew boss can check the shape of a sail to see how the crew are making adjustments without the crew being able to take time out during the race to discuss their performance. While we believe there are distinct advantages to having personal exchanges while monitoring, it is not critical to the definition of monitoring.

Leaders do not have to look as if they are monitoring. Leaders do not have to sniff for trouble, scrutinizing everything in sight. They can merely be in the vicinity, which allows them to perceive, however casually, what is going on. Supervisor Charlie did this often. Knowing the monotony of a good run, when the machines drone on and the packages drop uneventfully into the loading troughs, Charlie was known to make "visits" (Gellerman, 1976, p. 91), in which he would stop briefly to say a word or two to each operator, sometimes even encouraging "gentle ribbing and harmless jokes at his expense" (p. 91). Although he did not necessarily closely scrutinize their work, he had the opportunity to do so by virtue of his proximity; he would therefore be considered to be monitoring the operators' performance.

In short, performance monitoring is defined by two critical characteristics: (1) the *collection or gathering of information* (2) *about performance*. Other features can vary. Monitoring can have a number of variations: (a) The way in which it is delivered: it can be verbal or nonverbal, and it can be done via different methods, via work sampling, self-report, or secondary source, or by consulting archival records. (b) The awareness of its occurrence: subordinates may or may not be aware of the manager's monitoring. (c) The opportunity to interact while it is ongoing: followers may or may not have an opportunity to interact with the leader while the leader monitors. (d) The intent to monitor: leaders may or may not look as if they are scrutinizing people's work. Yet, in all of these circumstances, the action would be considered to be monitoring.

Performance consequences

Performance consequences, a well-established concept in the psychological literature, comprises an integral part of the model of effective supervision.

Expanding definition to include neutral consequences

Precedents have long existed for identifying consequences in applied settings. These investigators conceptualized them, however, only in terms of
their evaluative nature – as either positive or negative. Defining consequences as either *approving* or *disapproving*, for example, operant conditioners observed teachers and classified their behaviors (Cobb & Ray,
1976). When observing managers at work, Luthans, Rosenkrantz, and
Hennessey (1985) defined consequences as either *motivating/reinforcing*
events or as *disciplining/punishing* ones.

As we observed leaders, however, we ended up questioning whether a
reinforcing/punishing dichotomy would fully encompass the breadth of
consequences we had found. Some consequences were clearly positive or
negative. A stage director, thrilled that the stage manager had been able to
locate a "nonexistent" piece of equipment at the last minute, exclaimed, "In
the great record book in the sky, you deserve a gold star." The boss of the
training director mentioned in Chapter 1, after sitting through the screening
of a film he evidently hated, raged, "I wouldn't pay $500.00 for that piece of
crap!" Such visceral reactions left no room for doubt.

Other consequences, however, were more much subtle. Many leaders,
even if they felt as strongly as those above, did not express their feelings
as directly. Instead they would refer obliquely to unmet expectations:
"Weren't you supposed to get that report to me last week?" or "Don't
you remember you promised to do that for me?" Comments such as these,
while in hindsight clearly constituting a consequence for performance or the
lack thereof, we initially overlooked.

A consequence of a different sort that we missed at first is exemplified by
the way in which supervisor Charlie responded to his workers' performance
when they did not quite meet his standards. Gellerman (1976) describes him
moving down the production line, shaking workers' hands. But there's a
catch:

> Charlie told me that his practice was to announce the previous night's
> results at the beginning of each shift. He shakes hands, however, only when
> 500 or more cases have been produced. Below that figure, he is likely to say
> something like, "It wasn't too bad, but we can do better." (p. 90)

We could easily classify as positive his hand-shaking and his comments:
"Good running last night. Five hundred thirty-seven cases." But if we
adhered strictly to a positive–negative classification, it was not immediately
clear where to place the comment: "It wasn't too bad, but we can do
better." The first part of the statement – almost reassuring workers for
trying – seemed too harsh to be simply categorized as a "disciplining or
punishing" event. But the withholding of the handshake was far short of a
congratulatory gesture. Comments and actions such as these were not
atypical in the everyday interactions we witnessed.

Table 3.2b   Transcript of supervisor Charlie continued

Number	Statement/action
6	An operator had reluctantly thrown the emergency switch, indicating the pneumatic feed had broken down. Charlie immediately reassured the somewhat ambivalent operator, saying: " 'Okay, you did the right thing' " (p. 91).
7	A young man from the labor pool had just arrived. **Charlie patiently showed him how to use a small metal scoop to hand-feed the machine** (p. 92).
8	Then he instructed the operator to start up again [A].
9	As Charlie checked to make sure that the machine was operating correctly, the maintenance crew arrived [S or NC].
10	Charlie told the crew chief what had happened [W],
11	and then **returned to the hand-feeder, making sure that the young man was properly timing his delivery of ingredients into the hopper.**
12	Before he left, he cautioned the young man: **" 'I know you'd rather watch what those maintenance boys are doing, but I want you to keep your eyes at this level-marker in the hopper.' "**
13	Gellerman asked Charlie why the pneumatic feed had failed. "He grinned and said it was a preventable defect: 'But when a supervisor is running well, he doesn't want to shut down his line for preventive maintenance. It was just my turn to get caught tonight' ".

Note: The events have been separated and numbered to indicate the order in which they happened. The events in bold are part of an Antecedent–Monitor–Consequence sequence. The OSTI categories are noted in brackets: A = Antecedent, M = Monitor, C = Consequence, NC = Not communicating, S = Solitary, W = Work-related.

Source: Gellerman (1976, pp. 90–92). Copyright © by the President and Fellows of Harvard College. Reproduced by permission of *Harvard Business Review*.

Another comment made by Charlie raises a different issue. Charlie immediately reassured the operator who had triggered the emergency switch, saying: "Okay, you did the right thing" (6 in Table 3.2b). Even though the statement is short, it would probably be clear that it should be coded as a positive consequence. But what if Charlie merely said "Okay," without the explanation?

Many leaders simply murmur "okay" or "hmn" to indicate that the follower acted appropriately – without further explanation. Sometimes an "okay" means simply that they saw what the person did. The Marine Corps warrant officer described in Chapter 1 would sometimes simply say "okay" or "hmn" when a mechanic explained his actions. Occasionally, the officer described what the mechanic had done: "So you've already tried that." Should these brief "hmns" and "okays" constitute consequences? Should the comment: "So you've already tried that." count? We thought so. Although these comments are not distinctly positive or negative, we believed that there should be room in the definition for remarks such as these.

Restricting ourselves to a definition categorizing only positive or negative consequences would leave out this middle ground and make it more likely that only the "squeaky wheel" would be heard. If we waited for such wheels, we would probably wait a long time and, more importantly, run the risk of overlooking these more subtle, understated consequences, which in two studies (Brewer, Wilson, & Beck, 1994; Goltz, 1993) were estimated to be roughly one-half of all consequences.

To capture these less evaluative consequences, we revised and expanded upon the working definition to include consequences that are neutral and informational in character. Hence, performance consequences are defined as communicating an evaluation of or indicating knowledge of another's performance, where the indication can range from highly evaluative to neutral.

Examples of consequences by sign

Because we had some hypotheses about different signs of consequences, we divided them into those that are positive, negative, and neutral.

Neutral

A prevalent neutral consequence, defined as expressing neither approval nor disapproval, was often an "okay" or "hmn" said with little or no intonation. A trainer, in checking his jockey's weight, might mutter without much expression, "Okay." An administrative judge would ask her clerk: "Have you finished the filing?" Following the clerk's answer, the judge might simply nod and say: "Hmn." In these cases, the short phrases would indicate that the leader saw what the person had done, but the evaluation, if any, would not be apparent.

Often, these neutral comments were uttered while sampling the work. When making his "visits", supervisor Charlie might simply say to one of the operators, "Hmn," and walk on. Another occasion in which they frequently occurred was during a discussion of the follower's performance. A horse farm owner might inquire, "How's it going?" to which a barn hand would reply "All right, I guess," and the owner would then say, "okay."

A small minority of neutral consequences contain a mixture of both positive and negative components, such as the crew boss saying to a crew member who had been improperly making an adjustment: "Okay, you almost got it" (Table 3.1, see p. 38). Others we have heard are:

- "You've pleated so successfully the curtains don't meet" (Table 3.1).
- "That's a different way to sort."
- "I guess it's okay to do it that way."

In all of these statements, the leader acknowledges that the person had done something – pleating, doing it that way. At the same time, there was also some questioning of the way in which it was done: pleating "so successfully the curtains don't meet."

Another set of neutral consequences that we often overlooked were those merely describing what the follower had done, with no indication from the intonation or the context as to whether the behavior mentioned is positive or negative:

- The insurance manager might say to the auditor: "I noticed you showed the 1008 in your report."
- The post office supervisor to a clerk: "You've got some bundles (of envelopes) there."
- The same PO supervisor to another clerk: "You're starting by sorting by the first digit."
- The priest to the deacon: "He changed his hours."
- The government manager to the worker: "You have over 300 open cases" (Table 3.1).

As one can see, a whole host of consequences that may have gone unheralded are considered neutral. By including neutral consequences, we gain the benefit of capturing these often overlooked statements, and we flesh out what we mean by the concept of a consequence.

Positive

Positive consequences are ones in which leaders express a favorable evaluation or approval of a person's performance. Sometimes they are understandable without much context:

- "You saved us from making a very big mistake."
- "Taking initiative. I like that."

In the heat of a competition, sailboat skippers were trying to perform a complex maneuver with a chute, a sail, that is notorious for billowing out of control as they jibe and change the direction of the boat. In Table 3.3 (p. 55), at 6:02.25, the leaders had just given several orders (called an antecedent [A]): "Trim that chute!!! You gotta come down. Coming down. Go ahead centerline." After successfully accomplishing part of the maneuver, one of the leaders cried, "Looks great, guys!" (a positive consequence).

Many positive consequences, however, are not as easily recognizable and require close attention to the context in which they occur. For example, after the costume designer had shown the director sketches of costumes that had undergone change after change, the director finally approved the last one with a terse "okay." However brief this "okay," the context indicated that the designer had finally gotten it right and could proceed. Hence, it was coded a positive consequence.

Once the context is taken into consideration, some consequences are unmistakable. After hearing that a much-desired sponsor had requested a formal proposal, for example, a project director gave her staff a thumbs-up sign with a big smile.

Many consequences occur as the leader is monitoring via work-sampling or self-report. A bank vice president (VP) says to the director of personnel after a lengthy discussion of the director's difficulties in getting on-line with a new system: "That's all right, it'll come." This comment indicates, however subtly, that the VP recognizes and approves of the personnel director's efforts.

Most consequences, even the positive ones, are relatively impersonal, referring primarily to the person's performance and not to the person. Comments such as the director's to the stage manager – "In the great record book in the sky, you deserve a gold star" – are rare. It is much more likely that the only reference will be made to the work. The disheveled plumber announces that "(Apartment) 3E's done," to which the building superintendent replies: "Oh, it's finished already?" Or supervisor Charlie comments to his workers: "Good running last night. Five hundred thirty-seven cases." In both of these cases, the reference is not to the person, but to the task.

Negative

Negative consequences are similar to positive ones in that they, too, are largely impersonal. They are also evaluative, but they convey disapproval or doubt about another's work or indicate work that has not been done. Some of them can be quite intense. During the sailboat race, the crew are busy trying to make the proper adjustments to the sail or chute. The crew boss (B) yells out (in Table 3.3 at 6:03.25): "Okay, go ahead and jibe." But then someone noticed something amiss, asking, "What's going on?" (a monitor). And the crew boss started calling for adjustments: *Come on guys. Come on.* Then, even louder: "HARD! Now. HARD!" This last exclamation conveyed disapproval with the way in which the crew was adjusting the chute, and, hence, was coded a negative consequence.

Not all negative consequences, even in such a pressure-packed setting, are as volatile. A minute or so prior to this exchange (6:02.00), the order, "Pull forward...pull it forward a bit" (an antecedent) was given. Then one of the leaders looked at the sail (a monitor), and when he found that the line needed more adjustment, he noted, "Now bring it back a little bit." This command is a negative consequence because it indicates disapproval with the way in which the crew had performed, but it is not a severe or angry judgment. It merely indicates that adjustments need to be made that only the leaders, from their vantage point, can see.

The vast majority of negative consequences given are about corrections that need to be made:

● (Following a work sample monitor, the officer says:) "It helps if you do it this way."

- (As the technical director walks through the shop:) "No, you've got the door upside down."
- (A note inserted in Chapter 1 to the author from her editor:) PROPER USE OF "HOWEVER" IS TO INSERT IT BETWEEN CLAUSES RATHER THAN AT THE BEGINNING OR ENDING OF THE SENTENCE.

In these examples, the leader notices something amiss and indicates it – calmly, without animosity – to the person responsible. Rarely, if ever, are the consequences personally destructive.

From our observations, most negative consequences, at least those delivered by working adults, are relatively impersonal and typically tame. They are also similar to positive and neutral consequences in that they often occur when leaders are asking about performance or sampling work.

Consequences delivered directly and indirectly

Because we believed that consequences delivered indirectly might affect supervisory effectiveness, we instituted a classification by delivery that included both direct and indirect consequences.

Directly

When consequences are delivered straightaway to a person about his or her own performance, they are classified as direct. An example of such a direct consequence is when the government manager says to one of his staff: "You don't have to explain. This is quite all right." (Table 3.1, p. 38).

Indirectly

When consequences are delivered to a third party about someone else, they are classified as indirect. Supervisor Charlie, for instance, provided several indirect consequences when he talked about his cleaning crew to a third party, in this case, the author of the article. As Gellerman and Charlie watched, the cleaning crew gave a machine a regular wipe-down, after which the machine's operator and his helpers swept immediately back into position at their work stations. Charlie then said to Gellerman, "See that? They went right back into production without waiting to be told. These are good people" (p. 93). Gellerman then suggested that the workers may have done this for Charlie's benefit, to which Charlie replied with another indirect consequence: "Hell, no. There's no way you can run 500 cases with a lazy crew. You couldn't on this floor, anyway" (p. 93).

Additional examples of direct and indirect, and positive, negative, and neutral consequences, are illustrated in Table 3.1. Refer also to Komaki, Zlotnick, and Jensen (1986).

Essential characteristics

Communicating knowledge or indicating evaluation

Performance consequences have two critical attributes. The first is that leaders must *transmit* their knowledge or evaluation. It is not sufficient to have an opinion secretly. When a vehicle maintenance supervisor collects safety information but tucks it away in his desk drawer, he is not considered to have delivered a consequence because he has not communicated the information to anyone. He must tell what he knows.

Only information concerned with performance

Consequences, like monitors, deal exclusively with a person's performance. For example, in the case of the smiley face e-mail messages, coders sometimes miscategorized them as positive consequences. This was, in fact, only true of smiley faces that referred to someone else's performance. For example, when the writer referred to receiving a manual the programmer had done, noting, "It will be the highlight of my otherwise drab existence :-)", it was a positive consequence because it indicated knowledge of the programmer's perform-ance – finishing the manual. If, however, the smiley face referred instead to a jar of chocolate fudge he had just received from his partner for Christmas, it would not be correct to code it as a consequence, positive or otherwise.

To be classified as a performance consequence, the ":-)" must refer to performance: something for which followers are considered to be account-able, or for which there would be adverse organizational consequences for performance deficiencies or excesses.

Irrelevant attributes of consequences

Consequences do not necessarily have to be either positive or negative

It is not necessary for a consequence to be evaluative; this is an irrelevant characteristic. Hence, neutral comments indicating knowledge of perform-ance are considered consequences.

Consequences do not necessarily have to be delivered directly

Consequences can be transmitted to a third party, as when supervisor Charlie told Gellerman how he felt about his workers. Leaders do not need to transmit their reactions directly to the person or people involved.

Consequences can be delivered without monitoring

It is not necessary for a consequence to be preceded by a monitor in order to be considered a consequence, although we have found, as we shall discuss later, that the order is important for effectiveness. Leaders can and do provide consequences without having monitored. As we have seen, the executive in the *New Yorker* cartoon proclaims to a laboring worker, "Keep up the good work, whatever it is, whoever you are" (Stevenson, 1988).

Consequences are similar to monitors in focusing on performance. But, in this case, leaders are not seeking out information. They are instead displaying what they know. Consequences can be provided in different ways: (a) their sign: they can be positive, negative, or neutral. (b) the way in which they are delivered: they can be direct or indirect. (c) their accompaniment: they can be paired or not paired with monitoring.

Identifying monitors and consequences in context

Having explained the critical and the irrelevant features of each concept and provided some examples and non-examples, we will now present some practice and test cases. Two will be in a narrative format, and two will be actual transcripts of leaders at work.

We have tried to place each of these in its context: with the circumstances surrounding each incident, the reactions of the various parties, and the sequence of their interactions. Context provides valuable information with which to make critical inferences as to whether or not performance is involved, and whether a leader is obtaining (as opposed to displaying) knowledge of a follower's performance. To grasp the context, we recommend reading each in its entirety.

Supervisor Charlie

We return once again to Charlie, who is a supervisor in a packaging plant (Gellerman, 1976).

Identifying a monitor

On this particular shift, a machine operator had just alerted Charlie that the pneumatic feed line had broken down (6 in Table 3.2b). While waiting for a repair crew, Charlie had asked for a worker from the labor pool. The young man had just arrived, and Charlie checks the timing of ingredients into the hopper (11). Is Charlie's checking a monitor? Was he gathering information?[4] Did it involve performance?[5] For clues, look for evidence showing who was responsible for the timing of ingredients. Identify who is doing the task. Look at what Charlie said to the young man (7, 12) and to the operator (6) and make inferences. From these conversations, does the responsibility for the timing lie with the operator or the young man?[6]

Another indication of who is responsible is whether Charlie would have taken corrective action if the ingredients had not been properly hand-fed into the hopper. Did Charlie, in fact, take such action? If so, what did he do? with whom? Would this be another sign that the young man was responsible for the timing? Hence, is Charlie's checking of the timing a performance monitor?[7]

Ferreting out consequences

Is what Charlie does when cautioning the young man (12) a monitor or a consequence? Is he gathering information? Does he already know what the young man is doing or has done? Is he displaying his knowledge?[8]

Is the young man's performance involved? Why or why not? Can merely describing what has been done be a consequence? Has Charlie indicated approval or disapproval? Has he identified any performance deficiency? If so, what kind of consequence is this: positive, negative, or neutral?[9]

Distinguishing between monitoring performance and inspecting equipment

Turning now to the breakdown of the pneumatic feed, let us now discuss whether Charlie's checking of the feed lines (2 in Table 3.2a, p. 42) was a monitor. Was he gathering information? Did it involve someone else's – the operator's or young man's – performance?[10] Depending on who was responsible for the smooth running of the pneumatic feed, you can infer whether Charlie's scrutinizing the pneumatic feed is or is not a monitor.

To see whose performance is at stake, make use of every shred of information available to you (as our observers learn to do). Let's start first with the young man. What did Charlie say to (or do with) the young man? Was anything said or done to suggest that the young man was at fault for the breakdown?[11]

Was anything said or done to suggest that the operator was at fault (such as a statement denigrating the operator)? How did Charlie react when the operator alerted him to the breakdown? Hence, was it the operator's responsibility?[12]

Was there any indication that it was the supervisor's responsibility to check the feed lines and to call maintenance when the breakdown occurred? Did Charlie have a way of checking the operation of the machines? How did he do this?[13] Charlie also revealed his perception of why the line broke down. Where? To what did he attribute the breakdown? From this admission, you can infer who is responsible for the machine's operation.[14] Hence, is the checking of the feed lines a performance monitor for one of Charlie's employees? Why or why not?[15]

Based on your determination of who is responsible for the operation of the pneumatic feed, does Charlie's checking the hand-feeding machine (9) to see if it was operating properly constitute a monitor? Why or why not?[16]

Sailboat skippers

The next example is a transcript of actual conversations (Reynard & Komaki, 1995).

Recognizing different types of monitors and consequences

In the transcript, shown in Table 3.3, three leaders on a yacht are engaged in a sailboat race, as referred to earlier. Look at the beginning of the segment at 6:02.00. One of the leaders, the helmsman (H), gives an order, "Pull forward...pull forward." The pull forward, in this case, refers to a rope (or line) attached to the chute. The leaders want the crew members to pull forward on the line to adjust the shape of the sail.

The crew boss (B) then quickly looks up at the sail to see if the line has been pulled forward enough. This looking is considered a monitor (M) because the leader is gathering information about performance. He is checking to see if a crew member has made the adjustment as ordered. Performance is involved because the crew member is responsible for this action; if the proper adjustment is not made, the leaders can (and do) take corrective action. Given that the looking at the sail is a monitor, what type of monitor is it?[17]

Finding that the line has not been pulled back enough, the tactician calls out to the crew member: "Now bring it back a little bit." Does this statement involve performance? Whose performance? Is this person responsible for making the adjustment, in this case, bringing the line back "a little bit"? How do you know that?[18]

Does the statement: "Now bring it back a little bit." indicate the tactician knows how the crew has done? Would this be a consequence? Is it delivered directly or indirectly? What sign of consequence is this? Is an evaluation expressed? Therefore, we know it is not what type of consequence – positive, negative, neutral? Is the crew member doing it to the satisfaction of the tactician? Is the performance being done correctly? Therefore, it is what type of consequence – positive or negative? Why?[19]

Understanding the rationale for monitors and consequences

At 6:02.15, the helmsman orders: "Square back the pole." Almost immediately, the tactician asks: "Who's on the foreguy?" Both the pole position and the easing of the foreguy are integral to the positioning of the sail and to the performance of the team.

The question, "Who's on the foreguy?" is a monitor. Why? Does it meet the two essential characteristics of a monitor? What type of monitor is it?[20] Seconds later, the helmsman says, "Square back the pole more." Is this a monitor or a consequence? Why? Does it meet the essential characteristics of a consequence? What type is it?[21]

Table 3.3 Transcript of lackluster and effective leaders during sailboat races with leaders' behaviors classified by OSTI category and AMC sequence

Lackluster leaders[a]			Effective leaders[b]		
Time	Speaker	Statement/action	Time	Speaker	Statement/action
5:19.00	H	(Steering boat) **Guys, you gotta build up speed.** (A)	6:02.00	H	**Pull forward a** (unintelligible), **pull it forward a bit…yeah.** (A)
.05	T	Keep it fat until we get speed. (A)	.05	B	(Looking up at sail) (M)[2]
	T	Break 'em down a little bit and we'll go over faster. (A)		T	Now bring it back a little bit. (C)[6]
.10	H	(unintelligible) cross this (unintelligible). (CD)	.10	H	We're supposed to jibing again right here. (W)
.15		NSH	.15	H	Square back the pole. (A)
				T	Bring the pole back. (A)
				T	Back, back, back, back. (C)
				T	Square back the pole. Square back the pole. (C)
				H	Who's on the foreguy? Who's on the foreguy? (M)[3]
.20		NSH	.20	H	Square back the pole more. (C)[6]
.25	T	(Looking out over water) (S)	.25	T	That's why we're having trouble trimming chute. (W)
				H	**Trim that chute! You gotta come down.** (A)
.30	T	(Looking out over water) (S)	.30	H	Coming down. Go ahead centerline. (A)
.35	T	(Looking out over water) (S)	.35	H	Whew. (W)
.40		NSH	.40	T	Trip. (A)
.45		NSH		H	(Pulling rope through pulley at feet) (S)
			.45	T	Looks great, guys. (C)
				H	I know I don't. (OP)
.50		NSH	.50	T	Wait, wait, wait. (C)
.55		NSH	.55	H	(Camera wet)

Table 3.3 Continued

Time	Speaker	Statement/action	Time	Speaker	Statement/action
5:20.00	H	(Looking around over the water) (S)	6:03.00		(Camera wet)
.05	H	(Looking around over the water) (S)	.05	B	**(Looking at sail)** (M)[4,5]
	T	We're (unintelligible) that red mark. (W)			
.10	H	(Looking around over the water) (S)	.10		NSH
	T	(unintelligible) up. (CD)			
.15	H	(Looking around over the water) (S)	.15		NSH
.20	H	Allright. (unintelligible) what I was thinking (unintelligible). (CD)	.20	H	(Looking out over the water). (S)
	H	(unintelligible) jibe. (CD)			
.25	T	You gotta go high by Privateer so you don't get their gas. (W)	.25	B	(unintelligible) Okay, go ahead and jibe. (A)
	T				
.30	T	As long as you're coming in late, you might as well come in late fast. Ah shit we are moving. (C)	.30	T	(Looking out over the water) (S)
				H	Come down here. (A)
				H	(unintelligible) place. (CD)
				H	Main inside there. (A)
				H	Coming down. (A)
				T	(Adjusting rope in pulley at feet) (S)
.35		NSH	.35	T	(Adjusting rope) (S)
				H	Hold it, hold it. (C)[7]
.40	H	Ready about. (A)	.40	T	(Adjusting rope) (S)
.45	T	Helm's over! (whistles) All right guys, come on let's move. (C)	.45	H	Easy. What's going on? (M)
.50	T	Come on. Come on. Come on. Let's go. (C)	.50	B	Come on guys. Come on. We gotta move. Blow it! (C)
				B	Come on, guys. Come on. HARD! Now. HARD! Easy. (C)
				H	Watch the boom. Watch your head. Watch your head. (A)
				B	Go! (C)

Time		Transcript
.55	H	Let's go, Sam. Let's go, Mike. (C)
5:21.00	T	Skirt. (Whistles). (A)
.05	H	(Looking out over the water) (S)
.10	H	(Looking out over the water) (S)
.15	H	(Looking out over the water) (S)
.20	H	(unintelligible) you guys(unintelligible). (CD)
.25	T	Everybody's going forward, forward. (W)
.30	T	(Looking out over the water) (S)
.35	T	(Looking out over the water) (S)
.40		NSH
.45	T	The mark's up high.(unintelligible). (W)
.50		NSH
.55		NSH
5:22.00	H	Allright, we'll do a jibe set then. (W)
.05	H	Allright. Everybody understand that? When we come around this mark, we're going to jibe. (A)
.10	H	(Looking around over the water, steering) (S)
.10	T	John, we're going to jibe set. (A)
.15	H	(Looking around over the water, steering) (S)
.20	T	We're gonna tack, then we're gonna jibe. (W)
.25	T	Hold this, Tim. Tim, hold this. Come right in behind Skyway. (C).
.30	H	(Looking around over water) (S)

Time		Transcript
.55	M	(Looking around) (S)
6:04.00	H	(unintelligible). (CD)
.05	T	Hey Jeff, trim that chute, trim that chute. (A)
.10	T	Back on pole. (A)
.15	B	Jeff, on this, after we finish, let's drop that chute. (A)
	H	Where's our pin? (W)
.20	H	This is it right here. (W)
	H	Falling off here. (A)
.25	H	Coming down a little bit. Square back the pole. (A)
	B	(Looking around) (S)
	T	(Looking at sail) (M)
.30	M	(Looking around) (S)
	B	Okay guys, we're finished, let's drop the chute now. (A)
.35	H	Yeah. (W)
	T	(Listening to conversation) (NC)
	B	Just stay on this jibe. (A)
.40	H	No, we'll just – there's not much air. There's not much gas in the chute because(unintelligible). (W)
.45	H	Well, let's do it now and we'll hoist the jib later. (A)

End of tape

Table 3.3 Continued

Time	Speaker	Statement/action	Time	Speaker	Statement/action
.35	H	NSH			
.40	T	Tack. (A)			
		Ready about. Turn the boat. Tacking. (A)			
.45	H	NSH			
.50	H	NSH			
.55	T	NSH			
5:23.00	H	Allright, prepare to jibe. (A)			
.05	H	Down. (A)			
.10	H	Jibing. (A)			
	T	Jibing. (A)			
	H	John, put a little main on. (A)			
.15	H	Haul up some chute. (A)			
	T	Come on Sam. Come on. (A)			
.20	T	Come on Todd, let's go. Good, good, good. Ease the main. Going down. (C)			
.25		NSH			
.30	T	**(Watching crew get sail ready) (M)[5] Come on, guys. (C)[8]**			

Note: For each crew, in order from left to right are: (a) the time, to the five-second interval, (b) the speaker, one of the three leaders – the helmsman (abbreviated H), tactician (T), or crew boss (B) – calling out to the crew and speaking as a single voice, (c) the statement or action, and (d) in parentheses, the OSTI category, where A = Antecedent: conveying expectations of performance, M = Monitor, C = Consequence, W = Work-related: discussing the work but not performance, NC = Not communicating, S = Solitary, OP = Own performance. NSH = Not on screen and no statements heard. CD = Can't decipher: not enough of the statement could be understood to determine the category; unintelligible. AMC = Antecedent-Monitor-Consequence sequences. Horizontal lines separate AMC sequences.

[a] Mean AMC and AM duration for effective set of leaders = 53.0 secs

[b] Mean AMC duration for lackluster set of leaders in actual race = 275.0 secs

Source: Adapted from Reynard and Komaki (1995); Study 15

Table 3.4 Differences charted between lackluster and effective leaders during sailboat race

Lackluster leaders	Effective leaders

```
Lackluster leaders                          Effective leaders

    00  10  20  30  40  50              00  10  20  30  40  50
A   |-●--o---------------------         A   |-●--|----●--|-●----o---------
M   |------------------------          M   |-●--|---●--|---------------
C   |------------------------          C   |----●|---o--●|---------o--o----
OP  |------------------------          OP  |----|---------|----------o----
W   |------------------------          W   |----|-o----o|----o-----------
NC  |------------------------          NC  |----|-------|--------------
S   |------------------o--o--o------    S   |----|-------|----------o------

    00  10  20  30  40  50              00  10  20  30  40  50
A   -------------------------o--------- A   -------------o--o--|--------o----
M   ---------------------------------  M   ---●-----------------|---o-------
C   --------------------o-------o--o--o-C   -----------------------●|---o--o---
OP  ---------------------------------  OP  --------------------|-------
W   ---o-----------o---------------    W   --------------------|-------
NC  ---------------------------------  NC  --------------------|-------
S   -o--o--o--o-----------------------  S   ------------o--o--o--o|-o-------o-

    00  10  20  30  40  50             00  10  20  30  40
A   -o------------------------------    A   ---o--o--o--o--o--o--o----o-
M   ---------------------------------  M   ----------------o---------
C   ---------------------------------  C   --------------------------
OP  ---------------------------------  OP  --------------------------
W   --------------o---------o------    W   --------o--o-------o--o--o-
NC  ---------------------------------  NC  ----------------o---------
S   ---o--o--o--------o--o------------  S   -------------o--o---------

    00  10  20  30  40  50
A   ---o--o--o--------------o--------
M   ---------------------------------
C   --------------o-----------
OP  ---------------------------------
W   -o-----------o-----------------
NC  ---------------------------------
S   ------o--o--------o--------------

    00  10  20  30
A   -o--o--o--o--------|
M   ---------------●|
C   -----------o----●|
OP  ---------------|
W   ---------------|
NC  ---------------|
S   ---------------|
```

Note: Corresponds to transcript in Table 3.3. A = Antecedent, M = Monitor, C = Consequence, OP = Own performance, W = Work-related, NC = Not communicating, S = Solitary.

Tom Brand

In this example, portrayed by Terkel (1975) in his book, *Working*, Tom Brand is a plant manager at the Ford Assembly Division in Chicago. Tom describes his job in Table 3.5.

Discriminating monitors from non-monitors in management by walking around

Going out on the floor and touring the plant (2 to 6 in Table 3.5) is sometimes referred to as "management by walking around." This can be an ideal opportunity to monitor, but, as Yukl (1994) cautions, its success depends upon how the visit is conducted.

Even within the visit itself, not all of the interactions would be cataloged as monitoring. The fact that Brand stops to talk to foremen or to hourly

Table 3.5 Transcript of Tom Brand

Number	Statement/action
1	"You're responsible to make sure the car is built and built correctly. I rely on my quality control manager. Any defects, anything's wrong, we make sure it's repaired before it leaves the plant... we've got to build forty- seven an hour... 760 big Fords a day. These things go out the door to the customer.... If the customer comes in and says, 'I have a water leak,' the dealer'll write up an 1863 [form], and the company pays for that repair. Everybody's real interested in keeping this down.... In December, we beat $1.91. It's unheard of for a two-shift plant to beat $1.91 in the warranty" (p. 244).
2	The first thing that Tom does after reading the report from the production manager of the previous night's shift is to: "Go out on the floor, tour the plant.
3	We've got a million and a half square feet under the roof. I'll change my tour – so they can't tell every day I'm going to be in the same place at the same time.... I'm always stopping to talk to foremen or hourly fellas.
4	Or somebody'll stop me, 'I got a suggestion.'
5	I may see a water leak.
6	I say to the foreman, 'Did you call maintenance?' [I would] not do it myself, [I would] let him go do it.
7	Usually about nine-thirty I've looked at our audit cars. We take eight cars, drive 'em, rewater 'em, test 'em, put 'em on a hoist, check all the torque, take a visual check.... Then there's 40 more each day.
8	The federal government says you must provide ear protection for anybody in a high-noise-level area. We baffled all those.
9	Some of the fellas said, 'I'm not gonna wear 'em.'
10	We said, 'Either you wear 'em or you're not gonna work here'."

Note: The events have been separated and numbered to indicate the order in which they happened.

Source: Terkel (1975, pp. 244–246). Copyright 1975 Avon Books. Reproduced with permission.

employees (3) does not necessarily mean that he's always monitoring. For example, would seeing the water leak (5) constitute monitoring? Ask yourself if Brand is collecting information, and if the information is about workers' performance. What indication is there that workers' performance might *not* be involved in seeing the water leak?[22]

On the other hand, would asking the foreman, "Did you call maintenance?"(6), be considered a monitor? Is Brand displaying knowledge of the foreman's performance? Or is he gathering information? Is performance involved? Is the foreman responsible for calling maintenance? What would Tom Brand be likely to say if the foreman answered: "No, it's not my job"? How did Brand respond when some employees in high-level-noise areas refused to wear ear protection (10)?[23]

Differentiating between monitors and consequences

Would looking at audit cars every morning (7) be a monitor or a consequence? What type of monitor or consequence?[24]

Would noting that "in December, we beat $1.91. It's unheard of for a two-shift plant to beat $1.91 in the warranty" (1) be a monitor or a consequence? What type?[25]

Dr Roy and Project Team

This last transcript is one of a series in Honey's (1978) book, *Face to Face*. It depicts a portion of what was said during a monthly meeting in a research and development (R & D) division. Dr Roy is the project manager in R & D, and is meeting with four of his direct subordinates: Harold, Neil, Alan, and Steve. They meet monthly to check on the progress of various projects for which each is responsible. A typical sequence in the procuring of a project is to assess the potential client's needs and then, if interest is expressed, to prepare a proposal outlining what the R & D division can do and its proposed cost.

Spotting monitors and consequences in context

The following passages illustrate the subtle quality of many interactions among employees. In the first passage in Table 3.6a, the group has just finished talking about another project. How would you categorize Dr Roy's first question (1) and his second question (2)? Is he gathering information or indicating knowledge in the second question?[26] A hint can be found in what occurs after the question, in this case, Neil's reply.

Catching the subtleties

In this next passage in Table 3.6b, the group has just had a conversation about another one of Alan's projects. Dr Roy monitors twice. When? What

Table 3.6a Transcript of Dr Roy and his project team of engineers

Number	Speaker	Statement/action

Dr Roy then turns to Neil and asks:

1	*Dr Roy*:	What about the Permatract proposal, Neil?
	Neil:	Well, as you know, they accepted the feasibility study and that was followed up with a proposal worth about $20,000. They say the cash can't be raised this year and that they hope to fit it into next year's budget.
2	*Dr Roy*:	Oh, dear! Did you actually go and talk to them about it?
	Neil:	Well, no, it was done on the phone.
	Dr Roy:	So you've been spared that one now. And we have been spared $20,000 as well, it seems.

See note Table 3.6b

Table 3.6b Transcript of Dr Roy continued

Number	Speaker	Statement/action

Dr Roy says to Alan:

3	*Dr Roy*:	This next one is yours, too, Alan.
4	*Alan*:	Yes, well, some samples have been sent. I contacted them a month or so ago and they said they were still thinking about it.
5	*Dr Roy*:	You told us last time.
6	*Dr Roy*:	What, if anything, has happened since?
7	*Dr Roy*:	Wasn't Bert supposed to have asked them when he went to the other meeting a couple of weeks back?
8	*Alan*:	Yes; I'm not sure whether he did, though.
9	*Dr Roy*:	I think so.
10	*Dr Roy*:	I'm sure I saw a copy of a letter. I forget the context just now.
11	*Alan*:	Oh. Well, he must have, then.

Note: The events have been separated and numbered to indicate the order in which they happened.
Source: Honey (1978, pp. 129–30). Copyright 1978 Prentice Hall. Reproduced with permission.

type is each?[27] Did Dr Roy provide any consequences to Alan? When? If so, was it positive, negative, or neutral?[28]

How would you categorize Dr Roy's question about Bert (7)? Was performance involved? Was he seeking information, or did he already know? What evidence is there that he already knew?[29] What type of consequence was it? Why?[30]

Congratulations. You're an observer

This concludes our practice session. To check your answers, please turn to the notes to this chapter. By providing these examples, we hope we have given you an idea of how understated, embedded, and successful monitors and consequences can be in sustaining performance in research labs, at food processing plants, aboard sailboats, and on coffee farms.

OBSERVING SUPERVISORY BEHAVIOR USING THE OPERANT SUPERVISORY TAXONOMY AND INDEX (OSTI)

The preceding passages have provided perspective on defining what leaders do. This section describes the instrument we have developed to observe leaders monitoring and providing consequences. We call it the Operant Supervisory Taxonomy and Index, or OSTI. It consists of two parts: (a) a classification or taxonomy of eight major categories (and a number of subcategories) of leaders' behaviors, and (b) a method of observation. With the OSTI, we can describe what leaders actually say and do, as well as obtain precise information about the amount of time leaders spend on the various categories and sub-categories.

The OSTI, field-tested in a theater and a bank, has been found to be feasible, psychometrically sound, acceptably reliable, and sensitive to differences among leaders (Komaki, 1986). Furthermore, field-tests indicated the number of occasions necessary to obtain representative information. The OSTI has been successfully used in widely divergent settings – in for-profit (construction) and non-profit (university) organizations, in the financial (bank) and service (insurance) sectors, and in government (police), and the arts (theater).

Taxonomy of supervisory behaviors

Tailored to theory-based categories

The categories of leader behaviors in the OSTI were built around the cornerstones of the model, monitors and consequences, both of which draw their inspiration from the theory of operant conditioning. To round out what leaders do and say when they are not monitoring and providing consequences, six categories were added to the taxonomy: performance antecedents, own performance, work-related, non-work-related, not communicating, and solitary. Brief definitions and examples of all of the categories follow:

Performance monitors

Performance monitors, as we have said, involve the gathering of information about followers' performance.

Performance consequences

As mentioned earlier, when bosses evaluate or communicate knowledge of another person's performance, these events are classified as performance consequences.

Performance antecedents

When bosses deliver instructions or inspirational speeches, provide rules, training, or policy statements, or convey their expectations of desired or undesired performance, they are delivering performance antecedents. Supervisors in a medical insurance firm, for example, delivered the following antecedents: "You can just write 'no comment' in there if you want to," and "Let's try to coordinate these two if we can."

Own performance

When bosses refer to the way in which they themselves are performing, rather than the performance of their followers, this is classified as their own performance. For example, the bank VP might say about himself, "I need to check on those and then call bookkeeping", "Did you see anything wrong with my report?", or "I always screw that up."

Work-related

The work-related category refers to discussions of the work that do not concern anyone's performance. Supervisory personnel in charge of computers, for example, might say, "That screen should be able to print in the Tektronix mode," or "You can carry a lot of weight when you want [to buy] 6,000 of those puppies."

Non-work-related

When the leader is interacting, but the conversation is not about work, it is considered a non-work-related activity. A Marine Corps warrant officer, for instance, might make such statements as, "Yeah, did you see how he did in that last game?" or "Going racing this weekend?"

Not communicating

When the boss is interacting, but not contributing to the conversation, the boss is considered to be not communicating. For example when a worker stops Tom Brand on his tour of the plant, saying, "I got a suggestion" (4 in Table 3.5, p. 60), *and* Brand pauses to hear the recommendation, Brand would be classified as interacting but not communicating.

Solitary

When the leader is not interacting, he or she is considered to be "solitary." Carol Mosley-Braun, Senator from Illinois, would be classified as being solitary when she is drafting a speech alone, walking down the hall by herself, or reading daily briefings in her office.

Qualitatively rich subcategories

Believing that the manner in which leaders implement the categories is important,[31] we further divided five categories (except solitary, non-work-related, and not communicating) into sub-categories. These sub-categories, briefly presented below, allowed a fuller description of leaders on the job.

Monitors were subdivided by the method in which they are used to obtain performance information: whether the leader directly observes or inspects the work (*work sampling*), asks workers themselves (*self-report*), or relies upon other sources for this information (*secondary source*).

Consequences have two sub-categories: (a) delivery (whether the consequence is delivered *directly* to the worker whose performance is being discussed or *indirectly* to other workers about another's performance), and (b) evaluation (whether the consequences provided are *positive*, *negative*, or *neutral* in evaluation).

Antecedents were subdivided five ways, by: (a) delivery (whether the antecedent is delivered *directly* to the worker whose performance is being discussed or *indirectly* to other workers about another's performance), (b) planning (whether the antecedent refers to behavior that a leader expects another to carry out in response to some *current* objective or problem, or that he or she predicts will prevent an *anticipated* problem, (c) specificity (whether it is clear what is expected),[32] (d) type (leaders *inviting* or *not inviting* participation), and (e) responsibility (how *clear* or *unclear* it is who is specifically responsible for performing the behavior.

The own performance category was subdivided by the content of discussion about the leader's performance. Managers can provide information regarding three aspects of their performance: *consequences*, *monitors*, and *antecedents*.

Lastly, the work-related category was subdivided into comments *inviting* and *not inviting* participation.

Brief definitions and examples of the eight categories and their respective subcategories appear in Table 3.1 (p. 38). Refer as well to Komaki, Zlotnick, and Jensen (1986).

Exhaustive and mutually exclusive categories

In keeping with Fleishman and Quaintance's (1984) suggestions for taxonomies of human performance, we designed the OSTI's eight categories to

Manager's behavior

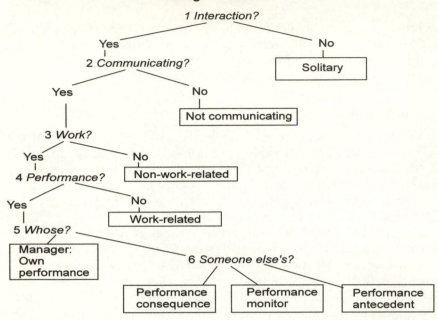

Figure 3.1 Decision tree listing questions posed by observers when using the OSTI to observe a manager

be *exhaustive*, that is, for virtually every behavior of a leader to be classifiable as belonging to one of the eight categories, and *mutually exclusive* so that any behavior falls into one, and only one, of the categories. To see how the OSTI meets these criteria, refer to the OSTI decision tree in Figure 3. 1. It lists the sequence of questions that an observer poses when collecting data and the decisions that must be made. At the top of the figure is the manager's behavior followed by a series of six questions. Let's say you are classifying the helmsman's statement to the crew, "Square back the pole." Beginning with this behavior:

1 The observer first asks, "Is the leader interacting?" (*In this case, the answer is yes.*) If no interactions are taking place, then the leader is classified as being "solitary."
2 If interactions are occurring, then the observer asks, "Is the leader communicating?" (*The answer is yes.*) If the leader is not contributing to the discussion, then the leader is categorized "not communicating."
3 When the leader is communicating, then we ask: "Are the communications related to *work* (where work is broadly defined as issues relating to the job, individual tasks, individuals in the work place, or even travel done for one's profession)?" (*The answer is yes.*) If the communications are not concerned with work, then the leader is classified as being involved in a "non-work-related" communication.

4 If the communication deals with work, then the question is, "Does the work communication concern anyone's *performance*?"[33] (*The answer is yes.*) If the communication has to do with work but does not concern anyone's performance, then it is classified as "work-related."
5 If the communication includes someone's performance, the observer asks, "*Whose* performance is involved? Is it the leader's?" (*The answer is no.*) If the communication concerns the leader's own performance, it is classified as the leader's "own performance." Is the performance someone else's? (*The answer is yes.*)
6 If *someone else's* performance is involved, these communications are further divided into performance consequences, monitors, or antecedents. Because the statement, "Square back the pole," conveyed an expectation of performance, it was classified as an antecedent.

As one can see, the observer must either decide that the behavior fits the category or move on to the next set of questions. Because the comment, "Square back the pole," did not fit into the categories of solitary, not communicating, non-work-related, work-related, own performance, consequences, or monitors, it ended up fitting into one and only one category, that of antecedents. In this way, the OSTI is mutually exclusive.

This decision-making process also shows how an observer can take virtually anything the leader says or does and classify it into one of the eight OSTI categories, hence, illustrating the exhaustiveness of the OSTI.

An observational index

Directly sampling face-to-face interactions

To collect data using the OSTI, observers went to the leaders' work sites and stood about five or six feet from the leader, out of sight but within hearing distance. They followed each leader like a shadow. When tracking the director, scenic designer, and stage manager for a spring production of "The Music Man", they observed from day to day, at different times, in a variety of situations (Komaki, Zlotnick, & Jensen, 1986). From pre-rehearsal to opening night, they recorded after late-night rehearsals, during costume fittings and formal meetings, and at the many chance gatherings outside cramped offices, inside the trap room, and backstage.

Equipped with a stopwatch, a clipboard, and a data sheet, each observer wrote down what the leader said and did for a thirty-minute stretch. Each minute was divided into a ten, forty, and ten-second period, as shown in Figure 3.2. During the first ten seconds of every minute, the observer watched the leader. For the next forty seconds, the observer wrote down what the leader did or said, verbatim, and then coded the statement or action into the appropriate category and subcategory. In the last ten seconds, the observer began listening for context, then took a deep breath and

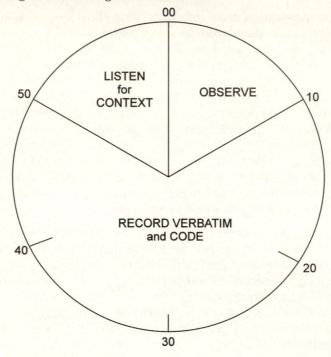

Figure 3.2 Illustration of how each minute during a thirty-minute observation period, using the OSTI, was divided into a 10–40–10-second sequence

started all over again. This breakneck ten–forty–ten-second sequence continued for the full thirty minutes. To obtain representative information, we observed each leader for twenty sessions of thirty minutes each, a total of ten hours.

Training and maintaining the behaviors of the observers

To train the observers, materials were specifically developed, consisting of definitions, observational procedures, instructions for summarizing data and conducting reliability checks, as well as data, summary, resummary, reliability, and reliability resummary sheets.

A minimum of forty hours was required to train observers – twenty in classroom instruction, practice, and discussion and twenty of practice in the field. Observers were considered to be trained only after passing the test of interrater reliability (described below). In practice, this meant that they had to obtain reliability scores of 90 percent or better on three consecutive, representative occasions before formally collecting data.

Once observers had been trained, the data collection process began, including the scheduling, directing, and maintaining of the observers' data collection efforts for extended periods of time. In one case, data collection lasted for seven months (Komaki, 1986). Clearly, the commitment of time and energy to observe leaders, using the OSTI, is not an inconsequential one.

Development and field test

Critical role of test of interrater reliability

<u>In defining categories</u>

In developing the OSTI, the definitions of terms such as "monitor" and "the first ten seconds of every minute" were first honed and the observational system sketched. Repeated interrater reliability tests were then conducted over a four-month period, first with transcripts (e.g., Honey, 1978), then with videotapes (e.g., Borman, 1978), and, finally, by observing leaders in action (Komaki, Zlotnick, & Jensen, 1986).

An interrater reliability test consists of two persons observing (or "rating") the same manager at the same time, independently coding the behaviors and then comparing their recordings to determine whether or not both raters agreed on the categorization. In the case of the OSTI, we used an interval-by-interval agreement system, looking to see if the two independent raters, or observers, agreed or disagreed on each and every ten-second interval. Using this system, reliability was calculated overall as:

$$\frac{\text{\# agreements}}{\text{\# intervals}} = \frac{29}{30}^{34,35} = 97\%$$

Each disagreement was used as a springboard for discussion on how to change the definitions or observational procedures to reduce judgmental differences among observers. For example, the work-related subcategory, inviting participation, was particularly troublesome. Arguments went on during many meetings. Eventually, we changed its definition from "communications which explicitly solicit opinions or ideas" to "communications which explicitly solicit a response other than a yes or no." Using the former definition, some observers thought that a manager was explicitly soliciting ideas when she said, "Plan A sounds great, don't you think?", whereas other observers felt that the manager was asking only for confirmation, not for alternative ideas. Using the revised definition, observers reliably noted that a question phrased as "Plan A or B, which do you think?" invited participation.

Hence, in developing definitions of terms, reliability was the benchmark for deciding whether or not a category was clearly conceptualized. Revisions of definitions and observational/recording procedures continued until 90 to 100 percent agreement was reached. When two independent observers agreed on the occurrence, frequency, duration, and/or quality of all terms, the categories were considered to be unambiguously defined. No matter how objective or straightforward the terms may appear, the proof is in the agreement between two independent raters. When this criterion is achieved, then and only then are the terms actually objectively defined and the instrument ready for use.

During observer training

To ensure the reliability of raters, we required that they too pass the IRR test. In observer training, reliability was the criterion for judging when training was successful.

Throughout data collection

To determine whether or not the data collected were dependable, we monitored observer reliability throughout the formal data collection period. A minimum of 10 percent sampling is suggested.

As one can see, in the development of the OSTI, the test of interrater reliability was essential in the definitional process, in training observers, and during data collection.

Field-testing the OSTI

The field test of the OSTI consisted of making 189 observations of thirty minutes each of seven theater leaders over a five-week period and 440 observations of thirty minutes of twenty bank leaders over a twelve-week period.

Feasibility

The mere completion – and duration – of these field tests indicated that it is indeed feasible to observe leaders over an extended period of time in their own work settings.

Reliability

The mean overall reliability scores for the OSTI in the theater and bank samples were both 91 percent, well within the limits of acceptability for both a new (80 percent) and an established (90 percent) measure (Miller, 1997). Furthermore, kappa[36] scores for the categories in both samples ranged between .65 and .98, well above the minimum acceptable estimate of .60 recommended (Hartmann, 1977). Subsequent data collections in other settings have also shown that the OSTI provides reliable data. The overall figures by setting, shown in Table 3.7, range from 91 percent in the theater and bank settings (Komaki, Zlotnick, & Jensen, 1986) to 98 percent in a computer center (Komaki & Newlin, 1990). These figures are particularly striking given our strict definition of reliability.[37]

Table 3.7 Overall interrater reliability scores

Setting	Reliability (%)
Bank[a]	91
Theater[b]	91
Insurance[c]	95
Newspaper[d]	96
Construction[e]	93, 90
Computer[f]	98

[a] Source: Komaki, Zlotnick, and Jensen (1986), Study 1a
[b] Source: Komaki, Zlotnick, and Jensen (1986), Study 1b
[c] Source: Komaki (1986), Study 2
[d] Source: Jensen and Komaki (1993), Study 3
[e] Source: Komaki, Hyttinen, and Immonen (1991), Study 5a and 5b
[f] Source: Komaki and Newlin (1990), Study 11

Sensitivity

The OSTI was also found to be sensitive to differences in behavior among leaders, as revealed in separate analyses of variance with repeated measures for each category. Results for the theater sample, for instance, indicated that the OSTI significantly discriminated among the seven leaders for all of the categories except non-work-related.

Empirically determining the frequency of sampling

At the onset, the OSTI was developed to directly sample leaders' behaviors, but it was always assumed that a single thirty-minute observation would not be sufficient. The question remained: how many times is it necessary to observe? Two times? Three? Five? Ten?

To find out, an empirical determination was made. The analytical procedure used was derived from generalizability theory (Cronbach, Gleser, Nanda, & Rajarathnam, 1972). Generalizability theory assumes that a particular observation or occasion of measurement is merely one occurrence in a universe of observations or occasions of measurement. The theory also assumes that variations between samples can arise from different sources (the persons being observed, the observers, the occasions of measurement, and so on).

To estimate the number of observations needed for obtaining representative information, we took the following steps: (a) We determined the contribution made by one source of variation (in this case, the persons observed) to the total variation in the obtained measurement sample. (b) We calculated an estimate of how well other possible measurement samples, from differing numbers of occasions, would generalize to the universe of measurement samples. We did this by examining (1) the coefficient of generalizability (the proportion of obtained score variance attributable to the person's universe score variance), and (2) the error of measurement (the estimated difference between the obtained score and the corresponding universe score).

The coefficients of generalizability and the error of measurement based on five, ten, fifteen, twenty, and twenty-five occasions of measurement for the theater and bank leaders, are shown in Komaki, Zlotnick, and Jensen (1986). With ten or fewer occasions, relatively little of the total variance was accounted for, and the error of measurement was unacceptably high on monitoring and consequences, the two categories of interest. With twenty occasions, at least 60 percent of the variance was accounted for, and the error of measurement was relatively low. For example, the coefficients of generalizability ranged in the theater department from .58 for consequences to .96 for monitors; the coefficients ranged in the bank from .65 for consequences to .68 for monitors. Given the fact that coefficients of generalizability of .60 to .70 have generally been regarded as acceptable (Coates & Thoresen, 1978; Mitchell & Gray, 1981) and the fact that the above results were found with two groups in two different settings at two different times, we decided that twenty occasions would result in reasonably representative information in the two categories of interest.

Given the results of the field test, we determined that it was necessary to collect a total of ten hours (twenty observation sessions of thirty minutes each) of information on each leader.

Output

Using the OSTI, we can quantify *how much time* leaders spend on the various categories and sub-categories. For example, we can determine that a leader spent 5.6 percent of her time providing performance consequences, with approximately one-third of those consequences being positive and directly delivered.

We can also obtain *verbatim accounts* of what leaders said and descriptions of what leaders did, as shown in Table 3.1 (p. 38). By identifying what leaders said in their own words, it was possible to better capture the short staccato sentences and the sometimes blooming confusion on board ship, in bank vaults, and backstage.

VARIATIONS ON THE OSTI

Five variations of the OSTI have followed. Like the OSTI itself, all include an assessment of monitors and consequences.

Operant Supervisory Team Taxonomy and Index (OSTTI)

We developed this version of the OSTI to reveal whether the model could be extended to leaders of teams conducting interdependent tasks (Komaki,

Desselles, & Bowman, 1989). The OSTTI retained the major categories of the OSTI, but the subcategory of team coordination was added because of our hypothesis about the importance of this subcategory.[38]

Our observers positioned themselves in the cabin area of a 24-foot boat, approximately 10 feet from the skipper. They recorded what the skippers said and did every fifty seconds on five categories and one subcategory, continuously without interruption. The OSTTI definitions, examples, and data sheet are presented in Komaki, Desselles, and Bowman (1989).

Operant Supervisor-Subordinate Taxonomy and Index (OSSTI)

In an effort to understand the impact of the leader's monitoring on the follower, we conducted an experiment looking at their interactions (Komaki & Citera, 1990). To assess their interactions, we developed a variation of the OSTI, called the Operant Supervisor-Subordinate Taxonomy and Index (OSSTI). The OSSTI retained the major categories of the OSTI. Coders watched the videotapes, categorizing behaviors every *five seconds*, first watching the leader and then watching the follower. The OSSTI definitions, examples, and data sheet are described in Komaki and Citera (1990).

Operant Supervisor-Subordinate Taxonomy and Index – Written Version (OSSTI-W)

This written version of the Operant Superior-Subordinate Taxonomy and Index stemmed from our looking at leaders and followers exchanging messages via electronic mail (Komaki & Newlin, 1990). The OSSTI-W is designed to be used in coding written communications, such as e-mail messages, correspondence, press releases, in-house reports, and policy statements.

Because of the unique characteristic of written messages, adjustments had to be made in the concept of a "unit." With spoken communications, one can divide them into five-second intervals as in the OSSTI, fifteen-second intervals as in the OSTTI, or the first ten-seconds of every minute as in the OSTI. For written communications, however, no such metric exists. Thus, we refined the concept of a "unit" for written messages. The following message, for example, contains two units:

To: jlk@purccvm
From: mhn@purccvm

Well, I have an answer,/but it is not a good one.

Dividing written messages in this way allows one to assess the percentage of units classified as monitors, consequences, antecedents, and so forth.

Operant Supervisory In-Basket Assessment (OSIBA)

Because of the extensive time commitment required to obtain information using the OSTI, we developed a faster alternative. Referred to as the Operant Supervisory In-Basket Assessment (OSIBA), it is a paper-and-pencil measure in which respondents take on a leadership role by handling items in their "in-basket." The twenty-two in-basket items range from telephone messages from department heads complaining about other departments to reports from accounting on production costs. Using forms that we provide, respondents can reply to whoever, and in whatever manner, they see fit. The only limitation is that they have one hour to respond.

The OSIBA and the OSTI are similar in that they both take context into consideration, and provide information about the quantity and quality of the monitors and consequences provided. Contrastingly, with the OSIBA, the leader has to spend an hour taking the test, and each coder typically spends two to three times that long scoring it. To ensure that no monitors and consequences embedded in the replies are missed, two coders should score each OSIBA. Thus, from five to six hours per leader are needed to obtain commensurate information using the OSIBA.

Validating Operant Supervisory In-Basket Assessment (OSIBA)

Given the potential time savings with the OSIBA, but the fallibility of having respondents write what they would do, the question naturally arises as to how OSIBA scores compare with the real actions of leaders on the job. To address this, a validation study was performed, scrutinizing the relationship between OSIBA and OSTI scores (Komaki & Newlin, 1990). Twelve leaders in a computer center at a large state university were each observed using the OSTI. Each leader took the OSIBA as well. Two persons scored each OSIBA. The interrater reliability for the OSIBA, calculated strictly, averaged 83.5 percent. For the final scores, each disagreement was reviewed and reconciled.

To assess whether OSIBA scores were positively related to the amount of time that leaders spent on these categories on the job, correlation coefficients were calculated. The OSIBA scores were highly and positively related to the amount of time that leaders spent on the job monitoring ($r = .57$, $p<.05$) and providing consequences ($r = .60$, $p<.05$). Based on these findings, it was concluded that the OSIBA might be an acceptable, but not necessarily preferred, alternative to the OSTI.

INCORPORATING TIME

The OSTI and each of its variations discussed thus far have aggregated the data into summary scores: the number of monitor points for the OSIBA, for example, or the percentage of time spent monitoring via work sampling for the OSTI, the OSTTI, the OSSTI, or the OSSTI-W.

Operant Supervisor-Subordinate Taxonomy and Index – By Sequences (OSSTI-S)

As we became increasingly convinced of the importance of behaviors unfolding over time, we developed the Operant Supervisor-Subordinate Taxonomy and Index – By Sequences (OSSTI-S). The OSSTI-S retains the same taxonomy of leader behavior as the OSTTI, but provides information about (a) the pacing or duration of sequences of behaviors, such as the number of seconds it takes for a leader to complete an AMC sequence discussed earlier, and (b) the placement of behaviors within these sequences, such as whether a monitor occurs before or after a consequence.

An example: Charlie and the young man

To see how we did this, look once again at the interaction between Charlie, the supervisor, and the young man who has just arrived from the labor pool (Gellerman, 1976).

Identifying pacing of AMC sequences

As one can see in Table 3.2b (p. 46), Charlie first delivers an antecedent (7 in bold beginning "Charlie patiently'). Then, after several interactions with the operator and the maintenance crew, Charlie monitors (11). Soon thereafter, he provides a consequence (12). This completes an AMC sequence.

To show the pacing of this AMC sequence over time, we plot it on a chart, akin to a musical score. The vertical lines denote the beginning and end of the AMC sequence. The time in intervals moves from left to right. The marker antecedent (in bold in position 7 in the Table) is plotted as • in the seventh position on the line marked A which stands for an antecedent.

```
      6    8   10    12
  A |----●-------------|
```

The marker monitor (also •) is the eleventh event and is plotted in position 11 on the M line signifying a monitor:

```
      6    8   10    12
  M |----------------●---|
```

The marker consequence (in bold) takes place as the twelfth event:

```
      6    8   10    12
  C |-----------------●|
```

Bringing them together, we can see that this entire AMC sequence takes place fairly quickly with marker A in position 7, M in position 11, and concluding with the C in position 12.

```
      6      8    10    12
 A |----●--------------|
 M |----------------●---|
 C |------------------●|
```

By identifying the duration of AMC sequences, in this case, five positions (12–75), we could test our hypothesis that effective leaders would provide quicker AMC sequences than not-so-effective leaders.

Determining placement of behaviors within AMC sequence

To assess the positioning or placement of various behaviors within the AMC sequence, we looked at what happened in the intervening positions. Interested in any antecedents that occurred between the marker antecedent and marker monitor, referred to as an AM sequence, we looked for any As. Finding one (8 beginning "Then he . . ."), we plotted it in position 8, as shown.

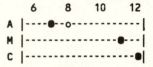

```
      6      8    10    12
 A |----●--o-----------|
 M |----------------●---|
 C |------------------●|
```

Given this addition to the score, we can now count for the AM sequence the number of intervals with As (in this case, one). Counting the number of intervals in the AM sequence in this way allowed us to assess whether the number would be higher or lower for the effective and not-so-effective leaders.

A live example: sailboat skippers

We used the OSSTI-S to assess the pacing and placement of behaviors of leaders (described earlier) during sailboat races (Reynard & Komaki, 1995).

Identifying pacing of AMC sequences

As one can see in Table 3.3 (p. 55), the marker antecedent (in bold, beginning "Pull forward") occurs during the 6:02.00 interval. In the same interval, the marker monitor (in bold) takes place, and in the next interval a consequence (in bold) occurs. For purposes of this analysis, the three leaders were assumed to be one voice. This AMC sequence is plotted with markers A and M under the 00-second interval and marker C under the next interval, as follows:

```
    00
 A |-●--|
 M |-●--|
 C |---●|
```

As shown, this particular sequence occurred rapidly in two intervals, for a total duration of ten seconds.

The same Table shows that the next AMC sequence begins at 6:02.15 and ends at 6:02.20. Like the previous one, it has a duration of ten seconds. Both of these ten-second sequences are portrayed – as the first and second sequences of the effective leaders under the 00- and 15-second intervals, respectively – in Table 3.4 (p. 59).

Seeing placement of behaviors within AMC sequence

The same scoring system is used to portray the positioning of behaviors within the AMC sequence. In its simplest form, the third AMC sequence in Table 3.3 can be plotted with only the marker antecedent, monitor, and consequence in the appropriate intervals:

```
        30    40    50    00    10    20    30
A  |-●--------------------------------------------|
M  |------------------------------●----------------|
C  |----------------------------------------------●|
```

Beginning at 6:02.25 and ending at 6:03.35, this AMC sequence takes place over 75 seconds or fifteen five-second intervals. This same 75-second sequence is portrayed in Table 3.4 as the third AMC sequence for the effective leaders.

To assess the placement of As, we can plot the number of intervals with As during the AM and MC sequences:

```
        30    40    50    00    10    20    30
A  |-●----o--------------------------------o--o---|
M  |------------------------------●----------------|
C  |-------------o--o-------------------------------●|
```

As shown, we can count one A (and two consequences) during the nine five-second intervals of this AM sequence, and two As during the seven intervals of the MC sequence.

We can do the same for sequences lasting much longer. Turning to the lackluster leaders in Tables 3.3 (p. 55) and 3.4 (p. 59), we can see that they completed only one AMC sequence in four-and-a-half minutes. It began at 5:19.00 with the marker antecedent (in bold, beginning "Guys") and ended at 5:23.30.

For this AM sequence (consisting of fifty-three five-second intervals), we can count the number of intervals with As that occurred during the first (1), second (1), third (1), and fourth (3) minutes, for a total of six out of fifty-three intervals.

We can also assess the placement of the other categories: own performance (OP), work related (W), not communicating (NC), and solitary (S). For solitary, for example, the lackluster leaders spent 3, 4, 5, and 3 intervals during the first, second, third, and fourth minutes respectively, for a total of fifteen intervals of solitary during the AM sequence.

In short, the OSSTI-S gave us a way to capture the pacing of AMC, AM, and MC sequences of behaviors, as well as the placement of behaviors within these sequences.

IN SUMMARY

The operant supervisory indices – the OSTI, the OSTTI, OSSTI, and the OSIBA – help to address the earlier mentioned concerns of Lewis and Stewart (1958) that we know shockingly little about the daily lives of leaders. The portrayal of what leaders do as musical scores and the expansion of consequences to include neutral as well as positive and negative consequences broadened our concept of what constituted effective supervision. At the same time, the data-gathering procedures we have employed make it possible to examine leaders' behavior in depth and detail. Direct sampling and the use of verbatim accounts make available more information about the denizens of executive suites. The identification of critical and optional attributes of the concepts aided us in providing precise data high in interrater reliability. And with this information at hand, we can pinpoint what effective leaders should actually do in motivating others, as we shall see in the next chapter.

4 Research on the model

Behaviors and effectiveness of leaders

In seeking the answer to what effective leaders really do, teams of researchers have carried out more than a decade of research on three continents, producing eighteen studies.[1, 2] As Figure 4.1 shows, the studies have shifted back and forth from the field to the laboratory, following a recommended triangulation approach (Runkel & McGrath, 1972). Initial studies were

Figure 4.1 Field and laboratory studies conducted in connection with the operant model of effective supervision: shifting from field to laboratory and back.

Initial field studies	Laboratory experiments	More refined field studies
1a *Komaki, Zlotnick, and Jensen* (1986) Bank		11 *Komaki and Newlin* (1990) Computer
1b *Komaki, Zlotnick, and Jensen* (1986) Theater		12 *Komaki* (1997) Theater
2 *Komaki* (1986) Insurance	7 *Komaki and Citera* (1990)	13 *Goltz* (1993) Reserve Officers Train. Corps
		14 *Komaki, Reynard, Lee, and Wallace* (1995) Sailboat racing
3 *Jensen and Komaki* (1993) Newspaper		15 *Reynard and Komaki* (1995) Sailboat racing
4 *Brewer, Wilson, and Beck* (1994) Police, Australia	8 *Larson and Callahan* (1990)	16 *Komaki and Reynard* (1995) Sailboat racing
5a *Komaki, Hyttinen, and Immonen* (1991) Construction, Finland	9 *Brewer* (1995)	17 *Gevgilili, Komaki, and Chu* (1996) Film
5b *Komaki, Hyttinen, and Immonen* (1991) Government, Finland	10 *Komaki, Desselles, and Schepman* (1988)	18 *Niehoff and Moorman* (1993) Movie theater
6 *Komaki, Desselles, and Bowman* (1989) Sailboat racing		

Key: Studies 1–18

1a,b Komaki, J. L., Zlotnick, S., & Jensen, M. (1986). Development of an operant-based taxonomy and observational index of supervisory behavior. *Journal of Applied Psychology*, *71*, 260–269.

2 Komaki, J. L. (1986). Toward effective supervision: An operant analysis and comparison of managers at work. *Journal of Applied Psychology*, *71*, 270–279.

3 Jensen, M., & Komaki, J. L. (1993, May). Beware of too many directives: Spotting a suppressor variable in the operant model of effective supervision. In J. Cannon-Bowers (Chair), *Optimizing team performance through team leader behavior*. Symposium conducted at the conference of the Society of Industrial and Organizational Psychology, San Francisco, CA.

4 Brewer, N., Wilson, C., & Beck, K. (1994). Supervisory behaviour and team performance amongst police patrol sergeants. *Journal of Occupational and Organizational Psychology*, *67*, 69–78.

5a,b Komaki, J. L., Hyttinen, M., & Immonen, S. (1991, August). Cross-cultural research in work and leader behavior. In K. R. Thompson (Chair), *Managing across cultures from a behavioral perspective: Theory and research*. Symposium conducted at the meeting of the Academy of Management, Atlanta, GA.

6 Komaki, J. L., Desselles, M. L., & Bowman, E. D. (1989). Definitely not a breeze: Extending an operant model of effective supervision to teams. *Journal of Applied Psychology*, *74*, 522–529.

7 Komaki, J. L., & Citera, M. (1990). Beyond effective supervision: Identifying key interactions between superior and subordinate. *Leadership Quarterly*, *1*, 91–105.

8 Larson, J. R., Jr., & Callahan, C. (1990). Performance monitoring: How it affects work productivity. *Journal of Applied Psychology*, *75*, 530–538.

9 Brewer, N. (1995). The effects of monitoring individual and group performance on the distribution of effort across tasks. *Journal of Applied Social Psychology*, *25*, 760–777.

10 Komaki, J. L., Desselles, M. L., & Schepman, S. (1988, October). *Testing critical linkages in the operant model of effective supervision: Assessing subordinate performance and attitudes*. Paper presented at the conference of the Society of Organizational Behavior, Worthington, OH.

11 Komaki, J. L., & Newlin, M. H. (1990, April). Walking on the wild side: Criterion-related validation of an in-basket exercise of supervisory behaviors. In M. H. Newlin (Chair), *Simulated performance assessment: Fact or fantasy?* Symposium conducted at the conference of the Society of Industrial and Organizational Psychology, Miami, FL.

12 Komaki, J. L. (1997). Behind the scenes: Fieldtesting a measure of effectiveness for theater teams. In M. T. Brannick, E. Salas, & C. Prince (eds), *Team performance assessment and measurement: Theory, methods and applications*. New York: Springer.

13 Goltz, S. M. (1993). Dynamic of leaders' and subordinates' performance-related discussions following monitoring by leaders in group meetings. *Leadership Quarterly, 4*, (2), 173–187.

14 Komaki, J. L., Reynard, M., Lee, C., & Wallace, J. (1995, October). *Apples and oranges at sea: Skippers' leadership styles make a difference*. Paper presented at the meeting of the Society of Organizational Behavior, Madison, WI.

15 Reynard, R., & Komaki, J. L. (1995, May). *The music of management: Rhythms of effective leaders*. Poster session presented at the conference of the Society of Industrial and Organizational Psychology, Orlando, FL.

16 Komaki, J. & Reynard, M. (1995, July). *Cross-currents at sea: A time-series analysis of leaders in action*. Poster session presented at the conference of the American Psychological Society, New York.

17 Gevgilili, A., Komaki, J., & Chu, S. (1996, March). Research in innovation. In D. A. Hantula (Chair), *Advances in organizational behavior analysis*. Symposium conducted at the meeting of the Eastern Psychological Association, Philadelphia, PA.

18 Niehoff, B. P. & Moorman, R. H. (1993). Justice as a mediator of the relationship between methods of monitoring and organizational citizenship behavior. *Academy of Management Journal*, *63*, 527–556.

conducted in naturally occurring settings, ranging from a medical insurance company in the midwestern USA (Study 2) to police departments in central Australia (Study 4). In these field studies, no attempts were made to alter the behaviors of leaders. Questions raised by the results of these studies, however, required further scrutiny in the precision of a laboratory setting (Studies 7, 8, 9, and 10). The findings of the laboratory studies, in turn, spurred investigators to return to the field (Studies 11 through 18).

Our researchers addressed four major issues: (a) *measuring leaders for their behaviors and their effectiveness*, (b) *testing hypotheses about leaders' effectiveness*, (c) *exploring why the model works*, and (d) *identifying boundaries of the model*. In this chapter, we discuss the ways in which we assessed leaders, and our testing of hypotheses about their effectiveness.

MEASURING LEADERS FOR SUPERVISORY BEHAVIORS

Our first task in testing the model was to develop a reliable, representative, and sensitive way of assessing how leaders supervised from day to day. We have developed two indices, as discussed in Chapter 2: (a) the Operant Supervisory Taxonomy and Index (OSTI) in which coders go to the leaders' places of work and observe them first-hand, and (b) a paper-and-pencil alternative, the Operant Supervisory In-Basket Assessment (OSIBA), in which leaders respond in writing to items in their "in-basket."

By observing in situ

Study 1 (Komaki, Zlotnick, & Jensen, 1986)

Psychometric properties of the operant supervisory taxonomy and index (OSTI)

Study 1 details the development and field-testing of the OSTI. To assess its psychometric properties, we collected data on twenty-seven managers, in a theater and in a bank. The results showed that it was feasible to observe managers in action, that the reliability of the observers was acceptably high, and that the OSTI was sensitive to differences among individual leaders. Results also showed that at least twenty observations of thirty minutes each were necessary to obtain reasonably representative information on a given manager's behavior.

Using an in-basket assessment

Study 11 (Komaki & Newlin, 1990)

Validating the operant supervisory in-basket assessment (OSIBA)

Study 11 is a criterion-related validity study of the OSIBA, in which twelve computer managers were observed, using the OSTI, and scored for their responses on the OSIBA. The results show that the amount of time managers spent monitoring and providing consequences was highly and positively correlated with their OSIBA scores.

MEASURING LEADERS FOR SUPERVISORY EFFECTIVENESS

The key to understanding how leaders lead is, of course, their behavior. But just as important is their effectiveness. We cannot pinpoint what effective leaders do without knowing which leaders are actually effective.

Continuing criterion problem

The assessment of success in motivating others, however, as with supervisory behaviors, poses a major challenge (Campbell, Dunnette, Lawler, & Weick, 1970; Dunnette, 1963; James, 1973; Schmitt & Klimoski, 1991; Smith, 1976; Stone, 1978). One obstacle, inherent to the task of managing, is that leaders typically make their contribution through their followers rather than by producing a tangible result themselves. Hence, it is necessary to assess their effectiveness by assessing the people they supervise. But, both practitioners and researchers agree, good measures of the effectiveness of groups are rare (Blake, Mouton, & Allen, 1987; Guzzo & Shea, 1992; Levine & Moreland, 1990; McGrath, 1984; Mitchell, 1982). Studies conducted with teams in ongoing organizations typically include only predictor variables about the team's inputs (e.g., group norms, the composition of the group), with occasional references to the group's dynamics or interactions. What is typically missing is how to judge the effectiveness of the group. In the almost exclusively descriptive studies of team-building (cited in Bettenhausen (1991)), for example, how the teams fared against one another is not known. Several authors recommend guidelines (e.g., Baker & Salas, 1992; Blum & Naylor, 1968; Campbell, Dunnette, Lawler, & Weick, 1970) or standards (Hackman, 1987). But, with the exception of behaviorally based checklists, few have been implemented. When investigators do assess group effectiveness, they rarely use actual outcomes, relying instead on superior's ratings (e.g., Tziner & Eden's (1985) ranking of tank crews by commanding officers), or assessments of emotional tone (e.g., Campion, Medsker, & Higgs's (1993) measure of employee satisfaction). Even leaders themselves have qualms about the ways in which they are appraised, as we shall see next.

Frustrations with purported evaluations of effectiveness

Some of the shortcomings of measuring leadership are most glaringly evident to the very leaders being rated. Directors in charge of theater production teams, for example, have strong opinions on this topic. Arvin Brown, former artistic director of the Long Wharf Theatre in New Haven, Connecticut, speaks from his own experience with theater critics:

I mean, if it were a matter of being damned for what you can't do well and being praised for what you do well, as much as anyone hates to be criticized, one could live with it .... [But] very often you're overpraised for things that you know damned well don't represent you or the other artists at their best, and you can be cruelly taken to task for things that are simply not true.

(Bartow, 1988, p. 34)

Theater director Brown points to two common complaints about evaluating effectiveness. One concerns extraneous factors over which leaders can exert *little control*. Such indices as critics' reviews and ticket sales are often seen as irrelevant, having to do with things "beyond what the manager can do himself to affect outcome" (Campbell, Dunnette, Lawler, & Weick, 1970, p. 107). Although Brown does not feel he has been particularly battered by critics, he likens the evaluation process to a "crap shoot" (Bartow, 1988, p. 34) – not a ringing endorsement of the evaluation process.

A second reservation concerns the extent to which the actions of the group as a whole are *comprehensively reflected*, what Campbell Dunnette, Lawler, and Weick (1970) refer to as the "sampling of the job behavior domain" (p. 111). This is particularly germane to the complexities of putting on a show. Lloyd Richards, famous for his direction of August Wilson's plays, compares the act of directing to Picasso's painting, *Guernica*. Picasso's genius, says Richards, was in "just where each little or big element existed in that picture – what shapes they began to take, where they appeared before they were finally in the right place" (Bartow, 1988, p. 259). Unfortunately, evaluations of directors are typically one-dimensional: the voice of a single critic or member of the cast or crew, or a single source such as ticket sales or the annual Tony Award.

Scholars, as well, have chastised such fickle measures of group performance. Hackman (1987) astutely points out that "most organizational tasks do not have clear right-or-wrong answers ... nor do they lend themselves to quantitative measures that validly indicate how well a group has done its work. Moreover, one needs to be concerned about more than raw productivity or decision quality" (p. 323). He recommends an evaluation composed of system-defined rather than researcher-defined assessments of a group's output. He also suggests that the process of interaction be included.

A final misgiving of theater professionals, reflecting both of the above problems, concerns the *lack of agreement among raters*. Rocco Landesman, president of Jujamcyn Theaters in New York, describes his peers as a diverse group, each with "his own ax to grind, his own vendettas and resentments" (Witchel, 1992, p. C2). Artistic points of view differ. In compiling interviews with American directors, Arthur Bartow (1988) notes:

even among those directors whose belief systems are similar, the work of each has its distinctiveness. Together, they serve to prove that there is no "correct" method of directing. As soon as one points to a

director whose technique results in success, one can then look to another
director whose method contradicts the first and whose work is also
recognized as significant. (p. xii)

Scholars too point out the vagaries of "response sets, chance response
tendencies, and differing expectations of observers" (Campbell, Dunnette,
Lawler, & Weick, 1970), indicating a dire need to return to the traditional
psychometric concern for interrater reliability.

Developing criteria for criteria

Study 12 (Komaki, 1997)

The CRU criteria for leaders of groups doing interdependent tasks

In response to these issues, Komaki (1997) proposed, in Study 12, a set of
standards that can be used to constructively judge existing criterion variables
and to improve future ones. The criteria were designed, in this case, for teams
doing interdependent tasks – tasks which, in the terminology of Thompson
(1967), are not pooled individual contributions, but reciprocally interdependent acts in which all parties depend upon one another to get the job done.

We refer to the criteria by the mnemonic CRU representing a fine wine:

"C" reflects the *complexity* of the team's effort: the interrelationship of the
product and process of the team (Hackman, 1987), multiple constituen-
cies (Schmitt & Klimoski, 1991), and/or components of the task requiring
coordination among team members (Komaki, Desselles, & Bowman,
1989).

"R" indicates that independent raters consistently agree on their recordings
and obtain interrater *reliability* scores of 90 percent or better during the
formal data collection period.

"U" means that the effort is primarily *under* the control of the team, is
responsive to their efforts, and is minimally affected by extraneous
factors.

The CRU criteria differ from previous criteria such as relevance, freedom
from bias, reliability, practicality (Bernardin & Beatty, 1984; DeVries,
Morrison, Shullman, & Gerlach, 1986; Fleishman & Quaintance, 1984;
Smith, 1976; Thorndike, 1949) and discriminability (e.g., Kane & Lawler,
1979) in that they: (a) are tailored for interdependent tasks, (b) address both
method *and* content, (c) function as a group, with no one criteria being
substitutable for one another, (d) favor neither outcomes nor behaviors (cf.
Gilbert, 1978), and e) take the leader's perspective rather than that of the
criterion developer or management, either of whom might value such
attributes as practicality and inexpensiveness over those of the CRU
criteria.

As judged by performance ratings

Of the fourteen field studies involving our model, eight have included one or more measures of effectiveness, in keeping with our aim of identifying what effective leaders do. Toward this end, we assessed both performance and attitudes of followers. This section focuses on performance.

One method of evaluating performance, the *ratings of superiors and subordinates*, was used in six of our studies. Another method, the *direct assessments of performance*, was used in four studies.

Studies 2, 3, 4, and 6 (Komaki, 1986; Jensen & Komaki, 1993; Brewer, Wilson, & Beck, 1994; Komaki, Desselles, & Bowman, 1989 respectively)

Using ratings of effectiveness by superior

One indicator of effectiveness is how the leaders themselves are evaluated, assuming that effective managers will be regarded accordingly. Ranking and rating managers by supervisory effectiveness can be done by superiors, sub-ordinates, and/or peers. The indicator in four studies was the judgments of superiors. Each Division Vice-President in Study 2, for example, ranked and rated each insurance manager in his division (e.g., Director, Unit Manager) in terms of "motivating others" on an A through F scale. We assessed only the dimension of "motivating others," because the broader scale of effectiveness can be influenced by many factors (e.g., technical expertise, entrepreneurial skills) not necessarily related to effectiveness in supervising others. We used the ratings and rankings to form two extreme groups: when the ratings were fairly homogeneous, only the highest- and lowest-ranked managers were selected, and when the ratings were more divergent, a higher proportion of managers was selected to be in each group.[3]

Brewer, Wilson, and Beck (1994) used a more elaborate in-house rating system when evaluating the effectiveness of patrol sergeants. Each ser-geant's supervisor in Study 4 completed a confidential performance rating, using a seven-point scale (with 1 being "very poor" and 7 "outstanding"), for each sergeant's team on thirteen dimensions (efficiency; field reports; local knowledge; legal/procedural knowledge; convictions; arrest ratio; arrest/report quality; citizen complaints; radio protocol; care/maintenance of equipment, property; concern with occupational safety issues; absentee-ism; evidence of principled behavior).

Another highly recommended possibility, however, is to use ratings from behaviorally anchored rating scales (BARS) (Campbell, Dunnette, Arvey, & Hellervik, 1973; Zedeck, Imparato, Krausz, & Oleno, 1974). BARS contain anchors illustrative of various degrees of supervisory performance. Despite its promise as a measure of supervisory effectiveness, we found BARS not to be feasible in Study 2, due to management's understandable reluctance to make available the considerable time needed to construct the scales and to rate all forty-five managers.

Studies 5a and 18 (Komaki, Hyttinen, & Immonen, 1991; Niehoff &
Moorman, 1993, respectively)

Using ratings of effectiveness by subordinate

Workers can also provide the assessment. In Study 5a, construction crews
rated their supervisors on how well they met "the demands of the job,"
indicating their responses on a five-point scale from very bad (1) to very
good (5). Each manager's average rating was his or her effectiveness score.[4]

Our decision to use performance ratings in the six studies, rather than the
highly recommended outcome approach, was largely due to the fact that no
single outcome existed by which these leaders could be reliably judged. In Study
18, for instance, the movie managers were responsible for a variety of activities
with few outcomes adequately reflecting the quality of their effectiveness. The
same was the case for Study 4. The activities for which police sergeants were
responsible ranged from their arrest ratio to evidence of principled behavior,
with few outcomes fairly representing the quality of their performance.

One advantage of performance ratings is that they can be used to compare managers whose subordinates perform dissimilar tasks. Performance
ratings were useful in Study 3, in a newspaper organization, for example,
where it was not possible to make meaningful comparisons among departments ranging from editorial to printing. And in Study 2, of an insurance
company, claims processing departments turned out to handle significantly
different types of claims and clients (e.g., large corporations versus government employees). The rating and ranking of managers, while indirect,
provides a viable alternative for assessing performance directly.

To the extent that a leader can take into consideration the complexity (C) of
the team's efforts, as well as extraneous factors that are not under (U) the
team's control, ratings by superiors can come close to meeting two of the three
CRU criteria. The disadvantage of such ratings, however, is that they are
subject to accusations of poor interrater reliability (R). With only one party
such as the publisher in Study 3 doing the rating, it is not possible to assess the
extent to which another observer would agree or disagree with the assessment
of the leader's behavior. All else being equal, actual assessments of performance are preferred over superior or subordinate ratings.

By directly assessing team performance

We have, to date, developed three ways of evaluating how well leaders
motivate teams.

Study 6 (Komaki, Desselles, & Bowman, 1989)

Sailing effectiveness measure (SEM)

The SEM is based on each skipper's series standings during a specially
designed round-robin regatta, or series of races. Since each skipper's stand-

ing is an integral part of the competition, the races lent themselves to this use of an outcome measure of effectiveness. Series standings were defined as the average number of points each skipper obtained per race. For each race, points were allotted, using the Low Point Scoring System (United States Yacht Racing Union, 1985): (a) "Each yacht *finishing* a race and *not* thereafter retiring or being disqualified shall score points equal to her finishing position, with one-quarter point off for first place" (p. 77). (b) "All other yachts, including a yacht which finishes and thereafter retires or is *disqualified*, shall score points equal to one more than the number of yachts registered for the series." (p. 77).

Critical variables were kept constant: (1) the model of boat (all were model J–24), (2) the number of crew members (three per boat), and (3) the sailing expertise of the crew (one person with high, one with medium, and one with low sailing expertise).

The round-robin regatta controlled for possibly misleading influences. Even though all boats in this case were the same model, some boats, while theoretically the "same," are faster than others. The same can be claimed for the expertise, compatibility, and experience of the crew in working together. Hence, boats (even though they were the same model), crew members, and observers were randomly assigned to skippers for each race; there were no intact crews.

SEM met some CRU requirements very well. It reflected the complexity (C) of the overall team's effort, closely approximating the conditions of normal yacht racing. And it minimized such extraneous factors as the composition and experience of the crew, assuring that results were more likely to be under (U) the control of the leaders.

One limitation, however, was that interrater reliability (R) could not be assessed because only one observer could be stationed per boat. Another problem was the overshadowing of the interdependent portion of the crews' work. Although we set up the race course to accentuate the team coordination aspect of raising and lowering one of the sails, crew members still spent less than 10 percent of their time on this part of the course. If one wanted to concentrate on team coordination, or if one could not arrange a random-assignment, round-robin format, then the STEM measure, described below, might be worth considering.

Studies 14 and 15 (Komaki, Reynard, Lee, & Wallace, 1995; Reynard & Komaki, 1995)

Sailing teamwork effectiveness measure (STEM)

The STEM differs from the SEM in that it emphasizes the coordination or teamwork aspects of racing, assessing the portion of the race – the hoisting of a particular sail, referred to as the "chute" – that requires five crew members to carry out jointly a minimum of six precisely-timed steps. The

Figure 4.2 Studies 13–15: sailboat racing course. Boats start at the downwind buoy or mark, travel to the upwind mark (at top of diagram), rounding it (while crew hoists the chute), and end again at the downwind mark

raising of the chute takes place as the boat makes a U-turn around a particular buoy or stationary mark (the upwind mark) as shown in the race course in Figure 4.2.

To judge how well the team did at hoisting its chute, we looked at the number of seconds (the metric used by all racers) the team required to accomplish the maneuver. We calculated this, as described in Table 4.1, by assessing when two events occurred: (a) the "upwind time" and (b) the "chute time." For example, with an upwind time of 5:51:33 and a chute time of 5:51:43, it took ten seconds to hoist the chute.

We accomplished this by videotaping the two relevant portions of the race from another boat. Coders then identified exactly when each event occurred. After extensive training of coders, involving the skipper of one of the boats, reliability scores averaging 94.4 percent were finally obtained.

On average, crews took 52.9 seconds (standard deviation [SD] = 39.6) to raise the chute successfully. The times ranged from a low of 10 to a high of 184 seconds, with a median score of 46.5 and a mode of 17.

STEM was a sensitive, reliable, independent assessment of how well teams coordinate under pressure. A shortcoming, however, was that STEM did not cancel out as many extraneous factors as SEM. Adjustments could be made, for example, for some boats having sails that took comparatively longer to hoist (Table 4.1, p.89), but not for other factors such as the composition of the leaders and crew.[5] Because of the differences and complexities among the boats involved, it was not safe to randomly assign skippers and crew to boats on every race.

Table 4.1 Study 14: measures of sailing effectiveness – sailing teamwork effectiveness measure (STEM) and sailing strategy measure (SSM)

Terms	Sailing Teamwork Effectiveness Measure Definition
Seconds to chute hoist	Number of seconds between the boat reaching the upwind mark and its chute or spinnaker being completely up and full *Formula*: Chute time minus upwind time (e.g., 5:51:33 − 5:51:43 = 10 secs).
Upwind time	Time at which the middle of the boat crosses the "midway point," where "midway point" is an imaginary line drawn between the upwind mark and the downwind mark
Chute time	Time at which the spinnaker or chute is first up and full (including all three corners of the chute) and continues to be full for at least three consecutive seconds
Adjustments[a]	*How calculated*
For type of set	By multiplying unadjusted time by a constant for a designated type of set. For a gibe set, the constant was .50, e.g., unadjusted time of 66 for gibe set ×.50 = 33
For designated boats	By multiplying unadjusted time by a constant (.90 or .95) for designated (slower) boats whose chutes were judged to take longer to hoist

Terms	Sailing Strategy Measure Definition
Seconds after start	Number of seconds boat's "nose" crosses imaginary line between the starting mark and the committee boat *Formula*: Actual start time minus potential start time (e.g., 5:39:56 − 5:39:54 = 2 seconds)
Potential start time	Five minutes after the coach gives the five-minute warning by sounding a horn or calling out "five-minute warning, 9, 8, 7, 6, 5, 4, 3, 2, 1"
Actual start time	Time at which any part of the boat's hull, crew, or equipment crosses the imaginary line drawn between the midpoint of the committee boat and the starting mark
Adjustments[a]	*How calculated*
For premature starters	A 30-second penalty was imposed

[a] Adjustments were also made for all cases in which the two tapes – the tape taken aboard the boat, referred to as the AB tape, and the tape taken on the committee boat, the CB tape – were not synchronized. To do this, the time for the CB tape was adjusted to coincide with the AB tape.

Another, perhaps prohibitive, problem with STEM is that it requires prodigious technical expertise and resources which were enabled by a contract to the author from the Army Research Institute. Though we are grateful for the opportunity, as researchers, we hardly presume it to be typical.

Study 12 (Komaki, 1997)

Theater teamwork effectiveness measure (TTEM)

The TTEM, like the STEM for sailboat crews, emphasized how well teams coordinated with one another to complete a task. In this case, the leaders were theater directors, responsible for melding the efforts of cast and crew members to create a performance. As Ives (1995), a playwright, describes the process:

> Over weeks of planning, weeks of rehearsal and weeks of performance, all the people in that group have to agree. This doesn't mean...they don't have political and philosophical or racial and religious differences. It doesn't mean there isn't a hierarchy of power.... It means that all those people have to work together and negotiate decisions... whether they like one another or not, in the interest of some agreed-upon greater good. (p. H13)

The TTEM included three aspects: (a) excellence in execution: whether production elements – e.g., lighting, sound, set, costumes, props – were in line with the standard operating procedures of any theater production, (b) fulfillment of the staff's vision: whether the director's discretionary wishes about the way the show looks, sounds, and feels are successfully implemented, and (c) factors affecting the morale of the group: elements such as whether the crew's time was productively spent, and the frequency of leaders' outbursts and gracious acts. These three aspects of execution, vision, and morale are multiplied for an overall TTEM score.[6]

Thus far, we have field-tested the TTEM in six theater productions: one in college and five Off-Off Broadway. Each production was of moderate technical sophistication. Six raters collected data during technical rehearsals and dress rehearsals when the following personnel were typically present – the director in charge of the entire production; a stage manager; lighting, costume, and sound designers, as well as their technical crews and running crews behind the scenes; and, on occasion, production crew members who built the sets and ran operations such as the ticket office. Since cast rehearsals in which the director works with just the cast were off-limits to the raters, interactions with the cast could not be included. Hence, the TTEM emphasizes the technical aspects of putting on a clean, tight show rather than its artistic merit.

The TTEM meets two of three CRU criteria in that it reflects the complexities (C) of putting on a production by including the three aspects of execution, vision, and morale. We took care to ensure that TTEM was minimally affected by extraneous factors and under (U) the control of the team. A team could operate on a shoestring budget of $15 (this actually happens) for the entire production, but still obtain a score of 100 percent for execution if all elements were in place. Similarly, vision could be expressed by the director, a designer, or even a cast or crew member; what mattered was that a decision was made to do it and that it could be done by dress rehearsal. If any member of the team objected, it was not counted as a vision. In the same way, morale did not depend upon the length of the rehearsals, but upon whether the time, however long or short, was spent productively. And an outburst did not in and of itself doom the team to a poor morale score. A volatile director who blew up, throwing a muffin in anger, could make up for this by acting graciously. In all cases, the emphasis was on assuring that all aspects of the TTEM were within the control of the team and not subject to extraneous influences.

Other extraneous factors that we eliminated were the choice of the play itself, the director's interpretation, and the acting by the cast. These aspects, classified under artistic merit, reflected a single person's vision rather than the work of the team as a whole. Critics could pan a show for its choice of material or the interpretation by the director and individual cast members, and the team could still meet the technical requirements of the production. Hence, we defined our excellence score to reflect whether the show, whatever its artistic content, was well-executed.

We also assessed TTEM for interrater reliability. To date, we have yet to attain satisfactory scores, and we continue to make revisions.

Our ongoing endeavors with TTEM illustrate how and why the CRU criteria are so important to the development of criterion variables. At the same time, however, like the sailing measures, TTEM requires considerable expenditure of time and resources, as well as great honing of expertise. We estimate that it necessitates twelve to twenty hours of observations per leader. Of course, no one ever promised that measuring leadership effectiveness would be easy.

As judged by follower attitudes

The effectiveness measures we have described so far concern performance: how well leaders motivated their teams, as assessed by ratings or actual outcomes. Attitudes, however, are also thought to be important for effective leadership.

Precedents for this dual emphasis can be found in both the operant conditioning and I/O literatures. Its value to operant conditioners can best be seen in their discussions of what they refer to as the "social validity" of treatment programs (Wolf, 1978). Each program, the argument goes, should be evaluated in terms of both performance and attitudes to be considered fully effective. Evaluations of a college course, for example, were based upon how much participants learned *and* liked the course (McMichael & Corey, 1969). A treatment for delinquent youths was assessed according to how much the youths improved *and* whether the youths thought the treatment programs were "fair" and that personnel were "concerned" about their welfare (Braukmann, Kirigin, & Wolf,

1976); in this case, the attitudinal ratings of these youths were actually shown to be negatively related to the number of offenses committed during and after the program, a critical outcome measure. Wolf and his colleagues (1996) go on further to describe how their dissemination efforts were severely hampered when they failed to assess the satisfaction not only of the delinquents themselves but key consumer groups (e.g., in legal and educational institutions) responsible for their welfare.

Including both performance and attitudes in the definition of effectiveness is a well-established practice in I/O psychology as well. Adams (1965) predicts that if sufficient tension arises from feelings of inequity, employees will change their inputs by increasing or decreasing their productivity and/ or they will change their attitudes by altering their perceptions of the situation. Similarly, Hackman and Oldham (1976), in their job characteristics model, designate both work performance and attitudes (such as satisfaction with one's job and with opportunities for personal growth) as indicators of effectiveness.

In testing our model, we assessed the attitudes of followers in Studies 5b, 10, and 18.

Study 5b (Komaki, Hyttinen, & Immonen, 1991)

A paper-and-pencil assessment of emotional tone

To see if Finnish government workers reacted to the amount of time managers spent monitoring and providing consequences, Immonen measured both satisfaction and well-being with questionnaires.

To assess satisfaction, she used the Job Diagnostic Survey, developed by the US psychologists Hackman and Oldham (1976). A few examples of the questions follow. For general satisfaction: "Generally speaking, I am very satisfied with this job." (1 = I disagree strongly with the statement, 7 = I agree strongly). For growth satisfaction: "How satisfied are you with the amount of independent thought and action you can exercise in your job?" For satisfaction with job security: "How secure do things look for you in the future in this organization?" For satisfaction with supervision: "How satisfied are you with the amount of support and guidance you receive from your supervisor?"

For mental well-being, Immonen used the Eigenzustandsskala (EZ-Scale) by the German sports psychologist Nitsch (1976). The EZ-Scale assesses a person's feelings, in this case, toward her job at a certain moment. Since these feelings are thought to be transient, measurement is typically repeated; in this study, it was administered at the beginning and the end of the work day. Here are some examples of questions. For sociability: "Do you now feel open-hearted?" "Do you now feel ready to interact with your co-workers?" For self-confidence: "Do you now feel superior to others?" "Do you now feel skilled?" For state of mind: "Do you now feel cheerful?"

"Do you now feel satisfied?" Workers rated themselves on a scale from one to six, with six being the most positive response.

Study 10 (Komaki, Desselles, & Schepman, 1988)

An observational measure of follower attitudes

The questionnaire has almost universally been the instrument of choice in assessing attitudes (Fiedler, 1967; Fleishman, 1973). As an alternative, we developed an observational measure of attitudes referred to as the Observational Follower Attitudes Measure (OFAM).

We assumed that individuals can exhibit their own attitudes, and that such statements portray a representative picture. We constructed OFAM specifically for Study 9, a laboratory experiment in which followers interacted with their bosses over a three-hour period. OFAM could, however, also be used in field settings.

We arranged group discussions in which three to four subordinates discussed their respective bosses; sometimes the moderator gently prodded reticent workers for their views. The discussions, averaging 8.8 minutes, were videotaped. Trained coders then watched the videotapes and coded what each subordinate said and did every five seconds; each of the twenty-five group discussions took approximately two hours to code.

Coders classified followers' actions into one of the following categories: (a) not communicating, (b) non-work-related, (c) work-related, and (d) personal comment about the boss. The last category constituted the measure of subordinates' attitudes, as shown in Table 4.2. Comments about bosses were further classified as being positive or negative. Positive (negative) attitudes were then calculated as the number of intervals in which a subordinate evaluated the manager positively (negatively) divided by the total number of intervals.

To assess reliability, two observers independently coded all twenty-four videotapes. Interrater reliability was defined as an interval-by-interval percentage agreement score, and averaged 86.4 percent with a range of 70.2 to 97.6 percent. At least one (but usually two) of the authors examined transcripts of the disputed intervals and/or watched the videotapes to reach a decision as to the appropriate category.

In short, we used a variety of methods to assess leaders' effectiveness: traditional ratings of performance, paper-and-pencil assessments of attitudes, direct assessments of team coordination, and an observational measure of followers' attitudes.

MEASURING OTHER DOMAINS

As described so far, our effectiveness measures have dealt with the motivational aspects of leaders' jobs. This emphasis was consistent with the model's aim. Questions arose, however, about how the model might shed

Table 4.2 Study 10: observational follower attitudes measure (OFAM): categories, definitions, and examples

Category	Definition	Example
1 Not communicating	Not conveying or seeking information, either verbally or nonverbally	Listening to peers talk. Reading evaluation form.
2 Non-work-related	Discussing topics other than work or the boss or task	"It's kind of cold in here." "Are you guys all from Indiana?"
3 Work-related	Referring to work in general or boss or task in particular, with exception of personal comments about boss/task	"I rated myself a lot higher than I got rated." (Following discussion about vague instructions): "Life is not fair, and you can't always expect it to be."
4 Personal comment about boss	Making statement reflecting opinion of party speaking	"I would definitely say she plays favorites." "If they would have told us at the beginning 'This is what needs to be done,' but she didn't give us any indication at all."
Positive	Expressing approval	"She was pretty good at prioritizing." "She knows what she is doing though, because she kept saying about the five–digits and all that stuff."
Negative	Expressing disapproval	"She came in so often and gave me instructions. 'Hey, look, man, these directions – they're in my blood.'" "She doesn't inspire me."

light on other aspects of a leader's job, such as making strategy decisions. To address this question, we developed two other indices: the Sailing Strategy Measure (SSM) and the Innovative Ideas Measure (IIM).

Direct assessment of decision-making

Studies 14 and 15 (Komaki, Reynard, Lee, & Wallace, 1995; Reynard & Komaki, 1995)

Sailing Strategy Measure (SSM)

The Sailing Strategy Measure (SSM) differs from the previous sailing measures in that it specifically assesses the decisional aspects of leadership.

To judge how effectively skippers made decisions, we looked at how well the skippers functioned at the very beginning of a race. The start was chosen because it requires making critical and rapid judgments, based on considerable technical information, within a five-minute countdown before the race begins. Among these decisions are: (a) where to start (referred to as the "favored end of the line"), (b) what tactic to use in starting (ranging from the commonly used Vanderbilt start to the dip start), (c) which boats to pass or follow, and where this places you in the first hundred yards, and (d) how to maneuver for optimal position. Skippers must also take into consideration: (a) "the puzzle of wind, weather, and current" (Conner & Levitt, 1992, p. 313), (b) the moves and countermoves of other boats, and (c) the rules, covering 134 pages, which Conner, winner of the America's Cup yacht competition, says are "as complex as our legal system" (p. 282).

To judge how well skippers handled the start, we looked at whether their boats crossed the starting line in a timely manner. Ideally, the number of seconds the boat crossed the line after the official start time would be zero. We identified two points in time, as described in Table 4.1 on p. 89: (a) the potential start time (five minutes after the coach gave the "five minutes to start" warning), and (b) the actual start time (the time at which the boat crossed the starting line). We calculated the number of seconds after the start as the actual start time minus the potential start time. For instance, with an actual start time of 5:41:31 and a potential start time of 5:41:30, the seconds after the start would be one.

Trained coders, referring to videotaped portions of the race, identified exactly when each of these events occurred. Interrater reliability scores averaged 90.0 percent.

The average number of seconds after the start was 16.0 seconds (standard deviation, or SD = 15.8). Scores ranged from zero to 54 seconds, with a median of 8 and a mode of 2. When we assessed the correlation between the SEM and the STEM, we found it was not significant, suggesting that the two were tapping fairly distinct or non-overlapping constructs, $r = .17$, $p = .40$.

Direct assessment of novel suggestions

Study 17 (Gevgilili, Komaki, & Chu, 1996)

Innovative Ideas Measure (IIM)

Facilitating innovation has become an important part of success for contemporary organizations. Regrettably, our knowledge of how to enhance *and* measure it borders on the archaic. Anderson and King (1993), in reviewing the literature, acknowledge the many process models (e.g., Amabile, 1988; Kanter, 1988), but conclude that "the proliferation of innovation process models is not matched by an abundance of empirical research examining their validity" (p. 16). When investigators have measured

Table 4.3   Study 17: transcript in which film director and director of photography express innovative ideas

---

Person: *Verbatim comment*

Administrative ideas

(Right after the shot)
DP: It was good for me!
  D: Thank you everybody, we have done it! Check the gate please, check the gate!
DP: Do you know what would be nice, **if the boom man could be here, working with me.**
  D: Why didn't we do that?
DP: I don't know.
  D: Ken said that the boom man should be behind the camera of course which is right...

....

(During set-up)
DP: At 2:30 we have to get this shot completely.
DP: Do you know.... Why don't we do something; **give me 10 minutes to set the shot, then we do rehearsal then I light...**
  D: That's good!

Technical ideas

(Right after the shot)
  D: That was beautiful!
DP: **Can I put a little light in here?** A little for her face. A lot of diffusion for her face here. I need to see her face when she is talking to Jim.
  D: Good for you! Could you do it, Dorothy, just a little bit?

....

(Before the shot, during the set up)
  D: I want to tell you that we have a whole shot with boxes and boxes.
DP: Do you want to see them first?
  D: No, not really. This is just the idea, if we don't see them it's fine.
DP: They will shake their hands here.... Oh no, not here, there.... Then go out of frame.
  D: Shaking their hands.... We have some movement. Shake hands and then one starts moving out and we get the POV of boxes.
DP: I don't know. I don't like the idea though.
DP: **I would like to end up near the boxes in the cut,** finally you might make them shake their hands here and go away, or he can stay like that and we get the boxes. I think this will work better.
  D: OK.

Note: Innovative ideas are in bold. D = Director and DP = Director of Photography

innovation, the "classic approach has been the use of attitude, and other scale measures and self-completion questionnaires, in cross-sectional designs" (Anderson & King, 1993, p. 8). Subjects, often scientists and engineers in research and development laboratories, rate each of their subordinates or co-workers on the extent to which he or she generates creative ideas, and searches out new technologies, processes, techniques, and/or product ideas. Besides the traditional measurement issues of halo and response bias, there is a problem with the sensitivity of the data. Respondents are often not able to make the fine distinctions necessary to discriminate among potential idea-generators. This can lead to reduced variability, creating the impression that everyone possesses and expresses innovative ideas at more or less the same rate.

To assess the generation of innovative ideas, we developed an index, referred to as the Innovative Ideas Measure (IIM). We observed potential idea-generators as they worked together over time and calculated their rate of innovative ideas as the number divided by the time the parties interacted with one another. So far, we have observed four pairs of leaders, the director and the director of photography, during eight-to-ten day film shoots, for five thirty-minute periods, making a total of 150 minutes per leader.

Among the ideas, as shown in Table 4.3, were those concerned with administrative matters and the technical aspects of shooting. Often ideas seemed to spring forth without ceremony or prompting. New ideas rarely went unnoticed. The way in which ideas unfolded and the reactions they provoked have provided material for further research.

IN SUMMARY

Besides the two measures of leader behavior – the OSTI and the Operant Supervisory In-Basket Assessment (OSIBA), our assessments of effectiveness included two performance measures for sailboat racing teams, the Sailing Effectiveness Measure (SEM) and Sailing Teamwork Effectiveness Measure (STEM), and one for theater production teams, the Theater Teamwork Effectiveness Measure (TTEM). Along with these measures of team performance, we have explored other domains as well, including an assessment of decision-making strategy, the Sailing Strategy Measure (SSM), and a measure of the generation of new ideas, the Innovative Ideas Measure (IIM).

Armed with these measures, we were finally ready to see what distinguishes between effective and lackluster leaders.

FIELD-TESTING HYPOTHESES ABOUT QUANTITY AND QUALITY OF EFFECTIVE LEADERS' BEHAVIORS

To date, we have addressed three different issues of the model. The first hypothesis, emphasizing the *quantity* and *quality* of behaviors, predicted that effective managers are likely to spend more time providing monitors (particularly work sampling) and consequences (of all kinds but not predominantly negative ones). The second hypothesis highlights the *conjunctive* nature of monitors and consequences and predicts that both are necessary for superior performance and for positive attitudes. The third and most recent hypothesis, which we discuss in the last section of this chapter, concerns the *timing* of these behaviors.

We have conducted five full tests (Studies 2, 3, 4, 5a, 5b, and 14) and two partial tests (Studies 6 and 18) of the first hypothesis. All tests measured leaders in the field who varied in effectiveness, and then compared their supervisory behaviors. Six of the tests used the OSTI or one of its variations as a measure of leaders' behaviors; one of the partial tests assessed only the major OSTI categories and none of the subcategories; the other partial test evaluated leader behavior, using a survey estimate that primarily tapped monitoring and its method; the remaining five tests included all categories and subcategories, enabling us to draw conclusions about the quantity and quality of the behaviors.

Three of our tests (Studies 2, 3, and 5a) used what is called a contrasted or *extreme groups* design (Meyers, 1972), as have studies in the areas of personality (Barron, 1955), educational assessment (Mager, 1982), and clinical assessment (Conger & Farrell, 1981; Cowan, Conger, & Conger, 1989). When there are specific, detectable behavioral differences between groups, with one group judged high along a particular dimension and another group thought to be low, one can identify how the groups differ by using an extreme groups design. Conger and Farrell (1981) used this design to determine if so-called "highly-skilled" and "poorly-skilled" individuals spent differing amounts of time conversing and making eye contact when interacting with members of the opposite sex. The extreme groups were composed of college males, judged to be the same in anxiety and conversational concern, but at opposite extremes in the frequency with which they went on dates. Using this extreme groups design, the investigators could identify what the highly-skilled individuals did that distinguished them from the poorly-skilled.

The extreme groups design is highly recommended for the exploratory phases of research programs. The contrasting of extremes also makes it easier to find differences with smaller sample sizes. Restricting the number of managers observed was critical in testing the model because of the extensive data collection required – a total of thirty twenty–minute observations per manager – to obtain representative information with the OSTI.

We describe each of the seven tests briefly.

Study 2 (Komaki, 1986)

We used an extreme groups design in the first test, comparing twelve effective insurance managers with twelve not-so-effective or lackluster managers, matched for organizational level and functional area, over a seven-month period.

Monitoring via work sampling distinguished between effective and lackluster managers

Monitoring was the critical behavior that distinguished between the two groups, as is shown in Table 4.4. Effective managers collected performance

Table 4.4 Studies 2, 3, 5a: means of OSTI categories and subcategories for extreme groups of insurance, newspaper, and construction managers

CATEGORIES (and sub-categories)		Study 2[a] Lackluster leaders	Effective leaders	Study 3[b] Lackluster leaders	Effective leaders	Study 5a[c] Lackluster leaders	Effective leaders
MONITOR		2.0	2.9##	5.1	4.9	8.9	11.5
Method:	Work Sample	0.1	0.5##	1.2	1.2		
	Self-report	1.5	1.9	3.3	3.0		
	Secondary Source	0.4	0.5				
CONSEQUENCE		5.8	5.7	4.4	6.4#	3.6	5.3#
Delivery:	Direct	2.2	2.4	1.6	2.0		
	Indirect	3.5	3.3	2.7	4.4		
Evaluation:	Positive	2.3	2.4	1.0	1.7		
	Negative	1.7	1.8	1.6	2.2		
	Neutral	1.7	1.6	1.8	2.6		
ANTECEDENTS		4.5	5.0	4.7	5.3	10.5	9.3
Delivery:	Indirect	0.5	0.4	0.7	0.9		
	Direct	4.0	4.0	4.0	4.4		
Specificity:	Action/condition	0.7	0.8				
	Action only	1.7	1.7				
	Outcome/condition	0.3	0.6				
	Outcome only	1.5	1.7				
	No outcome/no action	0.3	0.2				
	Specific[d]			1.1	1.7		
	General[d]			3.6	3.6		
Responsibility:	Clear	3.8	4.3	4.3	4.7		
	Unclear	0.6	0.7	0.4	0.5		
Planning:	Current	4.0	4.7	4.6	5.2		
	Anticipated	0.4	0.3	0.1	0.1		
Type:	Invited	0.2	0.1	0.1	0.04		
	Not invited	4.2	4.9	4.6	5.2		
OWN PERFORMANCE		3.7	3.5	3.1	3.6	3.6	6.2
Content:	Consequences	1.8	1.6	1.2	1.9		
	Monitors	0.2	0.1	0.2	0.2		
	Antecedents	1.7	1.8	1.6	1.5		
WORK-RELATED		40.8	44.1	37.6	37.1	20.9	22.7
Type:	Invited	1.3	1.3	2.0	2.1		
	Not invited	27.6	29.0	21.9	24.1		
NOT COMMUNICATING		11.9	13.9	13.8	10.9*		

Table 4.4 Continued

	Study 2[a]		Study 3[b]		Study 5a[c]	
CATEGORIES *(and sub-categories)*	Lackluster leaders	Effective leaders	Lackluster leaders	Effective leaders	Lackluster leaders	Effective leaders
NON-WORK-RELATED	1.3	1.6	2.4	2.7	2.9	4.7
SOLITARY	41.8	37.0	42.6	39.6	41.5	32.8

Note: OSTI = Operant Supervisory Taxonomy and Index. The mean time spent on each category as measured by the OSTI.
[a] Number in group = 12
[b] Number in group = 8
[c] Number in group = 8
[d] Used only in Study 3
*$p < .05$ for a nondirectional (two-tailed) test
#$p < .05$ for a directional (one-tailed) test
##$p < .01$ for a directional (one-tailed) test

information significantly more often ($M = 2.9$ percent) than the lackluster ones ($M = 2.0$ percent), $t = 2.59$, $p = .009$. Effective managers also more frequently used a particular method of monitoring: work sampling, $t = 3.32$, $p = .002$. Figure 4.3 shows that only four of the twelve marginally

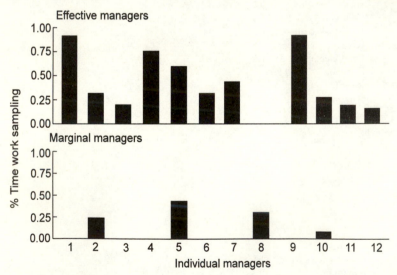

Figure 4.3 Study 2: work sampling and effectiveness. Bar charts showing percentage of time spent sampling the work by each insurance manager in the effective (portrayed on top) and lackluster (bottom) groups. Each manager is ranked according to the amount of time they spend monitoring overall.
Source: Komaki (1986). Copyright© 1986 the American Psychological Association. Reproduced with permission.

effective managers sampled the work, whereas eleven of the twelve effective managers did so.

What this meant, in day-to-day terms, was that besides monitoring via self-report (e.g., "Did you set up the rehab audit?") and secondary source (e.g., "Sonia, did Maryalice find them?"), effective managers also directly *sampled*: watching employees process claims, listening as employees spoke with clients, examining claim forms, and inspecting computer print-outs.

Consequences were positive, negative, and neutral

We found no differences in the amount of consequences delivered by effective ($M = 5.7$ percent) and marginal ($M = 5.8$ percent) groups, $t = -.14$, $p = .46$.

Effective managers did not necessarily deliver more positive or fewer negative consequences than marginal managers, as hypothesized. No differences appeared, even when the alpha level was raised to .30, in the provision of positive, negative, or neutral consequences by the two groups, $T2 = .18$, $p < .98$.

Table 4.4 shows that no other category or subcategory was related to effectiveness.

This set of data, as we state in our conclusion to the study, "provides an empirical basis on which to begin identifying what constitutes effective supervisory behaviors" (Komaki, 1986, pp. 277–278).

Study 3 (Jensen & Komaki, 1993)

The next study used the same extreme groups design, comparing roughly the top ($n = 8$) and bottom ($n = 8$) quarter of managers, matched for functional area and level within the organization. Jensen and Komaki (1993) conducted this study in a daily newspaper operation. With its frequent deadlines and highly visible product, the newspaper firm differed from Study 2's insurance company. Hence, we could see if the predictions of the model held in this setting as well.

Consequences distinguished between effective and lackluster managers.

The top-rated managers ($M = 6.4$ percent) spent more time providing consequences than did their less highly rated counterparts ($M = 4.4$ percent), $t = 3.42$, $p <.05$, as shown in Table 4.4. This meant that the effective managers were more likely to feed back results to their staffs, to make corrections, and to say such things as, "This is really good; you don't know how delighted I am that this went on [for] two pages."

Even though the newspaper firm had its own built-in consequences – the strong daily reactions of readers – these results reaffirmed the importance of providing periodic in-house recognition.

Consequences were positive, negative, and neutral.

As in Study 2, effective managers did not necessarily deliver more positive or fewer negative consequences than marginal managers. No differences were found in the provision of positive, negative, or neutral consequences by the two groups.

Not communicating also distinguished between effective and lackluster managers

Remaining silent while engaged in a face-to-face exchange distinguished between the top and bottom-rated groups as well. Not communicating was much more likely for the bottom-rated ($M = 13.8$ percent) than the top-rated ($M = 10.9$ percent) managers, $p < .05$.

No other category or subcategory, as is shown in Table 4.4, was related to effectiveness.

Antecedents as a classic suppressor

Orders or antecedents were found to fit the pattern of a classic suppressor (Conger & Jackson, 1972; Horst, 1966). The characteristics of a suppressor are: (a) a lack of association with the criterion, (b) a significant negative regression weight, and (c) a high intercorrelation with another predictor. As indicated in Table 4.5, we found an inverse relationship between effectiveness and antecedents, with antecedents receiving a negative weight, *Beta* $=-.47, p <.05$. In the correlations among effectiveness and the three predictor categories (in this case, we used the entire sample, $N = 33$), as shown in Table 4.6, antecedents were highly and positively related to consequences, $r = .69, p <.05$, but bore little or no relationship to effectiveness, $r = .01$.

Table 4.5 Study 3: multiple regression analysis for OSTI predictor categories and criterion of supervisory effectiveness for newspaper managers

Categories	Beta[a]	F
Antecedents	−.47	4.45*
Monitors	−.08	.23
Consequences	.71	9.76*

Note: The criterion was supervisory effectiveness; the predictors were the OSTI categories of antecedents, monitors, and consequences.
[a] Standardized regression coefficient
*$p < .05$

Table 4.6 Study 3: correlations between selected OSTI categories and rated
supervisory effectiveness of newspaper managers

Categories	Supervisory effectiveness	Antecedents	Monitors
Antecedents	.01		
Monitors	.03	.15	
Consequences	.37*	.69*	.25

Note: Degrees of freedom = 31
*$p < .05$

With a suppressor, "the irrelevant variance...is 'suppressed' by literally
subtracting its effects out of the regression equation" (Cascio, 1987, p. 276).
Horst (1941) found a similar pattern when he assessed the role of the verbal
score in selecting test pilots during World War II. The verbal score had a
very low positive correlation with the criterion, but a reasonably high
correlation with the mechanical, spatial, and numerical ability scores. The
regression weight for the verbal score was also negative, and when included
with the rest of the predictors, it increased the multiple correlation. Horst
(1966) explained this by suggesting that "verbal ability of a high order is not
essential for success. It *was* necessary, however, in order to perform successfully on the paper and pencil tests used to measure mechanical, spatial and
numerical ability" (p. 355). He concluded, "to include the verbal score with
a negative weight served to suppress or subtract the irrelevant ability, and to
discount the scores of those who did well on the test simply because of their
verbal ability" (p. 355).

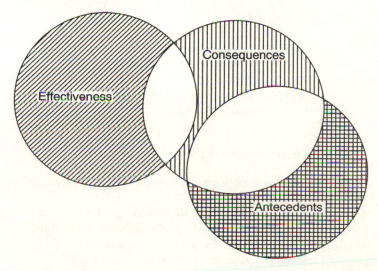

Figure 4.4 Study 3: Venn diagram showing antecedents as a suppressor variable

The Venn diagram in Figure 4.4 illustrates the relationship among the variables, with the irrelevant variance in the consequence score being suppressed by the antecedent score. Our finding that antecedents acted as a classic suppressor cast a new light on their role. These results were different from previous studies. Antecedents have consistently been shown, in Studies 2, 3, 4, 5a, and 14, to be unrelated to effectiveness.

Although difficulties have sometimes emerged in interpreting suppressors (Cascio, 1987; Dicken, 1963; Tzelgov & Henik, 1991), we identified a logically appealing explanation. The antecedent score in our study represents leaders' propensity to talk about workers' performance. Performance is implied or discussed, with leaders telling others about performance when they deliver both antecedents and consequences. Hence, this inclination to talk about performance could explain the high correlation between consequences and antecedents, $r = .69$. Yet, this penchant per se is probably *not* essential for being an effective manager. If we assume that this propensity is the irrelevant variance in the consequence score, then including the antecedent score in the regression equation serves to discount the scores of those who provide consequences, and it enhances the multiple correlation, $R = .50, p < .05$.

We conclude, in our study, that future researchers should look at the relationships among variables in the model[7] rather than focusing on each one in isolation. Based on the *Beta* weight in the regression equation for consequences, for example, managers should be encouraged to raise the level of their consequences without necessarily increasing their level of directives or monitors. Along the same lines, managers should refrain from increasing antecedents, particularly when no commensurate increases are made in monitors and consequences.

Study 4 (Brewer, Wilson, & Beck, 1994)

Study 4 examined the generality of our model in an Australian police force, with measures of supervisory behavior obtained on twenty police patrol sergeants. To prevent any purposeful bias in the observations, Brewer, Wilson, and Beck (1994) sampled across shifts and stations, and collected data over a three-to four-month period.

More effective sergeants monitored via self-report

Patrol sergeants of higher-performing teams spent more time monitoring the performance of their officers, $r = .40, p < .05$ (a directional, one-tailed test), *degrees of freedom* $(df) = 18$. Moreover, the highly rated sergeants more often used a particular method of monitoring – self-report – with the officers, $r = .47, p < .05$ (a non directional, two-tailed test). When sergeants monitored via self-report, more than 60 percent of the discussions revolved around the off-site patrol activities of officers. The authors note, "although sergeants rarely directly sampled their subordinates' performance on patrol, those with higher-rated teams [spent] more time collecting verbal reports on patrol activities" (p. 75).

More effective sergeants provided neutral consequences

Consequences in general were not associated with effectiveness, $r = .35$ ($p > .05$). But a particular type, a neutral consequence, was significantly related to effectiveness, $r = .51$, $p < .05$ (two-tailed test). This meant that supervisors of teams ranked higher for effectiveness were likely to provide more neutral consequences than their lackluster counterparts.

The authors conclude by noting that "[behavioral] observation using the OSTI confirmed that the supervisors' use of performance monitoring and consequences (neutral) were strongly associated with effective team performance" (p. 76).

Study 5a (Komaki, Hyttinen, & Immonen, 1991)

Another set of researchers looked at two sets of leaders in Finland. Hyttinen assessed thirty-one managers in the construction industry, and Immonen looked at sixteen supervisors in a government agency. We discuss each sub-study separately, beginning with that of Hyttinen.[8]

Monitors and consequences together distinguished between effective and lackluster construction supervisors

We used an extreme groups design and made comparisons between roughly the top and bottom quarter of managers, with eight people in each group.

To reflect the necessity of both monitors and consequences in effectively motivating others, we created a new variable by multiplying[9] each manager's monitor and consequence scores. The combination of monitoring and consequences (MONxCON) distinguished between the effective ($M = 59.8$ percent) and marginal ($M = 33.2$ percent) groups, $t = 1.9$, $p = .03$. The differences between the two groups in monitors, although in the predicted direction, were not statistically significant, $t = 1.5$, $p = .08$, as shown in Table 4.4 (p. 99). With consequences, the effective group spent significantly more time ($M = 5.3$ percent) providing feedback in contrast to the lackluster group ($M = 3.6$ percent), $t = 1.7$, $p = .05$.

Solitary behavior makes a difference on construction sites

Our results also pointed to an interesting difference concerning the "solitary" category. Although the results only approached significance, effective supervisors spent less time by themselves ($M = 32.8$ percent), while lackluster supervisors spent more time alone ($M = 41.5$ percent), $t = -1.9$, $p = .07$.

Study 5b (Komaki, Hyttinen, & Immonen, 1991)

The second sub-study aimed to see how Finnish followers reacted to managers who spent more or less time monitoring and providing consequences. Immonen assessed their satisfaction, as discussed earlier, using the Job Diagnostic Survey, and their well-being, using the Eigenzustandsskala.

Monitoring and consequences related to government workers' satisfaction and mental well-being

The correlations are shown in Table 4.7. With two exceptions, the relationships were positive. Managers who provided more monitors and consequences (MONxCON) had workers with greater well-being in terms of mental effort, self-confidence, state of mind, and tolerance, at either the beginning or the end of the day or both, $r = .71$ to $.80$. These managers also

Table 4.7 Study 5b: correlations between selected OSTI categories and subordinate attitudes in a Finnish government agency

	Supervisory behaviors			
ATTITUDES	*Monitors*	*Consequences*	*Monitors × consequences*	*Solitary*
SATISFACTION				
In general	.50	.33	.52	−.83*
With opportunities for growth	.23	.25	.26	−.74*
With job security	.82*	.59	.87**	−.72*
With supervision	.57	.17	.63	−.54
MENTAL WELL-BEING				
Mental effort {Beginning of day	.66	.71	.71*	−.88**
{End of day	.42	.83*	.72*	−.70
Sociability {Beginning of day	−.13	.81*	.20	−.53
{End of day	−.19	.77*	.24	−.35
Self-confidence {Beginning of day	.63	.82*	.75*	−.80*
{End of day	.38	.73*	.75*	−.32
State of mind {Beginning of day	.24	.84*	.55	−.60
{End of day	.39	.89**	.73*	−.45
Tolerance {Beginning of day	.84*	.52	.80*	−.86*
{End of day	.36	.68	.59	−.46

Note: OSTI Categories: each category was defined per department as percentage of time spent by manager + percentage time spent by assistant manager/2. Number of departments = 8. Degrees of freedom = 6. Attitudes: satisfaction as reported on the Job Diagnostic Survey (Hackman and Oldham, 1980), and mental well-being as reported on the Eigenzustandsskala (EZ-Scale) (Nitsch, 1976), where subordinate reports per department = sum of subordinate reports/ number of subordinates in each department.
* $p < .05$, two-tailed
** $p < .01$, two-tailed

had workers who were more satisfied with job security, particularly if the managers monitored more often, $r = .82$ to $.87$. We also found a positive relationship between managers who provided more consequences and workers' reported positive feelings about their mental effort, sociability, self-confidence, state of mind, and tolerance, $r = .73$ to $.89$.

Solitary behavior in government offices. While we found generally positive associations with monitors and consequences, we found the reverse with solitary. Negative relationships appeared, as shown in Table 4.7, between the time managers spent by themselves and workers' satisfaction and well-being, r's $= -.74$ to $-.88$. Managers who spent more time alone in their offices had workers who were dissatisfied in general, dissatisfied with their opportunities for growth, and dissatisfied with their job security. On the other hand, managers who spent more time with their workers had workers whose mental effort, self-confidence, and tolerance was higher at the beginning of the day.[10]

The authors acknowledge that these results regarding monitors and consequences had been predicted. What we did *not* anticipate were the exceedingly negative findings about solitary leaders.

Study 6 (Komaki, Desselles, & Bowman, 1989)

To see how leaders can orchestrate optimal team performance, Komaki, Desselles, and Bowman (1989) looked at leaders of teams – a skipper and three crew members competing in a specially designed regatta. Each of the nineteen skippers participated in two to four races, with an average of 3.2 races per skipper for the series. Due to the precarious positioning of the observers (and an occasional spray of salt water), the OSTI was modified so that no subcategories and a smaller number of categories were coded; hence, as noted earlier, we considered this study only a partial test. We used two methods of assessing effectiveness: the Sailing Effectiveness Measure and the ratings and rankings of leaders, as discussed earlier.

Effective sailboat skippers monitored more and provided more consequences

Series standings correlated significantly and negatively[11] with consequences, $r = -.47, p < .05$, and monitors, $r = -.51, p < .05$, during the races themselves.

When the coach's ratings and rankings of crew handling were substituted for series standings, monitoring was not significantly related to effectiveness, although it was in the predicted direction, $r = -.42$, while consequences were significantly correlated with effectiveness, $r = -.60, p < .05$.

This meant that the winning skippers did not neglect to monitor and provide consequences. They oversaw the efforts of their crews and let subordinates know when they were doing things correctly or incorrectly, despite the constant motion and incessant roar of the racing environment.

In conclusion, the authors note, "the viability of the original model was affirmed. That is, the key components of performance monitoring and consequences were found to be meaningfully related to leader success under conditions of realism and control using a clear-cut outcome" (p. 529).

Study 14 (Komaki, Reynard, Lee, & Wallace, 1995)

Study 14 was similar to the preceding study in that it, too, looked at leaders of teams on boats ($N = 28$) in a fleet racing competition. There were two or three leaders and eight to ten crew members aboard each forty-foot sailboat. The measure of effectiveness was the Sailboat Team Effectiveness Measure (STEM), discussed earlier, which focused on the interdependent portion of the race, the hoisting of a particular sail, the chute.

Faster sail hoists related to monitoring

Monitoring performance was associated with quicker STEM times, as shown in Table 4.8, $r = -.33^{12}, p < .05$. Effective leaders gathered information about the team, as illustrated in Tables 3.1 and 3.3 (on pp. 38 and 55), in a variety of different ways. They sampled team members as they adjusted equipment. They asked crew members: "Who's on the foreguy?", as well as asking

Table 4.8 Study 14: means and correlations between OSTI categories and teamwork and strategy measures of sailboat skippers

CATEGORIES			Teamwork		Strategy	
	Mean[a]	SD[b]	r[c]	p[d]	r[e]	p[d]
MONITOR	18.6	9.9	−.33[#]	.05[f]	.44*	.02
CONSEQUENCE	16.3	5.3	.01	.54[f]	−.20	.31
ANTECEDENTS	40.1	9.8	−.03	.90	−.33	.09
OWN PERFORMANCE	3.0	1.7	−.28	.14	−.19	.35
WORK-RELATED	32.1	8.8	−.16	.43	−.15	.44
NOT COMMUNICATING	2.0	1.9	.37	.05*	−.13	.53
NON-WORK-RELATED	.05	.28	.01	.96	.19	.34
SOLITARY	31.7	12.8	.07	.74	.12	.56

Note: OSTI = Operant Supervisory Taxonomy and Index
[a] Percentage of intervals spent on category during all observations for each manager/number of Managers in the group
[b] Standard deviation
[c] Pearson product–moment correlation with Sailing Teamwork Effectiveness Measure of chute time
[d] Probability of the result occurring for a nondirectional (two-tailed) test unless otherwise noted
[e] Pearson product–moment correlation with Sailing Teamwork Effectiveness Measure of start time
[f] Probability of the result occurring for a directional (one-tailed) test
*$p < .05$, two-tailed
#$p < .05$, one-tailed

other team members: "Why does he have to trim the guy?" They also used a particular method of monitoring – which we referred to as "monitoring the equipment" – in which leaders would look up at the sail to see the impact of the crew's actions. Leaders who monitored using one of these methods were more likely to have faster sail hoists than their slower counterparts.

The time spent by the leaders providing consequences (over three-quarters of which were negative) was not related to effectiveness, $r = .01$. Positive and neutral consequences were not correlated either, although together they were in the predicted direction, $r = -.18$, $p < .35$.

Slower chute hoists associated with not communicating

Not communicating was significantly and positively[13] related to effectiveness, $r = .37$, $p < .05$. What this meant was that lackluster skippers were more likely to remain silent while engaged in a face-to-face exchange than their more effective peers.

No other category or subcategory was related to effectiveness.

The authors conclude that although the leaders with the fastest sail hoists monitored more, it is possible that the predictive power lies, not just in the quantity or quality of the behaviors, but in their timing as well.

Study 18 (Niehoff & Moorman, 1993)

In contrast to the preceding studies, Niehoff and Moorman (1993) focused on monitoring via work sampling. They predicted that managers who sampled the work would be more likely to have subordinates that perceive their manager allocates rewards equitably and makes decisions fairly (what they refer to as distributive and procedural justice, respectively). They based this hypothesis on their view that "monitoring is one of the primary mechanisms available to managers for maintaining fairness in reward allocation decisions" (p. 531) and on the views of Folger and Greenberg (1985) who have written extensively on workplace fairness.

To test this hypothesis, they conducted a study in a national movie theater management company with eleven general managers who operated eleven theaters with a total of 213 employees. To assess the leaders' behaviors and employees' attitudes, employees completed a survey, indicating the quantity and quality of monitoring of the manager at their theater and, on the same survey, they tallied their perceptions of their manager.

Leaders who monitor via work sampling perceived to be more fair

Results of the structural equations modeling provided general support for the hypothesis. Niehoff and Moorman (1993) conclude that work sampling "had a positive influence through its effect on fairness" (p. 527).

IN SUMMARY

Looking at the results of the five full tests (Studies 2, 3, 4, 5a, 5b, and 14) and the two partial tests (Studies 6 and 18), we can draw several conclusions.

Hypotheses about Quantity and Quality of Leaders' Behaviors

Monitors or consequences, or both, distinguish between effective and marginal managers

The time leaders spent monitoring and providing consequences made a difference in every single test, across lines of nationality: with medical insurance managers (Study 2), newspaper managers (Study 3), and two different sets of sailboat skippers (Studies 6 and 14), all of these aforementioned settings being American, and with Australian police sergeants (Study 4), Finnish construction supervisors (Study 5a) and Finnish government workers (Study 5b). Followers whose leaders took the time to find out how they were doing and to provide feedback surpassed their counterparts. Not only were the quantity of monitors and consequences related to better performance ratings (Studies 2, 3, 4, and 5a) and better outcomes (Studies 6, 14), but they were also positively associated with how workers felt about their mental well-being and their jobs (Study 5b). Furthermore, monitoring via work sampling was related to employees' perceptions of their leaders' fairness (Study 18).

Monitoring via work sampling is related to supervisory effectiveness

As predicted, the quality of the monitors used also made a difference. Monitoring was related to effectiveness in six of the seven tests (Studies 2, 4, 5a, 5b, 6, 14, and 18). Furthermore, monitoring specifically via work sampling was positively associated with effectiveness in two of the tests. Managers who were perceived as being more accurate and fair in their judgments of employees' performance (Study 18) were estimated to spend more time monitoring via work sampling. In another test with insurance managers (Study 2), effective managers were those more likely to go to where their followers were working and see first-hand how they were doing; these insurance managers, for example, would pick up claim forms and look at them.

The bar chart in Figure 4.3 (p.100), showing the effective and lackluster insurance managers in Study 2 by work sampling, is particularly illuminating. With one exception, all of the effective managers sampled the work at one time or another. In contrast, only one-third of the marginal managers picked up a claim form even once. The complete absence of work sampling on the part of two-thirds of the lackluster managers is greatly revealing, given that each manager was observed up to twenty times over seven months, and given the overall similarity of the effective and lackluster groups (the groups were matched for organizational level and function). Furthermore, the two groups did not differ substantially in education, span of control, (i.e. number of subordinates for whom they were responsible), supervisory experience, or training.[14]

Effective leaders provided a mix of positive, negative, and neutral consequences

As predicted, effective leaders did not provide substantially more positive consequences than lackluster leaders. Instead, they distributed positive, negative, and neutral consequences more or less evenly. Rarely did positive or negative consequences account for more than 50 percent of the total. The sole exception was Study 14, in which sailboat skippers in the heat of competition gave more than three-quarters negative consequences. Not surprisingly, the relationship between effectiveness and consequences in general hovered near zero.

Hypothesis testing: conjunctive

The evidence for our conjunctive hypothesis was mixed. Effective leaders provided more monitors *and* more consequences in four of the seven tests: the Australian police sergeants (Study 4), the Finnish construction supervisors (Study 5a), the Finnish government workers (Study 5b), and the American sailboat skippers (Study 6). In the other three tests, however, either monitoring alone (Studies 2 and 14) or consequences alone (Study 3) distinguished between effective and marginal leaders. Given the latter results, we were not able to conclude that both monitors and consequences are necessary. This, in turn, propelled a search for a better way of testing the conjunctive hypothesis (Study 10) and an examination of the impact of monitoring alone (Studies 8, 9, and 10) and of consequences alone (Study 10).

Some positive and some negative signs

Several results were not predicted. None the less, we have used both hypothesized and non-hypothesized findings as a rich source of data to configure and reconfigure the model.

Neutral consequences were highlighted

The relatively new subcategory of neutral consequences was found in Study 4 to distinguish between effective and marginal police sergeants. Interestingly enough in this setting, described as having a rigid chain of command, more than half of the consequences delivered were neutral.

Precautionary notes about antecedents, not communicating, and solitary

While evidence remains sketchy, it should be noted that some dissonant notes were sounded for: (a) antecedents (in Study 3, where it was a classic suppressor variable), (b) not communicating (in Studies 3 and 14, where it was negatively related to effectiveness), and (c) solitary behavior (in Study 5a, where a negative relationship between effectiveness and solitary approached significance, and in Study 5b, where the amount of time managers spent alone was negatively related to followers' well-being and satisfaction).

Evidence from our seven tests, therefore, shows that the quantity and quality of monitors and consequences is predictive of effective leaders. The data also indicate that caution may be in order for the categories of antecedents, not communicating, and solitary. Still remaining unanswered, however, is the conjunctive question of whether both monitors and consequences are necessary.

TESTING HYPOTHESES ABOUT CAUSALITY IN THE LABORATORY

Each of the preceding seven tests took place in naturally occurring settings in which no attempts were made to alter leaders' behaviors. By disturbing their behaviors as little as possible, we could obtain, as qualitative researchers encourage (Lofland, 1971; Moos, 1973; Patton, 1980), a sense of the true way in which leaders talk about and carry out their day-to-day issues and concerns. Field studies have the advantage of providing a "matchless way of learning the variables, their ranges and combinations" (Runkel & McGrath, 1972, p. 94).

This strength of field studies, however, is at the same time their downfall. Precisely because field studies do not disturb the social systems in which they operate, they lack the rigor necessary to support confident conclusions about cause-and-effect relationships. Only field or laboratory experiments in which one or more variables are manipulated can permit the making of strong causal attributions. Better performing subordinates, for example, "may simply demand increased monitoring and consequences.... Perhaps supervisors of more effective teams had to spend more time vetting the increased paperwork associated with more productive police work" suggest Brewer, Wilson, and Beck (1994, pp. 76–77). At the same time, well coordinated sailboat crews, for example, could conceivably "cause" their leaders to provide more consequences particularly positive ones, rather than the other way around.[15] In the shifting world of a tossing yacht or a busy office, the arrow of causation can point in many directions.

Because the major aim of our model is to identify what effective leaders do, with the clear implication that these pinpointed actions will lead to improved effectiveness, it is critical to be able to draw the causal link. To make this crucial connection, we made use of four laboratory experiments.

Investigators manipulated leaders' behaviors, then evaluated their impact upon followers' performance (in Studies 8, 9, and 10), attitudes (in Study 10), and subsequent interactions with followers (in Study 7).[16] Studies 7 and 10 randomly assigned subjects to different experimental conditions, Study 8 randomly assigned groups to conditions, and Study 9 used a matching procedure before assigning groups to conditions.

By having both laboratory experiments and field studies in one program of research, we were better-equipped to face the "constant, three-horned dilemma" that all investigators must confront to balance the "trinity of desirable conditions – concreteness of behavioral systems, precision of control and measurement, and generality" (Runkel & McGrath, 1972, p. 115).

We describe Studies 8, 9, and 10.

Study 8 (Larson & Callahan, 1990)

Larson and Callahan (1990) looked at the role of monitoring alone, apart from that of consequences. They acknowledged that the act of monitoring has traditionally been assumed to influence people's work behavior only to the extent that it is accompanied by additional managerial action such as performance consequences. They hypothesized, however, that performance monitoring would also have an independent effect upon work behavior.[17]

To test this hypothesis, they used a 3 x 2 factorial design with ninety subjects working at two tasks for a total of two hours. Each subject was exposed to one of three different patterns of supervisory behavior: (a) in the *monitoring-only* condition, the experimenter came into the room every twenty minutes or so to collect their work and to answer any questions; (b) in the *monitoring plus consequences* condition, the experimenter monitored as above, but also provided subjects with information about their performance up to that point; and (c) in the *control* condition, the subjects worked continuously for two hours without interruption.

Providing consequences improved performance over and above that of monitoring alone

Subjects in the monitoring-plus-consequences condition ($M = .82$) completed significantly more work on the monitored task than did subjects in the monitoring-only condition, $t(84) = 2.41$, $p < .01$.

Monitoring alone improved performance

As hypothesized, the subjects' work output was significantly increased by monitoring alone. Subjects in the monitoring-only condition ($M = .33$) completed significantly more work on the monitored task than did subjects in the control condition ($M = -.12$), $t(84) = 2.15$, $p < .02$. As Larson and

Callahan (1990) state, "[t]he amount of work completed on the experimental tasks increased significantly when performance on those tasks was monitored (in comparison with when it was not)" (p. 536).

Study 9 (Brewer, 1995)

Brewer (1995) also examined the role of monitoring alone in a laboratory experiment. He hypothesized that performance monitoring would have an independent effect upon work behavior.[18]

To test this hypothesis, he set up an experiment similar to that of Larson and Callahan, with 124 subjects working at two different tasks for a total of ninety minutes. Each subject was exposed to one of two different patterns of supervisory behavior: (a) an *individual monitoring* condition, in which the supervisor placed the output in a folder marked with the subject's name; and (b) a *group monitoring* condition, in which the supervisor placed the output in a box marked "Group C," making sure to vary the order in which each individual's output was placed in the box on each monitoring occasion.

Monitoring alone improved performance

As hypothesized, the subjects produced more on the monitored task at the expense of the unmonitored task. But this result was limited to performance quantity rather than quality and to monitoring that was administered individually rather than in a group.

Study 10 (Komaki, Desselles, & Schepman, 1988)

In Study 10, we tested the conjunctive hypothesis to see whether both monitoring *and* consequences were necessary for superior performance and satisfactory attitudes. Borrowing from the chemistry laboratory, Komaki, Desselles, and Schepman (1988) believed that the linkage between the two was catalytic. Only when leaders monitor *and* provide consequences will supervisory effectiveness result. The outcome of both occurring will be substantially different from when either happens in isolation.

To test our conjunctive hypothesis, we designed a format in which seventy-three subjects were randomly assigned to work on a US Post Office bulk-mailing sorting task for three hours under one of three conditions:

(a) *Monitors and consequences*, in which the manager first delivered an antecedent, then monitored by sampling the completed bundles or by asking, "How many bundles have you sorted thus far?" Then the manager provided a consequence contingent upon the individual's performance. When the subordinate had done something wrong, the manager suggested how to correct the error (e.g., "No, you don't need to put a sticker on every envelope. Just one sticker per bundle.") When the work had been done correctly, the manager made a fairly general and mildly positive comment to parallel the consequence only condition.

(b) *Monitors-only*, in which the manager provided only monitors (e.g., examining the envelopes without making any comment, or asking, "How many bundles have you sorted thus far?" and then listening to the subordinate's answer, pausing, and delivering the next antecedent).

(c) *Consequences-only*, in which the manager followed the antecedent (e.g., "Don't forget to put the stickers in the lower right-hand corner of the envelope") with a mildly positive comment (e.g., "I'm sure you're doing that.") These consequences, though pleasantly offered, were necessarily vague because the manager had not monitored.[19]

Besides randomly assigning subjects to groups, we held the following constant: (1) the task and materials; (2) instructions about the task; (3) the number and duration of interactions with the manager (who remained the same for the entire experiment); (4) the gender of the manager and subordinates (all were female); and (5) the number and method of monitors and consequences.

There were two dependent variables: one related to the quality of subordinate performance on the sorting task, and one concerning the attitudes of subordinates toward the boss as measured by the Observational Followers' Attitudes Measure, described earlier (p. 93).

For performance, combination is better than consequences alone but not better than monitoring alone

Performance was substantially better when managers both monitored and provided consequences ($M = 94.2$ percent) rather than relying on consequences alone ($M = 82.8$ percent), as shown in Table 4.9. The monitors and consequences group, however, was not found to be superior to the monitors-only group ($M = 86.0$).

Providing both monitors and consequences results in more positive and fewer negative attitudes about the boss

Subordinates who received both monitors and consequences had consistently more positive and routinely fewer negative attitudes about the manager than their peers, as shown in Figure 4.5. When compared with managers who provided only consequences, managers who provided both monitors and consequences were four times as likely to be described in positive terms. The same was true when comparing them with managers who only monitored; managers who did both were nearly twice as likely to be discussed in a positive manner. An examination of the negative attitudes expressed about the boss showed a similar pattern, with the managers who only monitored or provided consequences being described almost twice as often in negative terms.

Table 4.9 Study 10: means of performance and attitudes of subjects by monitor only, consequence only, and monitor and consequence conditions

Effectiveness indices	*Experimental conditions*		
	Consequence only	*Monitor only*	*Monitor and consequence*
Performance			
Quality[a]	82.8[d]	86.0[e]	94.2[f]
	(24.7)	(17.3)	(4.3)
Attitudes			
Positive[b]	2.1[g]	4.3[h]	8.5[i]
	(3.3)	(3.9)	(6.4)
Negative[c]	16.6	14.5	8.4
	(9.9)	(7.9)	(6.5)

Note: Numbers in parentheses are the standard deviations
[a] Percentage of bundles correctly sorted and packaged
[b] Percentage of intervals during group discussion in which subordinate evaluated the manager positively
[c] Percentage of intervals during group discussion in which subordinate evaluated the manager negatively
[d] $n = 24$
[e] $n = 26$
[f] $n = 23$
[g] $n = 22$
[h] $n = 24$
[i] $n = 21$

The evidence in this study, then, supported our conjunctive hypothesis. Although monitoring by itself did not result in any discernible performance

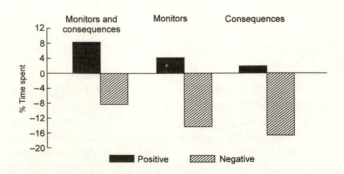

Figure 4.5 Study 5b: attitudes toward manager: proportion of positive and negative comments given by workers when manager provided monitors and consequences, monitors only, or consequences only

differences when compared with monitoring and providing consequences, it caused substantial decrements in followers' attitudes toward the boss. The authors therefore recommend the use of monitors and consequences in combination rather than monitoring alone.

IN SUMMARY

These three laboratory experiments demonstrate that bosses can and do have a meaningful impact upon the performance and attitudes of workers. Workers whose bosses monitored *and* provided consequences (in Study 10), however, outperformed those whose bosses only monitored (in Studies 8 and 10) and those who provided only consequences (in Study 10). Moreover, these workers (in Study 10) also made significantly more positive and substantially fewer negative comments about their bosses.

Because of the use of random assignment, individual differences were attenuated, meaning that these findings held regardless of differences in ability, personality, and demographics among followers. Furthermore, because influential factors (e.g., time spent interacting, the task, the number and type of instructions) were held constant across conditions, they could be ruled out as biasing performance and attitudes. Even when these situational factors were controlled, differences were evidenced.

To sum up, the studies described so far show that the quantity and quality of monitors and consequences make a difference, this supervisory combination is necessary, and this combination results in superior performance and more positive attitudes.

TESTING HYPOTHESES ABOUT THE TIMING OF EFFECTIVE LEADERS' BEHAVIORS IN THE FIELD

As we watched leaders in action, we began to discern some things that the summary scores[20] of the previous studies could not capture. With the racing skippers, for example, an exuberant, fast-paced picture emerged. As in a finely tuned trio, the tactician might bark out an order ("Square back the pole"), the helmsman follow with another ("Bring the pole back"), and the crew boss monitor in the background, while consequences – both negative ("Come on, guys. Come on. Hard! Hard!!") and positive ("Looks great, guys") consequences would be interlaced throughout. On other boats, however, the skippers would sometimes take considerable time before monitoring. They might deliver a welter of antecedents, with the helmsman giving a command ("Guys, you gotta build up speed"), followed immediately by the tactician's orders ("Keep it fat until we get speed. Break'em down a little bit.")

Speculating that the timing of leaders' behaviors was as critical as their quantity or quality, we began casting about for a more accurate vehicle for the patterns we were hearing, and we developed the Operant Supervisory Team Taxonomy and Index – by Sequence (OSTTI-S). This new measure enabled us to test our *pacing hypothesis* in which leaders interested in motivating their teams were expected to follow a cycle – first telling subordinates what to do (Antecedent), then finding out how they are doing (Monitor), and then letting them know how they have done (Consequence). We predicted that effective leaders would deliver these AMC sequences more quickly than their lackluster counterparts. Our rationale was that the more closely in time the elements of the sequence were delivered, the faster the leader could obtain information and then recognize or correct any errors.

Support for emphasizing the timing of behaviors can be found in both the experimental (Block, 1990) and the applied literature (Campbell, 1977; Dyer, 1984; Foushee, 1984; Herold & Parsons, 1985; McGrath, 1984; Yukl, 1992). Hackman and Morris (1975), for example, explicitly state that "the key to understanding the 'group effectiveness problem' is to be found in the ongoing interaction process" (p. 2). They specifically recommend that investigators deal with this interaction process as it "develops and changes over time" (p. 90). Rausch (cited in Hackman & Morris (1975))[21] also makes this point when discussing how to study chess players:

An understanding of successful chess play surely would not result from a study of the number of times players moved each of the chess pieces during games. Instead, one would almost certainly attempt to discern the sequences of moves players made in response to the particular status of the board at any given time (p. 57).

In fact, an assessment of what is needed shows that, at a minimum, data must be obtained uninterruptedly over time *and* then aggregated so as to reflect the patterns of behavior. To see what successful chess players do, for example, one needs to collect data continously throughout the game. Then one must summarize the data in such a way as to reflect the sequence of moves that the players make.

Unfortunately, few studies meet these criteria. Kelly and McGrath (1988) point out that "[m]ost social and behavioral scientists seem to have a natural tendency, when faced with repeated measures from successive trials or observation intervals, to add and average the data across those trials" (p. 60). This, they contend, results in "averaging away" minor fluctuations and masking any rhythmic patterns that should be the focus of research.

But these studies only go so far in looking at the process of interaction, since most of their data are aggregated into scores reflecting the frequency or rate of time spent interacting, with no indication of how the events occurred *in relation* to other events. For example, Foushee and Manos (1981) assess the operation of aircraft and the number of errors made; however, both are aggregated as summary scores.

One notable exception exists in the work by Kanki, Lozito, and Foushee (1989). They examined, closely and continuously, the patterns of communication between the captain and first officer during flight simulations. No clear pattern emerged for the pairs making the most errors, with the pairs showing "tremendous diversity in their behavioral profiles" (p. 60). But the pairs with the fewest errors were characterized as much more homogeneous in those communications, with more predictable (and they surmise more understandable) patterns between them; the captains initiated more commands and the first officers responded with more acknowledgments than would be expected.

Unfortunately, Kanki, Lozito, and Foushee's research remains an exception. Despite exhortations to apply tools and methods such as spectral analysis, Fourier transform analysis, and stochastic modeling techniques (e.g., Bakeman & Dabbs, 1976; Castellan, 1979; Dabbs, 1983; Faraone & Dorfman, 1987; Gottman, 1979; Gottman & Bakeman, 1979; Kelly & McGrath, 1988; Thomas & Malone, 1979; Warner, Kenny, & Stoto, 1979), relatively few researchers actually look at interactions between team members in any depth.

Study 15 (Reynard & Komaki, 1995)

Hence, to test the pacing hypothesis,[22] Reynard and Komaki (1995) conducted Study 15 as part of a larger research program, with the same subjects and setting (teams of leaders aboard twenty-eight boats during practice races) and the same measure of effectiveness, the Sailing Teamwork Effectiveness Measure (STEM), as Study 14, and the newly developed Operant Supervisory Team Taxonomy and Index–by Sequence (OSTTI–S).

We watched during a particularly intense nine-minute period of the race (totaling ninety-six five-second intervals, representing 31 percent of the average 29.3 total minutes of a race). During this period, the leaders dealt with two difficult maneuvers, rounding the upwind mark (as shown on Figure 4.2) and hoisting a particular type of sail, the chute.

Describing AMC sequences

To obtain data on AMC sequences, we again observed the leaders, this time every *five* seconds, using the OSTTI–S. The mean number of seconds per AMC sequence was 143.2, as shown in Table 4.10. The AM portion of the sequence was almost twice as long (94.2 seconds) as the MC portion (49.0 seconds).

Effective skippers provided quick AMC sequences

As shown in Table 4.10, the skippers with the fastest STEM times delivered AMC sequences more quickly, $r = .53$, $p < .001$. In other words, the faster a skipper delivered a sequence consisting of an Antecedent, a Monitor, and then a Consequence, the more effective the team's performance.

Table 4.10 Study 14: means and correlations of AMC, AM, and MC sequences of sailboat racing leaders

Sequences	M^a	SD	r
AMC	143.2	73.2	.53[###]
AM	94.2	77.6	.70[***]
MC	49.0	43.2	−.35

Note: AMC = sequence during which an antecedent (A) was followed by a monitor (M), which was then followed by a consequence (C). AM = the first portion of the AMC sequence, in which the antecedent is followed by the monitor. MC = the second portion of the AMC sequence, in which the monitor is followed by the consequence
[a] M = number of seconds on average it took for the sequence of behaviors to occur
[***] $p < .001$, two-tailed
[###] $p < .001$, one-tailed

We have plotted the actions of one of the most effective sets of leaders.[23] These leaders (depicted earlier in Chapter 3) completed their first two AMC sequences in ten seconds and their third in seventy-five seconds:

```
     00   10   20   30   40   50   00   10   20   30
A  |-●---|----●---|-●-----o----------------------------o--o---|
M  |-●---|----●---|------------------------------●-----------------|
C  |----●|-------●|-------------o--o--------------------------●|
```

As shown in Table 3.3, the third sequence began with the tactician shouting to the crew, "Trim that chute!" (A). The crew boss monitored by looking at the chute, and he cautioned the crew making adjustments: "Hold it, hold it." (C).

We have also plotted the actions of one of the lackluster set of leaders.[24] These leaders (shown in Tables 3.3 (p. 55) and 3.4 (p. 59)) took considerably longer – four and a half minutes – to complete a single AMC sequence.

Effective skippers provided quick AM sequences

A similar pattern was found with the AM sequences, as shown in Table 4.10. The effective skippers, once they gave an antecedent, rapidly monitored, $r = .70$, $p < .001$. The lackluster leaders, however, took much longer to monitor after giving an antecedent than their effective counterparts.

Effective leaders gave more leisurely MC sequences

In contrast, effective leaders, once they monitored, took more time before they gave a consequence. Although the results only approached significance, the MC sequences given by effective leaders were longer, $r = -.35$, $p < .07$. Lackluster leaders, on the other hand, were more brisk in letting their crews know how they had done.

Since this study is the first to show that the pacing of AM, MC, and AMC sequences is related to effectiveness, it would be critical to replicate these results. But they indicate that both the substance of leadership behaviors and their timing is important. Effective leaders provided rapid-fire AM and AMC sequences. They told subordinates what to do, checked what they were doing, and told them how they did. And they did it quickly.

LACKLUSTER LEADERS AND THE ROLE OF OTHER SUPERVISORY BEHAVIORS: ANTECEDENTS, WORK-RELATED, NOT COMMUNICATING, AND SOLITARY

Study 15 also sheds light on managers at the other end of the continuum, the lackluster leaders. It also drew attention to four behaviors: antecedents, work-related, not communicating, and solitary.

Study 15 (Reynard & Komaki, 1995)

Intrigued by the relatively nondescript (and, in one case, negative) impact of orders or antecedents in previous studies, Reynard and Komaki (1995) sought to understand better their role in effectively motivating others.

Antecedents have been relegated, since the model's inception (Komaki, Zlotnick, & Jensen 1986), to a secondary role. Originally, the rationale was that antecedents in the theory of operant conditioning fulfill informational or cuing functions (Kazdin, 1989; Krause, 1994; Miller, 1997; Whaley & Malott, 1971), but not a primary motivational one. To many operant conditioners, antecedents such as "instructions...[are] effective only if the specified responses made in their presence are reinforced, and only if the indicated response goes unreinforced when the instructions are absent" (Whaley & Malott, 1971, p. 248). A management consultant advising managers daily puts it succinctly: "Antecedents get us going: consequences keep us going" (Daniels, 1994, p. 22). In other words, changes in performance will not be sustained, unless antecedents are accompanied by consequences.

In tests of the model, neither the quantity nor the quality of antecedents has generally been predictive of effective leaders. Five of six tests of our model found that antecedents did *not* distinguish between effective and lackluster managers. This was the case in Studies 2, 3, 4, and 5a in insurance, newspaper, police, and construction settings, respectively; similarly, in Study 14 in a competitive racing situation, no relationships were found between effectiveness and antecedents, $r = -.03$.

Even when antecedents were divided by subcategories, no relationships were found with effectiveness in any of the five preceding studies. Antecedents have been subdivided by: (a) delivery: those that are delivered directly and those delivered indirectly; (b) responsibility: whether it is obvious or not obvious who is responsible for doing the antecedent; (c) planning: whether the antecedents anticipate the future or deal with the current situation; (d) teamsmanship: whether coordination is or is not a part; and (e) specificity: how clearly the antecedents identify what the leader expects.[25] The only study (Study 6) in which antecedents were positively related to effectiveness, $r = - .40, p < .05$, was conducted in a three-member team that had not previously worked together, with one of the members a neophyte. Because of the inexperience of one of the members and the lack of seasoning of the team, it was not unexpected that effective leaders would spend more time than usual telling people what to do.

Normally, however, antecedents have not played a distinguishing role when employees were both seasoned and knowledgeable. Neophytes were not doing the jobs of claims processor or auditor (Study 2), police officer (Study 4), construction crew (Study 5a), or racing crew aboard forty-foot boats (Study 14). One study (Study 3), done with employees publishing a daily newspaper, actually found that antecedents served as a suppressor variable.

Although evidence supports these contentions, relegating antecedents to a secondary role has not been without controversy. This stance flies in the face of conventional wisdom in the field of I/O psychology (e.g., Weiss, 1990). In reports of prominent industry leaders, for example, antecedents have traditionally been given a high profile. A former IBM executive was heralded as "a great leader, the ultimate motivator" and described as having a major impact on people so that "people not only understood what they needed to do, but were ready to charge a machine-gun nest to do it" (Rifkin, 1994, p. 8). Likewise, the most common recommendation when confronted with problems involving the work force is "to inform or exhort, or both" (Mager & Pipe, 1984, p. 1), both of which are antecedents. Training, another antecedent, is a ubiquitous solution (Goldstein, 1980; Latham, 1988; Tannenbaum & Yukl, 1992; Wexley, 1984).

These antecedent strategies appear as well throughout the leadership literature. One of the two major dimensions in the classic Ohio State Studies (Fleishman, 1973), initiating the structure of the task, is an antecedent. The inspirational speeches, exhortations, and confidently worded expectations of subordinate performance portrayed in the transformational work (Bass, 1985; House, 1977; Tichy & Ulrich, 1984) are antecedents. Goal-setting as expressed by managers in the work motivation literature is also an antecedent (Locke & Latham, 1990). Perhaps not surprisingly, given these ideological biases, evidence showing antecedents in a less than favorable light has not been warmly received.

Placement hypothesis

Seeking to explain why antecedents have had such a poor history in predicting effective managers, we posited that the frequency *per se* of antecedents may not be important; rather, it was when they occurred or their placement within the AMC sequence that mattered. Antecedents can occur before the monitor – during the AM portion of the sequence – or after the monitor – during the MC portion of the AMC sequence.

Lackluster leaders, we conjectured, are likely to be less attuned to followers and more self-absorbed. Because they are more egocentric, they do not necessarily find out what followers have done but, rather, continue to dwell on what they themselves know should be done. Effective leaders, on the other hand, we predict, would first find out about the followers before providing more antecedents. By monitoring, they would gain valuable information with which to generate more relevant antecedents and contingent consequences. Followers, we thought, would also perceive the subsequent antecedents as more credible and, perhaps, be more willing to accept them. Hence, we predicted in our *placement hypothesis* that lackluster leaders would be likelier than the effective leaders to deliver a string of antecedents *before* they monitored.

Describing antecedents during AM sequences

Using the OSTTI-S, we found that, before they monitored, leaders delivered antecedents during an average of 5.6 intervals.

Lackluster leaders provided more antecedents before they monitored

As we predicted, as shown in Table 4.11, the mediocre leaders had more intervals in which they gave antecedents *before* they monitored, whereas the effective ones had fewer during the same AM sequence, $r = .44$, $p < .05$.

Effective leaders gave more antecedents after they monitored

Interestingly, the opposite was found during the MC sequence. The effective leaders gave more antecedents but only *after* they had monitored. The more

Table 4.11 Study 15: frequency and correlations with effectiveness of sailboat racing leaders of selected OSTI categories

CATEGORIES	Placement within AM sequence	
	Mean	r
ANTECEDENTS	5.6	.44[#]
SOLITARY	6.4	.70**
NOT COMMUNICATING	.42	.43*
WORK-RELATED	4.0	.39*

Note: Mean = number of intervals in which OSTI category occurred. Correlation (r) with effectiveness of chute time

[#]p < .05, one-tailed
*p < .05, two-tailed
**p < .001, two-tailed

intervals with antecedents during the MC sequence, the faster the crew was able to raise the chute, $r = .44$, $p < .01$.

Charting these findings, the effective leaders provided more antecedents *after* they had monitored:

```
        00    10    20    30    40    50    00    10
A    |-●---------o-----o---------------------------o---
M    |----●----------------------------------------------
```

During the MC sequence, as one can see, the number of As is three. In contrast, no As occur during the AM sequence for the effective leaders.

Lackluster leaders, on the other hand, delivered more antecedents (in this case, three) *before* they monitored.

```
        00    10    20    30    40    50    00    10
A    |-●--o--o----------------------o--------------
M    |--------------------------------------●------
```

It is instructive to note that, in these charts, the number of intervals with an antecedent is the same for both effective and lackluster leaders. Three antecedents are given by the lackluster leaders during the AM sequence, and three are given by the effective leaders during the MC sequence. The difference is in their placement. This documented difference in placement helps explain why few differences have been found in the frequency of antecedents. Effective leaders do not necessarily provide more or fewer antecedents. Rather, what these findings suggest is that the difference is *when* they are given.

Based on the support obtained for our placement hypothesis, we did an *exploratory probe*. We wanted to see whether the positioning of other behaviors during the AM and MC portions of the sequences might also be predictive of effectiveness. Three behaviors were found to be related: solitary, not communicating, and work-related, as shown in Table 4.11.

Lackluster leaders were more likely to seek out solitude to work on their own tasks before they monitored

Lackluster leaders had more intervals in which they were solitary *before* they monitored, that is, during the AM sequence, whereas the effective ones had fewer, $r = .70$, $p < .001$. In the boat races, the lackluster leaders were more likely to be looking out over the water and steering the boat than interacting with the crew.

This finding was consistent with the findings of Study 5a, in which the lackluster leaders spent more time solitary, and Study 5b, in which the leaders who spent the most time solitary had subordinates who were the least satisfied and scored the lowest on mental well-being.

Lackluster leaders paid more attention to others talking about work details before they monitored

The greater the number of not communicating intervals *before* the Monitor in the AM sequence, the longer it took for the crew to raise the chute, $r = .43$, $p < .05$. The mediocre leaders were more likely to remain silent while engaged in a face-to-face exchange, for instance, than the effective ones. Discussion, when it happened, typically dealt with the work rather than performance.

This finding also supported previous findings in Studies 3 and 4 in which the lackluster leaders were more likely to not speak up while other workers talked about work details.

Lackluster leaders were more likely to shift from performance- to work-related discussions before they monitored

The skippers with the worst chute hoist times talked more about work details ("The mark's up high." "You gotta go high by Presley so you don't get their gas.") before they monitored performance, $r = .39$, $p < .05$.

The spotlighting of work-related was the first time that this category had been singled out as distinguishing between effective and lackluster leaders. It is consistent, however, with the previous finding about not communicating in which the lackluster leaders participated passively in many discussions of work detail.

In short, Study 15 revealed the important interplay between what leaders do and when they do it. These findings helped to clarify the previously nondescript findings about antecedents. The exploratory probes of Study 15 also cast light onto what the lackluster leaders did.

Study 16 (Komaki & Reynard, 1995)

Buoyed by our findings about the pacing and placement of leaders' behaviors, Komaki and Reynard (1995) continued to examine what leaders do over time. In this case, however, we conducted time-series analyses, looking for trends at various critical points on the race course. By plotting what leaders did every fifteen seconds during the race, we could see if leaders' actions remained more or less stable over time or if they shifted, perhaps increasing what they did as they approached a certain benchmark.

The importance of tracking trends was recently highlighted by the discovery of "a new way to think about AIDS" (Kolata, 1995, p. 2E). Previously, "little" was thought to be "happening during the 10–year period when an infected person is usually free of symptoms." But by looking at the virus and the immune system *daily*, a heretofore unknown pattern emerged. In discussing this research, Nowak and McMichael (1995) present a graph showing the evolution of the human immunodeficiency virus in the body every year over twelve years. It shows that during most of the period in which the patient has no symptoms, "the body's defenses remain strong...eradicating almost as much virus as is produced. At some point, however, the immune defenses lose control of the virus, which replicates wildly and leads to collapse of the immune system" (p. 61). Spotting this pattern can shed light on an innovative strategy for fighting the virus.

Although investigators interested in leaders recognize the significance of the process over time (e.g., Hackman and Morris (1975)), the traditional assessment methods rely on a typical one-time, cross-sectional survey. Rarely do we see data like those described above or by economist, Gali (1992), or biologists, Haussknecht and Kuenzer (1990). The latter present a graph for a shell-breeding fish (p. 132), showing the fish's activities every two minutes broken down by three critical phases in their lives: as they inspect, dig, and oversand their shells. A complex set of interactions was revealed, leading the authors to conclude: "the behavior sequence...is induced and controlled by the change in the external stimulus situation which is influenced by the performance of the building actions" (p. 141).

In Study 16, we did a time-series analysis of leaders over time at three periods of the race (a) the *start* (thirty-nine fifteen-second intervals), (b) the *upwind mark rounding* (thirty-three intervals), and (c) the *hoisting of the sail* (forty-one intervals). Like Studies 14 and 15, the leaders consisted of leaders aboard twenty-eight boats.

We were particularly interested in whether there were shifts in the leaders' behaviors as they grappled with the different events of the race. Given that skippers monitored the equipment 12.8 percent of the time, for example, we asked "Is this type of monitoring steady? Or does it change over the race course? If it does change, what event might precipitate this change?"

Calculating rate per boat during each interval

To see whether changes occurred over time, we calculated the rate per boat during a given fifteen-second interval. To do this, we (a) timed when the particular event occurred on each boat (e.g., we identified that boat fourteen with its team of leaders hoisted its sail at 6:04.13), (b) recorded what the leaders were doing during each fifteen-second interval (e.g., helmsman monitored the equipment and crew boss delivered a negative consequence during the 6:04.00 – 6:04.14 interval), and (c) aggregated OSTI scores across all boats for each interval. The rate per boat was defined as the number of boats in which a given OSTI category occurred during a given interval divided by the number of boats in which one or more categories occurred during that interval. A rate of .5 for antecedents meant that an instruction was delivered on half of the boats during that interval; a score of 1.0 indicates that an instruction was given on all boats.[26]

Describing what happened at different times during the race

Table 4.12 shows the rates of four categories: monitor (via equipment, work sample, and self-report), consequence (negative and positive/neutral), work-related, and antecedent. As shown, the rates varied with as many as two of

Table 4.12 Study 16: Auto-regressive moving averages analyses with sailboat skippers

Subcategories (and statistics)	Race phases					
	Before start	*After start*	*Before upwind rounding*	*After upwind rounding*	*Before sail hoist*	*After sail hoist*
Monitor: equipment						
Mean	5.3	16.8	7.9	26.1	9.3	25.3
Level Change[a]		ns		6.36**		2.92**
Slope Change[b]		.43		2.60*		.65
Monitor: work sample						
Mean	3.0	1.5	1.2	5.2	3.5	3.4
Level Change[a]		wn		wn		wn
Slope Change[b]		wn		wn		wn
Monitor: self-report						
Mean	1.8	3.6	4.1	6.1	4.4	5.5
Level Change[a]		wn		wn		wn
Slope Change[b]		wn		wn		wn
Consequences: negative						
Mean	9.9	14.4	16.0	33.8	20.6	28.9
Level Change[a]		.28		4.51**		− .27
Slope Change[b]		.69		1.63		.64
Consequences: positive/neutral						
Mean	2.5	7.3	5.3	10.2	6.3	8.9
Level Change[a]		wn		.96		wn
Slope Change[b]		wn		1.39		wn
Work related:						
Mean	66.1	53.7	58.6	61.3	54.3	66.1
Level Change[a]		−1.97[#]		− .41		1.05
Slope Change[b]		.88		1.60		1.62
Antecedents:						
Mean	57.6	41.0	50.2	63.6	54.1	57.7
Level Change[a]		− .28		.53		− .69
Slope Change[b]		− .28		− 1.81[#]		− 5 .10**

Note: wn = white noise. ns = no solution
[a] Probability of change as determined by a *t*-test comparison
[b] Probability of trend change as determined by a *t*-test comparison
*p < .05
**p < .01
[#]p < .10

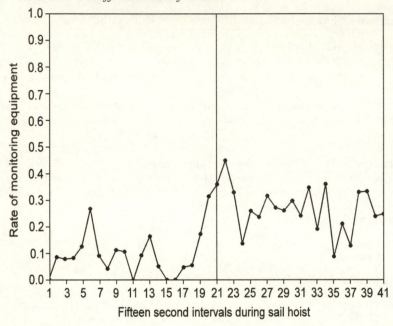

Figure 4.6 Study 16: Leaders' rate of monitoring equipment before and after chute hoist

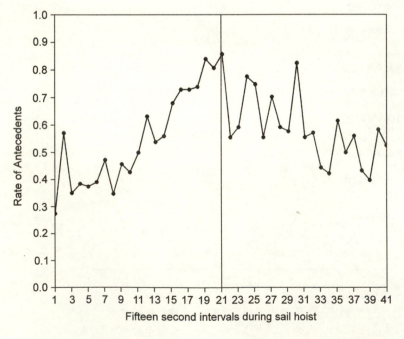

Figure 4.7 Study 16: Leaders' rate of antecedents before and after chute hoist

every three boats delivering antecedents before the start (.66) and after the sail hoist (.66).[27] Rates of positive/neutral consequences were much lower before the start (.03) and after the sail hoist (.09).

Figures 4.6 and 4.7 show the rate of monitoring and antecedents, respectively, five minutes before and after the sail hoist.

Level change

To see if leaders' behaviors remained more or less stable, we conducted an analysis appropriate for time-series data, the auto-regressive moving averages (ARIMA) analysis. An ARIMA analysis is designed for time-series data and removes any existing serial dependencies within the data through a series of transformations.

First, we looked to see if a level or mean shift occurred. As shown in Table 4.12, three significant shifts occurred, one for negative consequences and two for monitoring the equipment. When we compared before and after the chute hoist, for example, we found this type of monitoring tripled from .09 before the hoist to .25, $t = 2.92$, $p < .01$. As Figure 4.6 shows, leaders increased this particular type of monitoring; leaders on a quarter of the boats spent time watching the sail once the sail was raised.

Slope change

Two significant slope changes occurred, as shown in Table 4.12, one with monitoring the equipment and one with antecedents. For antecedents, the trend changed, with an ascending slope before the hoist and a descending one after it, $t = -5.10$, $p < .01$. Five minutes before the hoist, as shown in Figure 4.7 on interval one, the rate hovered near .3. As leaders got closer to raising the sail, however, they gave more and more orders ("Wait, wait, wait. There's too much halyard."). Antecedents eventually peaked at the midpoint (indicated by the vertical line at interval twenty-one) just as the sail soared, with orders ("Grind, grind, grind.") given on at least eight of ten boats. Once the sail was successfully hoisted, the instructions gradually declined so that five minutes after the hoist (intervals forty and forty-one) leaders were giving orders on half of the boats.

The conducting of a time-series analysis allowed us to see the currents as they undulated over time depending on what was happening during the race. Still yet to be explored is whether these currents distinguish between effective and mediocre groups of teams.[28]

IN SUMMARY

The studies discussed in this chapter show a vast array of findings. The first set of studies illustrate that leaders' behaviors can successfully be measured in the field using indices such as the Operant Supervisory Taxonomy and

Index and the Operant Supervisory In-basket Assessment. Further, we saw how specially developed measures were used to evaluate effectiveness of sailboat racing crews and theater production teams.

With these measures in hand, investigators could finally start to test hypotheses about the leaders' effectiveness. The second set of studies show that effective leaders have in common one or more behaviors: they either monitor or provide more consequences than their lackluster peers, and they are more likely to monitor via work sampling and to provide consequences of all kinds. The evidence also shows that both monitors and consequences are critical for effectively motivating others. Some data, in fact, suggest that using one or the other alone may be deleterious. The research demonstrates that leaders who monitor and provide consequences will have followers who perform better and have more positive attitudes about their leaders.

The results also suggest that the timing of leaders' behaviors makes a critical difference. Effective leaders are more likely to provide AM and AMC sequences quickly. Besides the pacing of the behaviors, their placement makes a difference. Finding that leaders who provide more antecedents after, rather than before, they monitor are more likely to be effective helped to clarify the previously nondescript findings about antecedents; perhaps effective leaders do not necessarily deliver more or fewer antecedents, rather their placement after monitoring makes a difference.

And, finally, the data suggest what the lackluster managers actually do. In contrast to the effective leaders, mediocre leaders spend more time before they monitor, doing such things as spending time solitary, being uncommunicative or laconic, providing antecedents, and detailing work-related rather than performance-related concerns. In short, the evidence from the studies identifies what leaders wishing to improve their supervisory effectiveness should do, when they should do it, and perhaps just as importantly, what they should try to avoid.

5 Research on the model
Why the model works

Seeing the powerful effect of the quantity, quality, and timing of leaders' behaviors on effectiveness raises a natural question: why is this so? Why are successful managers those who collect information by sampling the work? Is it the things they say, the things their subordinates say, or the things they think? Why does it matter that leaders go beyond giving directives, and actually let followers know how they are doing? Does it have to do with how subordinates react emotionally to receiving, or not receiving, feedback?

Specifying what a leader should do in a particular situation – which we have described in previous chapters – is only one step in the process of understanding leadership. Identifying the reasons why the individual should engage in a particular set of actions is an equally critical, yet often neglected, component in building models.

Here, we examine some of the underlying reasons beneath these central behaviors and leaders' effectiveness.

MONITORING AND ITS AFTERMATH

Most of the attention to date has focused on the information gathering aspect of the model. Monitoring alone in Study 2 was a feature distinguishing effective insurance managers from lackluster ones. We wondered why. This finding was particularly intriguing because of the relatively low overall frequency of monitoring; effective managers monitored only 2.9 percent of the time. Three teams of researchers went into the laboratory to try to establish the reasons: Komaki and Citera (1990), in Study 7, offered an explanation based upon the interactional perspective and group process literature; Larson and Callahan (1990), in Study 8, gave an information processing explanation of why monitoring works; and Brewer (1995), in Study 9, suggested an alternative mechanism dealing with evaluation concerns. We begin with Studies 8 and 9.

An information processing explanation

Study 8 (Larson & Callahan, 1990)

In trying to explain why performance monitoring may have an independent effect on work behavior, Larson and Callahan (1990) focused on the processing of information by the followers (Pfeffer, 1980; Salancik & Pfeffer, 1977; 1978). Their hypothesis was that managers, by monitoring, would influence the perceived importance of the task on the part of workers, and would also signal workers to expect pertinent consequences. These expectancies, known as "outcome expectancies," are a critical component in many cognitive models of work motivation (e.g., Naylor, Pritchard, & Ilgen, 1980; Porter & Lawler, 1968; Vroom, 1964) and they are assumed to guide behavior before (sometimes long before) the outcomes actually materialize.

To test this hypothesis,[1] Larson and Callahan set up three experimental groups ($N = 90$): one exposed to *monitoring only*, one exposed to *monitoring plus consequences*, and a *control* group that received neither. After the work session, subjects completed a questionnaire identifying the extent to which they felt it was important to do well on both the monitored and non-monitored tasks (1 = not at all important and 7 = very important).

Effect of monitoring alone was mediated by perceptions of task importance

Subjects generally perceived the monitored task to be more important than the non-monitored task. They judged the monitoring-plus-consequences tasks to be the most important ($M = 5.87$), monitoring-only tasks to be somewhat less important ($M = 4.79$), and tasks with no monitoring and no consequences (the control group) to be least important ($M = 4.07$).

To determine whether these task-importance perceptions were likely to have mediated the effects of independent variables on the quantity of work completed by subjects, the investigators conducted a hierarchical regression analysis. Among their findings was that the task-importance ratings accounted for a significant amount of variance, $F(1,78) = 33.46, p < .001$. A comparison between the monitoring-only and control conditions and the monitoring-only and monitoring-plus-consequences conditions was instructive in that the removal of the variance reduced the former to a non-significant level but not the latter. This led Larson and Callahan (1990) to conclude that "performance monitoring may also have an independent effect on work behavior by influencing the perceived importance of the monitored task" (p. 530).

A social comparison perspective

Study 9 (Brewer, 1995)

Brewer, Wilson, and Beck (1994), in Study 4, attempted to replicate the results of Studies 2 and 6. When they too found that effective police sergeants monitored more than their less effective counterparts, Brewer (1995) asked why monitoring was such a significant part of the supervisory process. He proposed an alternative theoretical perspective to that of Larson and Callahan (1990). Based on social comparison theory (e.g., Festinger, 1954), Brewer pointed to workers' concerns over the evaluation of their performance as underlying the effects of monitoring on performance. As an illustration, he noted studies demonstrating a phenomenon known as social loafing in which individuals whose efforts are pooled and hence indistinguishable from others decrease their performance in comparison with individuals whose efforts are clearly identifiable and attributable to each individual (Karau & Williams, 1993). Brewer hypothesized that individuals assigned to do two tasks would be differentially affected by the way in which supervisors monitored performance on those tasks.

To test this hypothesis,[2] he assigned groups to one condition in which the supervisor evaluated *individual* performance and one in which the supervisor assessed *group* performance. After the work session, subjects ($N = 124$) completed a question on a seven-point scale, ranging from most unlikely (1) to most likely (7), assessing whether the supervisor could evaluate their personal (individual) performance and whether the supervisor could compare their performance with that of other participants.

Effect of monitoring on performance was mediated by evaluation concerns associated with performance on each task

Subjects who were monitored individually rather than in a group considered it more likely that the supervisor could evaluate their personal contribution ($M = 5.1$ *versus* 3.2). To determine the impact of these perceptions of personal identifiability, Brewer conducted a path analysis. Among his findings was that changes to the quantity and quality of performance across the two tasks were mediated by adjustments in evaluation concern.

Brewer concluded that the results "supported the interpretation that the effects of monitoring on performance were mediated by evaluation concerns associated with performance on each task" (p. 760).

Based on the group process, leadership, and interactional literatures

Study 7 (Komaki & Citera, 1990)

Komaki and Citera (1990) took a different tack in elucidating the role of monitoring. Our focus was on the leader and follower and the process or interaction between them. Our prediction was that, within an ongoing dialogue, monitoring would prompt followers to talk about their own performance, and leaders to then deliver consequences, and that this exchange was what fueled the impact of monitoring.

Table 5.1 Transcript of Dr Roy's project team: avoiding performance issues by returning to work-related details

Number	Speaker	Statement/action
1	Harold	I'd like to talk about this manhole cover thing.
2	Dr Roy	Right. Fire away!
3	Harold	I've had a couple of preliminary conversations with them. At present, they use the normal eighteen by twenty-four-inch cast iron cover. Or rather, it's a cast iron basket really, filled with three or four inches of low grade concrete. The problem seems to be that they have to send out more men than are needed for inspection work simply because they are needed to lift the manhole covers! *They are asking if we can make manhole covers that are as durable, but light enough for one man to lift.*
4	Steve	Do you mean they literally wish us to make them? Or to do all the R & D involved in coming up with a new design?
5	Harold	Well, we couldn't make them, could we! We aren't in the production business.
6	Steve	**But do we want to do this?** Do we want to embark on a development program to construct and test an alternative cover?
7	Dr Roy	Why not? If there's money in it. How much do the current covers cost to make, Harold? (W)
8	Harold	The economics aren't straightforward. It isn't just a question of production costs. As I've explained, the present covers cost them indirectly in increased labor overheads. One man can't lift the present cover on his own, you see. Or so the unions claim, anyway! But they would, wouldn't they! It's back to "jobs for the boys again," basically!
9	Neil	Have you done any testing on the current covers, Harold? (W)
10	Harold	Well, we've broken a few using a six-inch steel pad to simulate the tire of a truck. The funny thing is that the concrete doesn't seem to make any difference to the strength.
11	Neil	Where *do* they break, in fact? (W)
12	Dr Roy	And under what conditions? Centrally loaded with the covers fully or partially supported? (W)
13	Harold	**Look!** They aren't going to be impressed with academic stuff! I can tell them enough about how the current ones break – rest assured!
14	Neil	If the concrete doesn't make any contribution, why don't they leave it out and turn them upside down? That would make them lighter. (W)
15	Harold	Ah! I've misled you there. The iron basket doesn't seem to have a bottom to it. The sides are slightly wedge shaped, you see, and that stops the concrete from falling through.
16	Dr Roy	It's St George's cross, is it, Harold? (W)
17	Harold	Yes, in cast iron, as I've explained.
18	Dr Roy	A St Andrew's cross would be stronger. I wonder why they don't use a St Andrew's cross. (W)
19	Harold	Because the present construction is strong enough! They want something equally strong but lighter.
20	Steve	Well, **I'd like to be clearer** about the criteria we need to use to decide whether to get involved in something like this.

21	Dr Roy	Suppose we kept the cast iron basket and found a replacement for the concrete filler? (W)
22	Neil	I think that if they just want us to replace concrete with a lighter fill, it's not a technical job for us.
23	Harold	Not technical? What do you mean? I'll remind you that de-technical is an emotive term around here, with respect, **I must disagree** totally with you. At least this work could mean we do something really practical and useful for once.
24	Dr Roy	Hmm. Must admit I'm still wondering if there is a credible alternative to concrete. (W)
25	Neil	Some kind of plastic dish, perhaps? (W)
26	Alan	Marine ply? (W)
27	Dr Roy	Yes, a sheet molded compound. What sort of density material could we offer as an alternative to concrete? (W)
28	Neil	I'd say two as opposed to about two point five for low grade concrete. (W)
29	Dr Roy	Is that all? Oh, well! (W)
30	Neil	I think you ought to find out if they would accept the same breaking load as now; what the current covers cost to make; what it will save to have a lighter one, and so on. When we know all this, we can sit down and do some unsophisticated calculations. (W)
31	Dr Roy	If we are talking about two as opposed to two point five, it is certainly a question of redesigning the whole thing, not just replacing the filler with something lighter, that's for sure. (W)
32	Harold	Anyway. **None of this is helping me much!** I'm meeting them early next week. What should I say? Are we interested or not?

Source: Honey (1978, pp. 132–4). Copyright © 1978 Prentice Hall. Reproduced with permission.
Note: Attempts to get conversation back to performance are highlighted in bold. W = Work-related

Exchanges in general have been highlighted by investigators taking an inter-actional perspective (Bandura, 1986; Magnusson, 1988; Patterson, 1982), as well as leadership scholars (Gardner, 1990; Gabarro, 1987; Graen & Uhl-Bien, 1995; Hollander & Offerman, 1990) & group researchers (Foushee, 1984; Hackman & Morris, 1975; Herold & Parsons, 1985; McGrath, 1984). To our knowledge though, investigators have rarely examined, in a continuous con-versation stream, how the actions of one party affect another.

We also proposed that the content of the exchanges would make a difference. This hypothesis we derived inductively from listening to coun-ter-productive conversations, some of which went on at great length about the minutiae of work detail. We predicted that monitoring would "funnel" subsequent exchanges to be performance-related – centering on discussions of what each party had to *do* to accomplish a task – rather than work-related – dealing with the technical details of the work itself.[3] The transcript in Table 5.1 illustrates how performance-related concerns can be deflected by dwelling on work-related details. In the transcript, Dr Roy (presented earlier) is discussing a potential project with his team of engineers. Two members of the group, Harold and Steve, want to discuss their performance, in this case, their plan for obtaining revenue for future projects. The others, including the group's head, Dr Roy, consistently deflect these two engineers' concerns (as shown in statements 6, 13, 20, 23, and 32) by returning again and again to details of the work: materials for manhole covers, why not use a St George's or a St Andrew's cross, and so on.

To test these process-oriented and content-based hypotheses, we conducted a laboratory experiment with sixty superior–subordinate pairs (in which superior or subordinate status was randomly assigned). Using the OSSTI, coders watched and recorded data from four five-minute exchanges per pair, for a total of 240 videotaped exchanges. The mean interrater reliability scores for the superior and subordinate were 88.6 and 96.2 percent, respectively.

LAG SEQUENTIAL ANALYSIS

Monitoring enables followers to discuss their performance and leaders to deliver consequences

We used two approaches. The *lag sequential approach* examined what happened every five seconds. To determine whether certain sequences of events tended to be repeated over time, we compared lag and expected probabilities, using the binomial z-test (Sackett, 1977; 1978).

We found a reciprocal interaction between the leader and the follower. When managers monitored, subordinates were more likely to respond by talking about their own performance, which, in turn, set into motion a chain of events in which the boss was likely to provide a consequence or to monitor again.

Three interactions are of particular note:

(a) *Manager monitoring followed by subordinate's own performance* As shown in Figure 5.1, the lag probability for subordinate own performance following manager monitoring, .109 (the number along the pathway), was significantly higher than the expected probability of .020 (the number in parentheses) for subordinate own performance. This was a five-fold increase in predictability, $z = 13.0$, $p < .01$, meaning that followers were five times more likely to talk about their own performance following a monitor than after any other behavior on the part of the leader.

(b) *Subordinate own performance followed by manager monitoring and consequences* The lag probability for manager consequences following the subordinate's own performance (.051) was significantly higher than the expected probability for the manager providing consequences (.017). The lag probability for manager monitoring following subordinate own performance (.107) was significantly higher than the expected probability for manager monitoring (.039).

(c) *Manager monitoring followed by consequences* The lag probability for manager consequences following manager monitoring (.124) was significantly higher than the expected probability (.017) for manager consequences, a seven-fold increase in predictability, $z = 16.83$, p $< .01$.

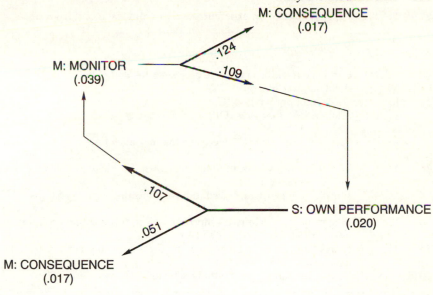

Figure 5.1 Key interactions between superior and subordinate as revealed by the lag sequential analysis. Numbers in parentheses refer to the expected probability [*p*(B| criterion event A)] and numbers along pathway (not in parentheses) refer to the lag probability [*p*(B| criterion event A)]. M = manager, S = subordinate
Source: Komaki and Citera (1990). Copyright © 1990 JAI Press. Reproduced with permission.

A transcript in Table 5.2 illustrates how one pair from the monitor group interacted. The manager monitored (M) during the first two five-second intervals (beginning "Can I see..."). In the next five seconds, the manager nodded approvingly (C). We can plot their exchange:

```
        00    10    20    30    40    50
M  -o--o----------------------------------
C  -------o--------------------------------
```

In the next five seconds, the follower (*F*) started to talk about her own performance (OP), saying "*I have a list of all your...*"

```
        00    10    20    30    40    50
F OP  -------o--------------------------------
```

In the next interval, the subordinate finished discussing her own perform-ance ("...*meetings*") and the manager said "Okay" (C). Bringing the charts together, the score looks like:

```
        00    10    20    30    40    50
M  -o--o----------------------------------
C  -------o--o----------------------------
F OP  -------o--o----------------------------
```

Table 5.2 Study 7: transcript of an experimental pair from the monitor group

Time	Speaker	Statement/action
00	M	**Can I see the itinerary you're preparing for me? (M)**
05	M	**(Looking over itinerary) (M)**
10	M	(Nodding approvingly) (C)
	S	*I have a list of all your* (OP)
15	S	*meetings.* (OP)
	M	Okay (in response) (C). Here are the messages I've been given so far.[a]
20	M	I don't know if you want to jot this down, but these are the messages I've got here. (W)
25	M	While I'm in Chicago, I need to have a meeting with Jay Swanson. If possible, I'd (A)
30	M	Like to be there Thursday morning before this meeting (pointing at information sheet). Although (A)
35	M	it says here, please arrange to come for a morning meeting and lunch, so... (A)
40	S	Okay, you don't have anything scheduled for your lunch. (W)

Note: M = Manager, S = Subordinate, (M) = Monitor, (C) = Consequence, (OP) = Own Performance, (W) = Work-related
[a] When two or more categories (in this case, a consequence and a work-related) occurred in the same interval, we used the priority rule and coded the higher priority category (in this case, the consequence).
Source: Komaki and Citera (1990, p. 101). Copyright © 1990. JAI Press. Reproduced with permission.

As shown, the back-and-forth exchanges beginning with monitoring seem to "invite" the subordinate to talk about her performance. It is as if showing interest in what the subordinate is doing provokes the follower to describe the list she has made – with no overt prompting. The follower's offering information about what she has done, in turn, provides an occasion for the boss to continue discussing performance, in this case, providing a consequence. This series of M–OP and OP–C (and OP–M) interactions we have seen again and again.[4] A cascade of behaviors initiated by monitoring occurs, with the resulting flow, almost inevitable in nature, of reciprocal interactions between leader and follower.

The lag sequential results also indicate the critical, but often overlooked, role of the subordinate in the supervisory process. The authors note: "That superiors influence subordinates was not particularly surprising. What was striking was that the reverse was shown to be true. The results showed that subordinates had a discernible impact on the subsequent behavior of managers" (p. 102).

Table 5.3 Study 7: events facilitating and inhibiting monitors and consequences based on lag sequential results

To facilitate:	To dampen:

MONITORING

Encourage followers who discuss their own performance	Encourage followers to talk about minutiae of work detail

```
        00   10   20   30   40   50              00   10   20   30   40   50
 F OP  -o----o----o----o----o----o----    F W  -o----o----o----o----o----o----

 M      ---o----o----o----o----o----o-    M    --------------------------------
```

CONSEQUENCES

Select, train, and motivate leaders to monitor	Select, train, and motivate leaders to provide antecedents

```
        00   10   20   30   40   50              00   10   20   30   40   50
 M     -o----o----o----o----o----o----    A    -o----o----o----o----o----o----

 C      ---o----o----o----o----o----o-    C    --------------------------------
```

Note: M = Monitor, C = Consequence, OP = Own Performance, A = Antecedent, W = Work-related, *F* = Follower

Subordinates' work-related discussions and managers' antecedents warnings of inhibition

The next set of results, illustrated in Table 5.3, shed light on the circumstances under which managers would and, perhaps more importantly, would not be likely to provide monitors and consequences. The lag probability for manager monitoring following subordinate work-related (.019) was significantly lower than the expected probability (.039) for manager monitoring, indicating that when followers talked about work- rather than performance-details, managers were much *less* likely to monitor. Likewise, the lag probability for manager consequences following manager antecedents (.006) was significantly lower than the expected probability for manager consequences (.017, $z = -3.51$, $p < .01$). Managers would be much *less* likely (2.8) to provide consequences after providing an antecedent than after displaying any other behavior.[5]

Monitoring is enhanced by subordinates talking about their own performance, but inhibited by their talking about work-related matters, as illustrated in Table 5.3. Perhaps the fact that monitors are more responsive to what the subordinate does is not surprising, given their invitational (and more interactive) mode. Consequences, on the other hand, are better predicted by the manager's actions; the manager's antecedents inhibit, and the manager's monitoring facilitates, the providing of consequences.

Although these lag sequential results are illuminating, there are limits to what we can conclude. Finding a sequential relationship does not necessarily mean that we can call it a cause-and-effect one. Monitoring, for example, could be a prior condition rather than a determinant of own performance. Because our model aims to identify what effective leaders do, with the implication that any facilitating strategies should be pointed out as well, it is critical to be able to establish a causal link. It is the randomized design of this study that permits us to draw causal conclusions, as described below, with confidence.

EXPERIMENTAL RESULTS

Monitoring resulted in more subordinates' discussions of their own performance

We also conducted, in Study 7, a randomized two-group experiment with a *monitor* condition, in which the manager gathered information via work sampling or self-report, and an *antecedent* condition, in which the manager reminded the subordinate about various aspects of the task. The number and timing of the exchanges, as well as the topics of the messages, were held constant between the conditions.

As hypothesized, subordinates discussed their own performance more in the monitor, rather than the antecedent, group, $t = 3.14$, $p < .05$. When managers started an exchange by monitoring, subordinates were twice as likely on average to discuss what they had been doing ($M = 2.9$ percent) than subordinates in the antecedent group ($M = 1.4$ percent).

Monitoring resulted in leaders providing more consequences

Managers provided significantly more consequences when they began an exchange by monitoring, $t = 7.81$, $p < .01$. Managers in the monitor group spent twice as much time indicating knowledge of subordinates' performance ($M = 2.6$ percent) as managers in the antecedent group ($M = 1.1$ percent).

Hence, we can conclude that monitoring contributes to the success of effective managers by actually promoting subordinates' discussion of their own performance, as well as enhancing the manager's providing consequences. The cause–effect relationship between monitoring and consequences is particularly noteworthy, given the problems that exist in getting managers to provide consequences on a regular and timely basis. Researchers (Fisher, 1979; Ilgen & Knowlton, 1980; Larson, 1986; Tesser & Rosen, 1975) and managers themselves (Longenecker, Sims, & Gioia, 1987) attest to how hard it is for leaders to do this.

In a review of the literature on the "MUM effect" (i.e., the tendency to keep mum about unpleasant messages), Tesser and Rosen (1975) detail the ubiquity of this response. They note that people, in general, dislike transmitting negative information to a person who is directly affected by the message. In study after study, they show that the phenomenon occurs over a wide variety of "settings, communicators, recipients, messages, and indices of transmission" (p. 200).

I/O psychologists report similar findings, particularly with subordinates who have performed poorly (Fisher, 1979; Ilgen & Knowlton, 1980; Larson, 1986). Besides being less likely to pass on the information at all, bosses were also found to minimize, or even distort, its negative aspects. Larson (1986) reports that "supervisors sometimes gave positive feedback even when the subordinate performed poorly...this happened much more often than would be expected as the result of innocent computational or procedural errors" (pp. 404–405).

Larson (1986) comments that few empirical studies identify why leaders are reluctant to give negative feedback.[6] He speculates that followers' reactions might be a factor, and that this could be because a leader does not want to discourage a follower or because the leader wants to avoid the follower's negative reactions. Anecdotal accounts from upper-level executives indicate that both play a role (Longenecker, Sims, & Gioia, 1987). One executive admitted, "Almost every executive has dreaded performance appraisals at some time or other. They hate to give them and they hate to receive them" (p. 183). Another executive noted:

> There is really no getting around the fact that whenever I evaluate one of my people, I stop and think about the impact – the ramifications of my decisions on my relationship with the guy and his future here. I'd be stupid not to. Call it being politically-minded, or using managerial discretion, or fine-tuning the guy's ratings, but in the end I've got to live with him, and I'm not going to rate a guy without thinking about the fall-out. (p. 183)

Even Miss Manners, the famed etiquette columnist, relates that she is often asked about the best way of indicating wrong doings to family and friends. At issue here is one of the thorniest dilemmas faced by managers: how to deliver bad news. Miss Manners' succinct advice is that it is difficult to do, at least politely. For this reason Miss Manners relates bad news only when asked. Managers, of course, do not typically have this luxury.

The results of Study 7, showing what is likely to spur managers to provide consequences, are of particular relevance. Further research needs to be done, however, to see whether the effect is restricted to primarily positive consequences.

While Study 7 went beyond the one-dimensional perspective typically implied in the leadership literature (cf., Sims & Manz, 1984; Fairhurst, Green, & Snavely, 1984), it suffered from a lack of generalizability. Its sample, 120 females in a laboratory experiment with no histories of working together and no expectations for continued interaction, raised questions about the extent to which similar results would be found in an ongoing setting.

Study 13 (Goltz, 1993)

To see if the work history of employees makes a difference, Goltz (1993) con\ducted a field study, replicating the laboratory results of Study 7. She videotaped and coded interactions during twenty-eight organizational meetings of a Reserve Officers' Training Corps. At any one meeting, at least two or three persons represented each of two or more tiers of the organization's hierarchy: (a) a major or equivalent, (b) one or more lieutenants, or equivalent, who reported to a major, (c) one or more sergeants, or equivalent, who reported to a lieutenant, and (d) one or more students who reported to a sergeant. Similarly to Study 7, Goltz used the OSSTI to code leaders' behavior every five seconds, and also performed lag sequential analyses.

Monitoring did not set consequences into motion overall

The finding of Study 7 that monitoring seemed to stimulate managers to provide consequences in the next five-second interval was not replicated.[7]

A preponderance of neutral consequences

Of the consequences given, slightly more than half (51.6 percent) were neutral, as shown in the second conversation in Table 5.4, with positive (24.7 percent) and negative (23.7 percent) consequences being approximately the same.

Followers describing performance as positive or negative stimulated leaders to provide matching consequences

Leaders were likely to follow subordinates' negative reports of their own performance with negative consequences, and subordinates' positive reports of others' performances with positive consequences. This finding was greater than would be expected from the overall frequency of positive and negative consequences.

Monitoring stimulated subordinates to discuss their own performance as well as that of others

After leaders monitored, the lag probability for subordinates' communicating about their own performance (.053) was three times higher than the expected probability (.156), $z = 7.72$, $p < .001$. The lag probability for subordinates' communicating about their reportees' performance, following leader monitoring, was also significantly higher than the expected probability for this category (expected $= .163$, lag $= .263$, $z = 4.59$, $p < .001$). In this respect, results paralleled those of Study 7. Following a

Table 5.4 Study 13: transcript of discussions in ROTC group

Time	Speaker	Statement/action
7:30.00	L	**Um. Did you get a copy of attendance to Sharon?** (M)
	S2	*Uh huh.* (OP)
.05	L	'Cause Carl isn't going to return 'til Sunday. (W)
	S2	*I gave her a copy today.* (OP)
	L	Good. (C)
12:00.00	S3	Um…National Security Weekend Team T-shirts. (W)
	L	We got those. (C)
	S3	Alright. (W)
.05	S3	Where did you get them? (W)
	L	We had some. Um, because they're not very high-ranked. Sorry to say that. (W)

Note: L = Leader, S1 = Subordinate 1, S2 = Subordinate 2, S3 = Subordinate 3
Source: Goltz (1993, p. 178). Copyright © 1993 by JAI Press. Reproduced with permission.

leader's monitoring, followers talked more about their own performance as well as that of their reportees.[8]

A transcript, shown in Table 5.4, illustrates how similar their exchanges during the group meetings were to those between the experimental pair in Table 5.2 (p.138). The leader's monitor (beginning, "Did you get…?") set the stage for the subordinate to talk about his own performance ("…*I gave her a copy today*"), which, in turn, stimulated the manager to, in this case, provide a consequence ("Good").

The second conversation, however, shows a different pattern. Once the conversation turns to work details, the parties are much more likely to continue this work-related discussion.[9]

In short, the results reaffirm one of the major findings of Study 7: that leaders who monitor stimulate followers to talk about their own and, in this case, their reportees', performance. This study, taking place in an ongoing work setting, also highlights the performance-related content of the exchanges between followers and leaders.

Study 17 (Gevgilili, Komaki, & Chu, 1996)

Gevgilili, Komaki, and Chu (1996) also assessed interactions among team members, hypothesizing, as earlier, that these give-and-take exchanges facilitated the exchange of innovative ideas.[10] Some investigators, notably Sayles (1979) and his associate, Chapple, talk about this process of synchronization in which the contacts between leader and follower are "reasonably evenly distributed" (p. 66) and essentially tailored to the cadences of the follower. Although Sayles suggests a tie to motivation, we hypothesized that this type of exchange is also conducive to the generation of novel strategies.

Table 5.5 Study 17: transcript of two leaders on a film shoot in give-and-take exchanges on an innovative idea

Time	Speaker	Statement/action
		(D and DP are discussing how to set up the last frame of the movie.)
5:04.00	D	I'm saying that even though this is a very nice frame... we don't need... we don't want... and we have to cut! (W)
	DP	The big one? (W)
	D	(Answering someone else's question) We are waiting for the food people, then we are going to have a sit-down dinner. (DP walks away, and the director follows him)
.30	D	Okay, Ken, sorry. (W)
	D	We need to go back. (A)
	D	Okay, Ken so, after this right? (W)
	DP	Uhmm. (W)
.45	D	After his... she walks down here. Options: either we dolly here... (W)
	DP	Uhmm. (W)
.00	D	...and we follow his re-entry and we have her, light on her and then she blows and all the lights behind go off which means that the last image is her. (W)
	DP	I love that! (W)
.15	D	...or we can cover it from there, pain in the neck, if we are not going to use it, cheat it right? The other thing is to shoot here – we watch her arriving... (W)
	DP	Yes. (W)
.30	D	We have seen him reacting to something coming. I think that is nicer, because you have the space. (W)
	DP	Wait, wait! I think, I think this last movement has to be very intense. (W)
	D	So, we shouldn't cut? (W)
	DP	No, no. You should cut! (W)
.45	DP	You cover it from here and we have this angle of conversation and we can cut exactly from both angles. (W)
	D	Yes, I cover it from both angles. (W)
.00	DP	Yes, the main dolly comes from here and you cover it from both angles. So you have this, this and this... and the last one... (W)
	D	...will be his close up. (W)
	DP	...or could be her close up, 'cause who blows the lights? She... (W)
	D	This, I always thought about. (W)
	DP	I might stay here or come back here. (W)
	D	Basically we should cover from both angles. (W)
.15	D	It is such an important movement, I don't want to risk getting one angle. (W)
	DP	We can cheat. (W)
.30	D	This and that, they are the summary of the film. We need to summarize the film, pull it together. (W)
	DP	Yes. (W)
.45	DP	Okay. Then we can do that, we can cheat when she goes like that and it's easy... (W)
	D	Yes, and then the film is finished. (W)
	DP	I wish! (W)

Note: D = Director, DP = Director of Photography.

Many have conjectured about how the process of innovating gets started (e.g., Anderson & King, 1993; Kanter, 1988), but little, if any, data exist. As a first step, we observed in a setting (a film shoot) renowned for seeking out novel ideas. Videotaping the director and the director of photography (DP), we were able to track their interactions over the course of an eight-to-ten-day film shoot. To date, we have collected data on four such pairs.[11]

We calculated give-and-take exchanges as a percentage figure, with the numerator being the number of fifteen-second intervals in which both leader and follower actually interacted, and the denominator being the number of intervals in which they had an *opportunity* to interact.

Quantifying time spent in give-and-take

Give-and-take scores among the four pairs ranged from a low of .21 to a high of .35. The lowest scoring pair spent less than a quarter of their time having exchanges in which reciprocal communication occurred, while the highest pair spent more than one-third of their time in mutual give-and-take.

Portraying the depth of exchanges

A transcript in Table 5.5 shows the director and the DP discussing the final frame of the film, ultimately deciding to go ahead with an idea proposed by the DP. The process went as follows. The director describes one option, to which the DP exclaims: "I love that!" After the director mentions two other options, the DP suddenly exclaims: "Wait, wait! I think . . . this last movement has to be very intense." They then jockey back and forth – "So, we shouldn't cut?" "No, no. You should cut!" – with the DP making a suggestion and the director agreeing: "Yes . . ." The DP confirms, "Yes . . . and the last one . . ." and the director finishes the DP's sentence: ". . . will be his close up."

This active, fluid discussion of ideas between two seemingly equal partners went on throughout the exchange. Their communication was strikingly balanced, with both parties contributing something virtually every fifteen seconds. Because of this equality of exchange, their give-and-take score was calculated as 12/12, for a score of 1.00. The transcript, in effect, serves as a model for how fulfilling and productive the exchange between leader and follower can be.[12]

This study, portraying a series of subtle but sumptuous interactions, further enriches our ideas about leaders and followers. In fact, we predict that this fertile exchange of ideas may not need to be related to performance. The process of dialogue *per se* may be a critical ingredient in a healthy working relationship. Having the ability to talk freely and openly *and* to respond to one another enables both parties to negotiate inevitable misunderstandings and to cement the relationship.

As we can see, these six studies (7, 8, 9, 13, 15, and 17) depict the subtle and sometimes surprising interactions between leaders and followers that occur as one or more of the aftermaths of monitoring. The next set of studies focuses on the other cornerstone of the model.

CONTRIBUTION OF CONSEQUENCES

What accounts for the criticalness of consequences? This, and a related question – why does reinforcement work? – have been the subject of highly charged but inconclusive debate. Many years ago Thorndike (1898) suggested that events were reinforcing because they were "satisfying." Considerable debate ensued, however, over exactly what it meant to be satisfying. One definition was that it meant things we liked. Further probing revealed that this could be boiled down to things that we would work for, or, put another way, events that had a special effect on our behavior. We therefore ended up with the functional definition of a consequence (or, more technically, a positive reinforcer) as an event that increased the probability of the behavior it follows – not an altogether "satisfying" answer to the original question.[13]

An affective explanation

Study 5b (Komaki, Hyttinen, & Immonen, 1991)

None of the studies associated with the model have tried to directly address this question about consequences. We do know from Study 5b[14] that managers who provide more consequences have workers who report more positive feelings about their mental effort, sociability, self-confidence, state of mind, and tolerance, r ranging between .73 and .89. So we know the workers respond positively but we do not know why. Few empirical studies exist (Millenson, 1967).

Study 10 (Komaki, Desselles, & Schepman, 1988)

Our Study 10, however, in prompting workers to speak candidly about how they felt about their bosses, led us to our most speculative explanation for why our model works. In this study, Komaki, Desselles, and Schepman (1988) exposed subjects ($N = 75$) to one of three conditions in which the experimenter provided: (a) *consequences only*, (b) *monitors only*, or (c) *both*. To assess effectiveness, we looked at both performance and attitudes. Using the Observational Followers Attitude Measure (OFAM), we listened to what participants had to say about how their boss treated them. The attitudinal results paralleled the performance findings, with one exception. Both performance and attitudes were substantially better when the manager monitored and provided consequences, and both performance and attitudes suffered when only consequences were provided. When the manager provided only monitors, performance did not significantly decline; however, attitudes did. Subordinates were twice as likely to describe their manager in negative terms despite the fact that there were no decrements in their performance. What this suggests is that, at least in the ways in which we operationalized them, subordinates' attitudes may shed a more discerning light than the index of performance.

The most revealing comments were made when participants felt that the manager breached the obligatory AMC-sequence "contract." When the manager omitted consequences, subordinates complained ("I get zip feedback"). Likewise, when the manager failed to monitor, they griped (e.g., "She says it's okay without really checking"). Some objections were very insistent ("If they would have told us at the beginning, 'This is what needs to be done,' but she didn't give us any indication at all"). These comments suggested that participants had strong expectations of an AMC sequence. Once participants received an antecedent, they anticipated receiving monitors and consequences, in that order, particularly when they attempted to carry out the antecedent.

Complaints also went beyond the behaviors of the boss. Some concerned the boss's intentions ("We have no way of knowing what she is thinking") or personality ("I would definitely say she plays favorites"). Some raised credibility issues ("I felt she didn't know what she was talking about"). One person actually said, "She makes me want to get up and hit her."

Hearing the intensity of some of these comments[15] – keeping in mind that this was only a three-hour laboratory experiment with subjects who had little, if any, previous experience with the task or the boss – led us to focus on the emotional reactions that are evoked during the supervisory process. Similar anecdotal evidence for the power of feelings can be found in Terkel's (1975) graphic and moving accounts of workers with their glowingly positive attitudes as well as seethingly negative ones.

A variety of emotions can be evoked, including the three primary ones (Plutchik, 1962): (a) rage, anger, and annoyance, (b) ecstasy, elation, and pleasure, and (c) terror, anxiety, and apprehension. The latter two emotions have been documented in laboratory experiments in which a chain of behavior was abruptly broken,[16] with a resulting display of extreme agitation, violent excitement, and aggression (e.g., Azrin, Hutchinson, & Hake, 1966). In another study, college students identified circumstances that caused them to become angry – having requests refused, being delayed on buses, losing money (each of which indicates the breaking of a behavior chain) – and described their reactions: making verbal retorts, physically injuring someone else, damaging objects, withdrawing from the situation, screaming and swearing (Gates, 1926).

In the literature, these emotional outbursts have been defined as instinctive. Darwin (1872) speculated that fear served to evoke caution, thus saving the life of many an animal. Anger, too, he thought, was probably useful in destroying physical barriers to a desired goal. Other emotions, such as joy, he suggested, may have signaled to other animals that no aggressive action would be forthcoming and therefore cleared the way for cooperative and sexual behaviors or both. Millenson (1967) likens these reactions to "primitive behaviors whose potentialities are built in" (p. 451). He concludes that these affective responses are probably not useful now,[17] although they may well have been for our ancestors.

Affective hypothesis

Put in the terms of our model, we predict that receiving and responding to antecedents sets into motion instinctive, visceral reactions depending upon whether the AMC sequence is intact.[18]

When the antecedent provider (in work settings, the boss) does not monitor, we predict that respondents will experience apprehension or insecurity.[19] When few, if any consequences, are provided, the respondent may become annoyed or angry. When followers find their expectations thwarted or unfulfilled, then the negative affect workers feel may make them less likely to communicate with their bosses, thus cutting short a potentially valuable bridge to productivity and satisfaction.

When managers provide both, followers' expectations are more likely to be met or exceeded. Sayles (1979) speculates that such exchanges fulfill basic social needs. He suggests that "the essence of being human is the need for social intercourse...know[ing] that others care enough to tell you what they think" (p. 68). He contends that these fulfilling exchanges promote workers to "be more willing and more able to [talk about]...the real problems that have been worrying them, the embedded anxieties and criticisms" (p. 67). The result is a follower describing her manager with more positive emotions: "I thought she did a pretty good job. I put the wrong sticker on, and she was so nice about it. She's like, 'I'm sure you didn't mean to do this'".

Thus, we propose that people's emotional response to their bosses depend upon whether the receiver attempts to carry out the instructions implicit in the antecedent, and whether the provider fulfills the implied AMC contract. Study 10, however, is only a first step. We encourage future researchers to assess how feelings may color and eventually influence whether and how workers approach and interact with their bosses. Further investigation will move us closer to answering a perennial question: why does reinforcement work, as well as revealing what managers should do.

Future research

Interestingly, the most frequent explanation for the importance of monitoring is the least well documented. We have portrayed monitoring as having a ripple effect which, at its conclusion, influences the quality of the consequences provided. Managers who first monitor are thought more likely to obtain accurate information about subordinates' performance, and are therefore more likely to provide consequences that are contingent. Such contingent consequences have been identified as critical to motivation by operant psychologists (Daniels, 1989; Kazdin, 1989; Miller, 1997; Skinner, 1974; Sulzer-Arazoff & Mayer, 1991), as well as I-O psychologists (House & Mitchell, 1974; Podsakoff, Todor, & Skov, 1982; Scott & Podsakoff, 1985).

Evidence lacking on contingent consequences

The idea that monitoring is an important precursor to consequences is both logically and intuitively appealing. At least five well controlled experiments have demonstrated that contingent, rather than non-contingent, consequences result in significant improvements in performance (Cherrington, Reitz, & Scott, 1971; Jorgenson, Dunnette, & Pritchard, 1973; Komaki, Waddell, & Pearce, 1977; Orpen, 1974; Pierce & Risley, 1974).

Close examination, however, reveals that these studies cannot provide definitive evidence supporting or refuting this precursor hypothesis, because the research looks at the *impact* of contingent consequences rather than what *leads* to contingent consequences. That is, the studies examine whether contingent consequences have an effect on performance rather than whether managers who monitor are more likely to provide contingent consequences.

What needs to be done? To test the idea, one needs a clear definition and a sensitive measure of monitoring, and contingent consequences in the field.

To gauge monitoring, one can use the Operant Supervisory Taxonomy and Index. For contingent consequences, however, neither the definition nor the measurement is clear. The critical features of a contingent consequence are that a particular consequence (consequence A) should be delivered *only* when a particular performance (performance A) occurs; consequence A should *not* be delivered when performance A does not occur (Ferster & Culbertson, 1982). Unfortunately, given these two critical features and the subtlety and variety with which consequences occur, it is a formidable task to determine whether a particular consequence is contingent. One might easily see, for example, the relationship between performance and the following consequences, delivered by managers in the field (Komaki, 1986; Komaki, Zlotnick, & Jensen, 1986):

"Thanks for getting here on time."
"Carol made the call."
"No, you've got the door upside down."
"Jim, we don't have any overtime schedules."

But in the following examples, the relationship between performance and consequences is not nearly as clear:

"So far, we are not putting enough claims through."
"Most of them had it memorized."
"You're late."
"I have a cast that has trouble picturing things."

One problem here is that one needs to know what it means for a cast to "picture things," how late is "late," how many is "most," how far back is "so far." Unfortunately, this is difficult to determine reliably in ongoing work situations. Another problem is that one must establish whether consequence A is delivered when performance A occurs and if consequence A is *not* delivered when performance A does not occur. Besides knowing that a relationship exists between performance and the consequence delivered at time X, one also needs to know whether the same (or a similar) consequence might have been delivered at time Y when the relevant performance did not occur. Short of tracking the manager constantly, it would be difficult to assess this. Until these definitional and observational problems are resolved, it will be hard empirically to assess whether managers who monitor are more likely to provide contingent consequences in ongoing work settings.

These definitional and measurement problems may be why researchers, interested in capturing what occurs in day-to-day work interactions, have used an indirect index of contingent reinforcement. Podsakoff and Schriesheim (1985), for example, rely on subordinates' questionnaires; they ask subordinates to rate the contingency of the consequences they receive, and they then assess the relationships between the perceived contingency of consequences and their performance and attitudes. Given the questions raised about the accuracy of questionnaires (Borman, 1983; Campbell, 1977; Luthans, 1979; Mintzberg (1973); Rush, Thomas, & Lord, 1977; Sims & Manz, 1984) and evidence showing the lack of correspondence between questionnaires and what managers actually do (Bernard, Killworth, and Sailer, 1979/1980; Burns, 1954; Hammer, 1985; Lewis & Dahl, 1976), questionnaire responses are not recommended as an accurate measure of managers' behavior.

We encourage future researchers to devote their efforts to generating a definition and a measure of contingent consequences which takes into consideration the complexity and depth of interactions in the workplace. Doing so will improve our understanding of the precursors of contingent consequences, as well as a host of other issues.

Doing this would enable future researchers to look at the interaction between the contingency and the sign (e.g., positive or negative) of consequences for both performance and attitudes. The following other questions would be interesting to address. Do negative contingent consequences have a more beneficial impact on performance than positive non-contingent ones? Are negative contingent consequences more likely to be perceived as non-contingent than positive contingent consequences? Does the order in which contingent consequences are provided – e.g., first positive, then negative, ending with a positive – make a difference?

IN SUMMARY

The results of Studies 5b, 7, 8, 9, 10, 13, 15, and 17 suggest no single answer as to why our model works, but they provide at least four reasons: (a) the recurring, sometimes reciprocal set of behaviors that result between leaders and followers when one of the model's cornerstones, monitoring, occurs, (b) the performance-related content of the behaviors that monitoring sets into motion, (c) the shifts in followers' perceptions of the importance of a task and their evaluation concerns that take place when the leader monitors, and (d) the affective reactions of followers that are evoked when antecedents are followed (or not followed) by expected AMC sequences. We have derived the affective and content explanations inductively, from the verbatim comments of workers concerning their responses to their supervisors and from listening to managers talking about work minutiae and avoiding discussions of performance. We have derived the other two explanations from the group process, interactional, information processing, and social comparison literatures; in doing this, we have gone considerably beyond the operant conditioning theory that inspired our model.

As revealed by our research, the elements that function together in leader–follower interactions combine to paint a broad, and varied, picture of why our model works. We encourage further work on these intriguing questions concerning the process of interaction as well as our emotional and cognitive reactions to our bosses.

6 Research on the model
Boundaries and breadth of the model

Glimpsing what effective managers do and why, we began asking where we can and cannot venture in trying to forge a path for leaders. Does the model apply to all managers regardless of level, personality, and interpersonal skills? Will it work with the vast majority of subordinates, even those who are disaffected? Can we profitably extend the model to decision-making tasks as well as tasks of execution?

These questions concerning the boundaries and the breadth of the model are the topic of this chapter. We begin by discussing the limitations of the model.

BOUNDARIES OF THE MODEL

Identifying a model's boundaries, as pointed out by philosophers of science (e.g., Dubin, 1969; Hempel, 1966), is as critical to constructing a model as are its building blocks or units. Just as we have specified the basic units of the model and the relationships between AMC sequences and leaders' effectiveness, we need to map out where we can and cannot apply the model.

Moderators of the model

We have identified five boundaries of our model:[1] (a) the knowledge, skills, and abilities of followers and their satisfaction with the context of their job, (b) the knowledge, skills, and abilities of leaders, (c) the sufficiency of the organization's resources, (d) the stage of the motivational process, and (e) the type of task. Only when the level[2] of these moderators is sufficient will the predictions about the relationships between the outcomes and the behaviors and sequences of the model hold.

These limits are what I/O psychologists refer to as moderators: they influence or moderate the relationship between the leaders' behaviors and their effectiveness. A substantial precedent exists in I/O psychology. Prominent theories – contingency theory, job characteristics, and goal-setting – identify their limitations.

A central theme in Fiedler's contingency theory, for example, is the importance of the situation as a moderator in what type of leader will be effective. Fiedler (1967) extensively describes features of situations that influence their favorability (e.g., the position power of the leader) and relationship to a preferred leadership style. Likewise, goal-setting theorists have begun to identify various moderators (e.g., feedback, ability, demo-graphic variables, personality, task complexity, situational constraints) that influence the relationship between setting goals and performance (Locke & Latham, 1990). From the start, Hackman and Oldham (1980) recognized, in job characteristics theory, that individual differences among people influence how they respond to redesigned jobs. They stipulated that those with high growth need strength, relatively good contextual satisfaction, and the requi-site knowledge and skills to perform the job were more likely to respond positively to enriched jobs.

Knowledge, skills, and abilities of followers, as well as context satisfactions

The first moderator of our model concerns the characteristics of the sub-ordinate. Only when followers know a job's technical aspects, possess the necessary verbal and psycho-motor skills, and have the potential to learn what is needed, will the relationship between leaders' behaviors and effect-iveness be sustained. The quickest of AMC sequences will not elicit a polished manuscript from a secretary who cannot execute rudimentary indenting commands, for instance. Along the same lines, subordinates who are dissatisfied with their jobs (e.g., because of duties, salary, location, peers) are not likely to maintain either high levels of performance or positive attitudes. Extended back-and-forth discussions about performance, for example, will not measurably improve the productivity or attitude of a CD salesperson who really wants to be performing music instead of selling it.

Knowledge, skills, and abilities of leaders

Just as the knowledge, skills, and abilities of subordinates are critical, so are they for superiors. Unless managers have what it takes to do the job, the model will not work. Managers must have detailed knowledge of the people they work with and the structure they work within; they must know how to get things done.

This know-how is not limited to technical expertise. While it is important that managers know the "business," it is also critical that they possess adequate analytical skills. After monitoring, for instance, managers need to make sense of the information they have obtained, use these data to generate hypotheses about what is going on, and then put what they have learned into action; without these diagnostic and hypothesis-testing skills, they will not be able to correctly process and act on the information they have obtained from monitoring.

Another integral area concerns that of interpersonal interactions. Managers must be able to develop good working relationships with a wide variety of people, particularly given the increasing diversity in the work force, where many backgrounds, temperaments, and values are represented (Thompson & Di Tomaso, 1988; Triandis, Kurowski, & Gelfand, 1994). To use our model effectively, bosses should be able to confront problems as they occur, working constructively until the problems are resolved satisfactorily. Unfortunately, as we have discussed earlier, the MUM effect still prevails, in which supervisors tend to avoid transmitting negative information to workers.[3] Without these communication and negotiation skills, managers will not be able to implement the model successfully.

Resources of organization

No matter how skillfully managers provide AMC sequences and no matter how capable subordinates may be, the job will not get done if equipment does not exist for employees – be they keyboard operators, football players, or rock stars – to do their work properly. Similarly, when school principals "find their budget chipped away by the mayor, governor and Uncle Sam alike, when many buildings are in ruinous condition, when class size is rising and teachers lack books and supplies" – a recent description of New York City's schools (Finn, 1996, p. A23), then the model is also limited in the amount of support it can provide.

The above three boundaries are not unique to our model. Material resources and subordinates' knowledge, skills, and abilities have been highlighted by Hackman and his colleagues (Hackman & Oldham, 1976; Hackman & Walton, 1986). The importance of the interpersonal skills of leaders has been emphasized as well by a number of writers (Daniels, 1989; Hackman & Walton, 1986; Kotter, 1982). Mintzberg (1973), for instance, singles out the interpersonal as one of three critical roles that managers play. Kotter (1982) describes each of the managers in his study, chosen because they were performing well in their jobs, as being "personable and good at developing relationships with people" (p. 38). Hackman and Walton (1986) talk about the importance of negotiation and problem-solving skills.

The following two boundaries, however, are specific to our model.

Stage of the motivational process

In developing the model, we specifically limited it to only one stage of the motivational process, the maintaining of behavior (Komaki, Zlotnick, & Jensen, 1986). To clarify how the maintenance stage is different from other stages, we developed a Taxonomy of Motivational Stages (TMS) based on distinctions made in the basic (Cofer & Appley, 1968) and the applied (Steers & Porter, 1990) motivation literature. As shown in Table 6.1, the TMS classifies what leaders attempt to do when motivating others: (a) to

Table 6.1 Taxonomy of Motivational Stages

Purposes of leaders	*Typical status of followers*	*OSTI categories best suited*[a]	*Motivational and leadership theories best suited*[a]
To initiate	Recruitees; at a cross road	Antecedents, e.g., exhortations, persuasive influence	Need Need for achievement Charismatic
To direct	Newly hired; neophytes at task	Antecedents, e.g., rules, reminders, training	Goal-setting Ohio State: initiating structure
To maintain	Experienced, having done the job properly; recalcitrant	Monitors, e.g., work sampling, self-report Consequences, e.g., feedback	Operant conditioning Path-goal: expectations about

[a] to leaders' purposes and followers' status

initiate or energize, (b) to *direct* or channel, or (c) to *maintain* or sustain existing behaviors over extended periods of time.

Leaders who *initiate* behavior attempt to get subordinates stimulated to do something that they are not currently doing. The heroic Trojan warrior Hector, for example, stirring his troops to battle with his calls for greatness, bravery, and glory in the face of death and a strong enemy, would be attempting to energize behavior. Contemporary examples would be managers' needing to get potential recruits to join a particular cause, to attract candidates to join the organization, or to convince newly hired employees to work in a particular division.

In *directing* behavior, leaders guide staffs to learn a particular set of skills. A welding supervisor might show newly hired employees how to mig-weld two parts together, or they might demonstrate to experienced employees on that section of the line how to grind off extra weld. That same supervisor might also structure the task, rearranging the sub-tasks, so that employees at the end of the line – assembling the parts – would receive them in the order in which they needed them.

In *maintaining* behavior, the focus shifts from those behaviors not known to those that employees are already carrying out on a regular basis. In these cases, followers know what to do and in many cases have been performing these tasks regularly. The emphasis is therefore on sustaining these behaviors over time; the duration can be a payroll period, a season, a year, or more. Managers might want to ensure, for example, that employees continue to operate a system, follow existing directions, or pursue a task that is underway – be it mig-welding, building airplanes, or tending coffee plants.

These stages describing the goals of leaders correspond to the status of followers. Managers who wish to initiate behavior, for example, would attempt to get recruitees energized to join the organization. On the other hand, leaders interested in maintaining performance would be addressing experienced rather than newly hired employees.

We can use the TMS to identify categories in the OSTI that would be most appropriate. For Hector to stir his troops to battle, we would recommend antecedents, particularly those exhorting his troops to bravery in the face of death. For supervisors wishing to channel performance, antecedents in the form of instructions, rules, and reminders would be appropriate. For leaders needing to sustain performance, we have suggested monitors and consequences. Recalcitrant employees, on the other hand, might require a combination of categories, from antecedents such as persuasive entreaties to consequences such as rebukes and feedback for improvements.

With the TMS, we can also group theories, identifying the purpose for which each might be most appropriate. The charismatic approach to leadership (Bass, 1985; Burns, 1984; House, 1977; Tichy & Ulrich, 1984) encourages leaders to propel followers onto untrodden paths. As an inspirational theory involving "the arousal and heightening of motivation among followers" (Bass, 1985, p. 35), it is considered a theory whose purpose might be best suited to helping leaders *initiate* behavior. Other theories that might be appropriate for energizing employees are need theory and, perhaps, the need achievement theory of McClelland, Atkinson, Clark, and Lowell (1953).

The concept of initiating structure in the Ohio State studies (Fleishman, 1953) seems most appropriate for *directing* behaviors. A leader who "initiates structure" organizes and defines group activities, defines the role she expects each member to assume, assigns tasks, plans ahead, and establishes ways of getting things done. That is, she assists in steering followers toward one alternative rather than another. Other theories that also seem most appropriate for directing behavior are Locke and Latham's (1990) goal setting theory.

The TMS differs from previous classification systems such as those making distinctions between process and content (Campbell, Dunnette, Lawler, & Weick, 1970) and explanation and change (Pinder, 1984)[4] in that it enables practicing managers to choose among theories depending on their purposes. Depending on the stage, managers need to do different things to attain each of the different purposes. An airline manager might conclude that the transformational leadership approach, for example, might be best in recruiting mechanics to join the organization. He might, however, look to path-goal theory when trying to sustain mechanics' follow through on the equipment. Similarly, the head of a coffee plantation might use goal-setting theory to urge workers to use a new drying method at the beginning of the season. To ensure that workers tend coffee plants all season, however, we would recommend that she use our operant model.

Tasks in which execution is primary

The last moderator is the execution-type task in which the leader, having already decided what to do and how to do it, is primarily concerned with ensuring that the task gets done.

This type of task corresponds to the fourth classification in McGrath's (1984) taxonomy. He distinguishes among tasks in which organizational members: (a) generate alternatives, coming up with plans or ideas about what to do, (b) choose among alternatives, solving problems or making decisions to use one tactic rather than another, (c) negotiate under conditions in which there are conflicts of viewpoint and/or interest, and/or (d) actually execute the task. For the fourth task, McGrath (1984) makes a further distinction between contests and performance. By this definition, contests are execution-type tasks in which the group is in competition, and how well the team does is often interpreted in terms of winning and losing. Performances also involve task execution, but instead of competition they emphasize trying to meet a standard of excellence.

It is on this level, in the actual completion of tasks, that many managers today need help. Such tasks, says McGrath, "are very heavily represented in the workaday world and, against that base rate, are quite under represented in research on groups" (McGrath, 1984, p. 65). These are precisely the tasks that our model is tailored to address. Not that other tasks, such as decision-making, are unimportant; they are significant as well. Our findings to date, however, allow us to make one clear prediction: that leaders who want to execute tasks more effectively will find our model's recommendations to be profitable. By identifying the limitations of our model, one can see when our model can and cannot be successfully applied.

Evidence to date

How correct are we about the boundaries we have identified so far? Although a number of studies have tested our model, only limited evidence exists about its boundaries. The one exception is the task moderator. This moderator originates in Study 14, showing that following the model's recommendations without taking into consideration the nature of the task can be counterproductive.

Study 14 (Komaki, Reynard, Lee, & Wallace, 1995)[5]

One of the goals of Study 14 was to see whether the nature of the task made a difference. To do this, we gathered information about two tasks, one requiring leaders to make split-second judgments and the other involving the timely completion of a complex maneuver. With the latter, execution-type task, we predicted we could successfully apply the model.

The study was conducted with twenty-eight teams of leaders aboard forty-foot sailboats during races. The racing setting lent itself well to testing the hypothesis. To race sailboats competitively requires that leaders do well at two key points during the race: the start and the upwind mark.[6] At the start, leaders must take into account a clamor of input – the time, the other boats, the wind, the weather, the current – and then make a series of judgments about how and where to start so that the boat can cross the line just as the starting gun goes off (Conner & Levitt, 1992).

The task changes as the boat rounds the upwind mark, from decision-making to executing a change, by the crew, from one sail to another. Some sail changes, such as the spinnaker or chute hoist, are notoriously difficult to execute (Ross, 1989). Raising the chute, for example, requires multiple crew members to complete a series of precisely-timed steps, any one of which can go afoul and cause precious time to be lost.

Both tasks are complex, timed, and bound by an intricate series of rules. But they make different requirements of a leader. Steps in hoisting the chute, while intricate, are more or less fixed. Leaders do not need to make decisions about how the crew hoists the chute. Instead, they need to guide the crew to hoist the chute. For the start of the race, however, leaders must adjust to a rapidly changing set of circumstances, each of which demands their split-second decision-making.

To assess how well leaders did on these two tasks, we gathered information via the Sailing Strategy Measure (SSM), assessing the number of seconds after the starting gun that the boat crossed the start line (and, by inference, the quality of the judgments made by the leader), and the Sailing Effectiveness Measure (STEM), assessing how long it took the crew to hoist the chute. With these measures, we could see if the behaviors predicted by the model would be associated with the STEM but might *not* be associated

Faster sail boats related to feedback

As predicted, we found that with an execution-type task, the ... 8, $p < .05$. Refer to Table

Slower sail starts related to monitoring

A dramatically different picture emerged, however, during the start of the race. Leaders with the slowest start times monitored the most, $r = .44$, $p < .01$. Conversely, leaders who were the best at making decisions about which strategies to use in the face of rapidly changing external conditions monitored their crew the least.

Monitoring, then, was positively related to execution-type tasks, but negatively related to making split-second decisions. These findings provide support for the concept of the task moderator. At the same time, the data suggest that when the task requires swift decision-making, monitoring the performance of one's crew may not be the most prudent use of one's time; in some cases, it may even be detrimental. These results shed light not only on what leaders should do, but on what they should *not* do.

Recommended research

Since the above study is the only one bearing on the boundaries of the model, we recommend further research, and we suggest two strategies.

Conducting field studies to test the moderators

Our best recommendation is to conduct more field studies such as Study 14. James and Brett (1984), in their article on moderator variables, give similar advice, suggesting that investigators obtain information on the level of "x", "y", and "z", where "x" and "y" are the limits of the model and "z" is the moderator. The moderators can include the type of task, as in Study 14, or one of the other moderators – subordinates' backgrounds, the sufficiency of organizational resources, the interpersonal skills of leaders, or the step in the motivational process. With data on "x", "y", and "z", researchers can then determine if "the relationship between two or more variables, say x and y, is a function of the level of z" (p. 310). For instance, to test whether or not the disaffection of subordinates' feelings about their jobs moderates the relationship between the units of the model, we would seek out a situation in which subordinates exhibited a range of attitudes and managers provided AMC sequences at various speeds. If we found a non-additive, linear relationship between "x" and "z" where "y" is regarded as a function of "x" and "z", then we would conclude that, in this situation, the predicted relationship between effectiveness and supervisory behaviors would be limited by the negativity of the attitudes on the part of subordinates. We would also conclude that managers who act in accordance with the model, but who have more disaffected subordinates, would be less effective than those managers with more satisfied subordinates.

Using experimental block design to illuminate limitations of the model

Another strategy is to use a block design (Liebert & Liebert, 1995). This combines both experimental and correlational approaches. As shown in Table 6.2, there is at least one manipulated variable and one classificatory variable. One could classify leaders into those in departments characterized as high, medium, and low on the level of organizational resources. Using this blocking, one could then randomly assign leaders with low, medium, and high levels of resources to training in the model (e.g., providing quick AMC sequences). The remainder would get another type of training (e.g., delivering direct, anticipated, and clear antecedents).

One advantage of using this block design is that we can obtain both "correlational and experimental evidence simultaneously, as two separate sources of variability on a given measure" (Liebert & Liebert, 1995, p. 149). That is, we can draw conclusions about causality with confidence, assessing

Table 6.2 Using block design to illuminate limitations of model

Treatment groups	Level of organizational resources		
	Low	Medium	High
Training A: On the model[a]			
Training B[b]			

Note: Level of organizational resources is the classificatory variable, the training treatment the experimental one. Performance and attitudes of the followers are the dependent variables.
[a] Providing quick AMC sequences and engaging in extended performance-related discussions
[b] For example, providing clear, anticipated, and direct antecedents

whether the treatment results in improvements in effectiveness. At the same time, we can also shed light on the limitations of the treatment. If effectiveness sinks when resources are low, then we would have evidence that a minimal level of resources was necessary for the model to work.

Another advantage of the block design is that it increases the likelihood that we will find differences when they exist. If we did not divide organizational resources into three levels, but instead lumped all the managers together, we might find that treatment did not improve effectiveness. This failure to detect an effect might be because of the large within-group variability (or error variance) that we incurred by grouping leaders, regardless of resources, together. By conducting a block design, we increase the likelihood of detecting effects that might have otherwise been masked.

We recommend further research to shed light on these intriguing but, as of yet, largely undocumented possibilities concerning the boundaries of our model.

BREADTH OF THE MODEL

Controversies about the sweep of theories

The idea of theories having limitations is fairly well accepted. Deciding how far to go in extending a model, however, is more controversial. This is particularly the case in extending theories involving leaders and followers. Leaders' styles and personalities are thought to be so different as to preclude any generalizations about what the effective ones do. The situations in which they operate – white or blue collar, high-tech or smokestack – are purportedly so distinctive as to rule out any general statements about good leadership. Some leadership scholars do, indeed, heed differences more than commonalities. Vroom (1976), in talking about his model of decision-making, for instance, says, "I do not see any form of leader behavior as optimal for all situations." True to his word, he differentiates among problem-solving situations (e.g., whether or not the problems possess a quality requirement) and then specifies how leaders should modify their behaviors in accordance with the characteristics of each situation.

Other leadership scholars downplay differences (Kotter, 1982; Mintzberg, 1975). By emphasizing the similarities among leaders and in the situations in which they operate, they conclude that meaningful generalizations can be made across people, doing different tasks, at different times, and in different settings and situations.

Mintzberg, for instance, points to commonalities in the role of managers as leaders, and how this role influences all subsequent interactions between bosses and workers. He contends that persons in a supervisory capacity share many characteristics, whether they are "chief executive officers, vice presidents, bishops, foremen, hockey coaches, [or] prime ministers. For an important starting point, all are vested with formal authority over an organizational unit.... Formal authority vests [them] with great potential power" (p. 54). By virtue of being in charge, managers are responsible for work being delegated and done, and what they do comprises the role of a leader.

After completing his classic study in which he tracked five top-level managers for a week each, Mintzberg identified ten managerial roles (e.g., figurehead, disturbance handler, leader) that transcend the person's particular position, setting, style, and personality. Managers can exercise their role directly by, for instance, selecting and training their own staffs. But they can also do it indirectly, as Mintzberg notes:

> Every manager must motivate and encourage his employees, somehow reconciling their individual needs with the goals of the organization. In virtually every contact the manager has with his employees, subordinates seeking leadership clues probe his actions: "Does he approve?" "How would he like the report to turn out?" "Is he more interested in market share than high profits?". (p. 55)

In talking about managers' direct and indirect exercise of their role as leader in motivating their employees which, in turn, affects the way in which followers are likely to respond, Mintzberg focuses on the similarities of managers.

Kotter (1982) also points to "identifiable regularities" (p. 9). After completing an in-depth look at fifteen general managers, with an average compensation (in 1978) of approximately $150,000 per year, he acknowledges that "the data show a complexity which often makes many managerial textbook concepts seem woefully inadequate" (p. 9). Underlying it all, however, he finds patterns among executives; he calls them "understandable complexity." His conclusion: "It is possible to generalize" (Kotter, 1982, p. 9).

Kotter (1982) gives a fairly detailed description of two general managers, Tom Long and Richard Papolis. They hold comparable positions, are well regarded, and work in the same organization, International Computers (IC). Yet, in terms of their backgrounds, philosophies, and styles, as Kotter characterizes them, they are at opposite ends of the spectrum. Tom, who at 36 years of age was one of the youngest people at his level, had risen rapidly from assistant sales representative to eastern regional general manager. Richard, on the other hand, came to IC upon the purchase of Datatrack, a company he and three others had founded a few years previously; IC set up Datatrack as an autonomous division with Richard as president. In interviews conducted by Kotter, the two men's philosophies on supervising others also seem quite different. Richard described his job as one in which he "order[s] no one to do anything.... It is much like sailing.... When I go sailing, I go with the wind" (p. 114). In contrast, a colleague described Tom as taking hold of the organization and aggressively directing and pushing it to "perform" at a very high level. Their styles also seem at odds. Richard never wore a suit and tie. He arrived at work between 8:30 and 9 a.m. and left at 5 or 5:30. On a typical day, he spent his time talking to people, usually in both large and small unscheduled meetings. In contrast, Tom dressed in conservative business suits. He estimated that he worked an average of sixty-five hours a week. He spent most of the day in his office or in the adjacent conference room in scheduled meetings.

Despite Kotter's characterization of Tom and Richard as being "somewhat extreme examples of differences in behavior, at least among the participants in this study" (p. 116), we found that there were many more similarities than differences when we examined the way in which they supervise. We drew our conclusions not from descriptions of their philosophies but from the actual samples, provided by Kotter (1982), of their daily behavior. For Tom, a typical internal memo sent to his region's senior staff after a regular staff meeting (p. 105) was reprinted; it is partially reproduced in Table 6.3. For Richard, Kotter summarized his notes about the large and small unscheduled meetings Richard had during the time Kotter was with him; these notes are partially reproduced in Table 6.3.

Although Tom's meetings were more formal and were scheduled in advance, Tom, like Richard, monitored and provided both positive and negative consequences. When Tom presided over a meeting with one of his reportees, he set up a meeting for a week later so he could continue to monitor. At the same meeting, he evaluated a particular reporting system, describing it as "unnecessary and confusing" (p. 105), and he referred non-judgmentally to the manpower plans that had recently been revised by one of his staff, thus providing both negative and neutral consequences. Kotter further describes Tom as "skillfully using both carrots and sticks. He praised and pushed, recognized and intimidated, motivated and drove people to achieve" (p. 104).

Richard, on the other hand, though described as supervising more inform-ally, also spent a fair amount of time monitoring. He initiated discussions with his vice president of manufacturing to "clarify what the problems were and how they should be addressed," listened and asked questions about a new product in the development stage, and inquired about a demonstration of a new product the vice president of systems development and two of his people had completed. Intermingled with Richard's monitoring via self-report and work sampling, he also is shown providing consequences, expressing "enthusiasm over most of the ideas presented" and praising "them for a job well done" (p. 116). Though Kotter describes Richard's interactions as "all characterized by lots of humor (initiated by everyone, but especially by Richard) as well as a good deal of directness, warmth, and informality" (p. 116), Richard also let it be known that he would not shy away from using the ultimate stick: "I'm also not afraid of firing people, although that rarely happens" (p. 115). He follows up that remark by describing how "many people have thanked me for terminating them" (p. 115). And in spite of saying, "I order no one to do anything" (p. 114), he makes it clear how he judges himself (and what he expects of others): "Effort doesn't count. Results count" (p. 115).

Table 6.3 Ways in which two managers in an international computer company
interacted with their staffs

A typical memo from Tom Long[a]

INTERNAL MEMO

TO: Region Senior Staff   FROM: T. R. Long
SUBJECT: Senior Staff Meeting   DATE: September 14, 1977
Sept. 12 Follow-up Action

---

1 Jack Lynch is responsible for providing us with an integrated schedule of events
   for our Spring HRP update. This schedule of events should be *reviewed* with us at
   our September 19th Staff Meeting.
2 It was generally agreed that the performance reporting system for branch profit
   and loss performances is *unnecessary* and *confusing* at this time. Mike Lewis
   agreed to *follow-up* with Gary O'Connell on delaying this program due to its
   inconsistency with current strategies.
7 Paul Thompson is responsible for communicating the revised 1200 manpower
   plans to our branches reducing our plan to 95. This correspondence should be
   communicated by Friday, September 16th.

Notes taken by interviewer on a series of encounters between Richard and his staff

- In three discussions with his vice president of manufacturing, Richard initiated
  two of these discussions and worked with the managers to *clarify what the
  problems were and how they should be addressed.*
- For much of the meeting of the officer group, Richard refereed an obvious fight
  between his marketing and manufacturing vice presidents.
- In two discussions with the vice president of marketing, Richard spent much of
  the time trying to calm the man down and to get him to see things from
  manufacturing's point of view.
- In a meeting of about 10 people on the major new product Datatrack was
  developing, Richard spent most of the meeting listening. He asked a few questions
  and left early.
- In a meeting of about 12 people on a new product they were just starting to
  develop, Richard *listened*, *asked questions*, and *expressed enthusiasm* over most of
  the ideas presented.
- In a meeting with the vice president of systems development and two of his people
  to *look at a demonstration* of a new product, Richard *asked questions* and *praised*
  them for a job well done.

Note: Italic is ours, [a] Excerpts from a memo typical of those Tom sends out after each regular
staff meeting.
Source: Kotter (1982, pp. 105, 115–116). Copyright © 1982 by Macmillan Publishing Co.
Reproduced with permission.

Again, when we looked at what Richard and Tom did when interacting
with their staffs, we could see that each spent time monitoring. Both
gathered information, sometimes via self report and often by direct sampling. Both Tom and Richard also provided consequences, recognizing
others for performing well, but neither were loath to let people know
when they were displeased with their performance. In other words, not all
effective managers say exactly the same thing, but they do say things that

fall under broad umbrellas. Tom may monitor by calling for a follow-up meeting, while Richard may monitor by dropping in on spontaneous discussion around the water cooler. The important thing is that they gather information about performance.

Had we riveted our attention on Tom's and Richard's disparate "styles," "philosophies," and "personalities", we could easily have let these differences obscure the very real similarities between them. As Table 6.3 shows, while each may have gone about it in a different way, both ended up gathering information and providing feedback to their staffs about their performance.

Sweep of the model

Similar observations on our part, as well as our belief in the universality of the demands of getting work done through others (Mintzberg, 1975), led us to conclude that a common managerial denominator exists that transcends differences in the persons, tasks, and settings involved, and that it is possible (and desirable) to make general statements on what managers should do. Hence, within the boundaries of the necessary characteristics of leader, follower, resources, tasks, and motivational stage, we contend that the model of effective supervision holds broadly across individuals at different levels and in varying aggregations, as well as different jobs, organizations, and cultures.

The model's recommendations do not differ according to whether managers operate informally or formally. This is true across the range from Chief Executive Officers (CEOs) to first-line supervisors. While the direct reports of a first-line supervisor will differ from those of a CEO, each is in charge of a particular unit and responsible for ensuring that the work gets done. To ensure that this occurs, both should provide quick AMC sequences. This is also true for managers of individuals and those of groups, and for interdependent and independent tasks. Tasks that are accomplished through the coordination of efforts by several individuals require the same basic managerial behaviors as do tasks accomplished through independent effort.

Challenges of bringing evidence to bear

What evidence is there that the expansive sweep we have identified for the model is true? This is a difficult question to answer, in part because of the youth of the model, with the first articles having appeared in 1986, and the relatively small number of field studies done.

A second difficulty has to do with the nature of the question itself. The issue of generalizability or external validity does not lend itself to straight forward solutions. Unlike internal validity, which can be accomplished by using a randomized control group design considered the quintessential internally valid design, there are no comparable samples of subjects, settings, tasks, or situations to guarantee external validity. Any one study, even with hundreds of subjects, is still limited to the setting in which it is conducted, to the managers being observed, to the subordinates and the tasks that they supervise, and to the investigators conducting the research. Bringing definitive evidence to bear in any one study is difficult. As Runkel and McGrath (1972) note in their research design text, there is no straightforward way of extending the generalizability of a model. "Within a fixed number of observations, everything we do to increase precision . . . tends to decrease generalizability . . . and vice versa" (p. 170). If we make 400 observations of 100 managers ranging in personal and organizational characteristics but do not impose any manipulations, we enhance external but not internal validity. We increase the extent to which we can draw conclusions about the generalizability of our findings, but minimize the precision with which we can make statements about the relationships between effectiveness and leader behavior. On the other hand, if we make 400 observations of 100 students acting as managers after randomly assigning them to one of four treatment groups in a laboratory experiment, we increase internal but not external validity. That is, we add to the confidence with which we can draw causal conclusions about the treatments, but we do not appreciably contribute to the generalizability of the treatments.

Ways of generalizing across types of people, settings, times, and tasks

Are there reasonable ways of increasing external validity? The answer remains an elusive one. Cook and Campbell (1979), however, make a series of constructive suggestions for increasing one type of generalizability, that of generalizing *across* types of people, settings, times, and tasks.

They make a distinction between "generalizing *to* particular target persons, settings, and times" and "generalizing *across* types of people, settings, and times" (p. 71). In the former, investigators first identify the target population (e.g., police sergeants in central Australia), then draw samples from the population with known probabilities, thus obtaining a formally representative sample. After the study is complete, they judge whether the goals of the research have been met for the specified population.

In contrast, in generalizing *across* types, no formally representative sample is obtained. Instead, investigators draw from a variety of different populations, for instance, police sergeants in Adelaide, executives in three minority-owned banks in southcentral Los Angeles, and Off-Off Broadway theater directors. After obtaining and analyzing the data, researchers then see whether their hypotheses held *across* these haphazard instances. They see whether the hypothesized results were obtained with the particular achieved samples of managers, irrespective of how well the achieved population can be specified. That is, they generalize not to, but across, their achieved samples.

This emphasis on generalizing across reflects the status quo in research. "Formal random sampling for representativeness is rare in field research," as Cook and Campbell (1979) point out, "so that strict generalizing to targets of external validity is rare" (p. 73). Given the fact that few investigators have the luxury of generalizing *to* target populations, we recommend they emphasize generalizing *across*. To this end, the threats Cook and Campbell (1979) identify to external validity – the interaction of selection and treatment, setting and treatment, history and treatment – reflect this emphasis. Hence, we now know what to watch for. Knowing, for instance, that we need to be vigilant about the way we recruit samples (selection), about the characteristics of the people in the places where we conduct our research (settings), and about the particular period and chain of events (history) helps us to avoid pitfalls in generalizing *across* types of people, settings, and times.

Conducting replications

Even better than identifying these threats to external validity, however, is Cook and Campbell's (1979) constructive path to generalizing across people, settings, and tasks. "In the final analysis," they state, external validity is "a matter of replication" (p. 78). Replicating or repeating the findings of previous studies in different settings, with different tasks, and so on increases external validity. It also shows that the results are not limited to a single instance, but can be generalized to instances other than the original case in which they were found.

Deliberately sampling for heterogeneity

One can conduct these replications by simply taking whatever samples are convenient. Or, preferably, one can purposively choose samples, what Cook and Campbell (1979) refer to as "deliberate sampling for heterogeneity"(p. 75). The critical difference is in the planning. To sample intentionally, one would first identify the particular category of persons, tasks, or settings across which one would like to generalize. Is it managers at the lowest and the highest levels in the organization? Is it tasks requiring coordination among team members? Is it leaders in artistic endeavors? Then one would plot how to obtain samples with these characteristics. If one were interested in interdependent tasks, then one would seek out situations in which leaders were responsible for these types of tasks. This proactive stance makes it less likely that one is inadvertently restricted to samples of secondary interest.

To do this, Cook and Campbell (1979) talk about (but give no citations of) multiple replications within the same study. One could seek out leaders in the artistic and corporate community and see if the same relationships would hold with both groups. We did this, though inadvertently, when we included in Study 1 samples of theater and bank managers. Another possibility is to do multiple replications, not within the same study but in individual studies. We have also done this, as described below. In fact, Cook and Campbell (1979) note: "a strong case can be made that external validity is enhanced more by many heterogeneous small experiments than by one or two large experiments'' (p. 80).

In either case, investigators would seek out instances across which they wished to generalize. Ideally, the samples should be as disparate as possible. One might choose to do one study in a small, intimate group with salubrious and long-standing relationships among the members and another study done in a multinational organization with newly constituted groups formed from those left after massive downsizing. Doing this, one could conclude that the relationships they found hold across the particular variety of samples of persons, settings, and tasks that were under study. Given these extreme cases, one could also expect that the model would probably hold in many other kinds of groups.

Evidence to date

Field studies

To date, fourteen studies connected with our model have been conducted in the field.

Ranging from theater production staff to ROTC officers

The subjects and settings have included:
- managers at a bank (Study 1a)
- theater production staff (Study 1b)
- managers at a large medical insurance firm (Study 2)
- managers in a daily newspaper operation (Study 3)
- sergeants at police headquarters (Study 4)
- supervisors on construction sites (Study 5a)
- managers in a government agency (Study 5b)
- skippers aboard twenty-four-foot boats in a sailboat regatta (Study 6)
- computer managers in a university-based center (Study 11)
- stage directors of Off-Off Broadway productions (Study 12)
- ROTC officers at a university (Study 13)
- leaders aboard forty-foot boats (Studies 14–16)
- film directors and directors of photography on film shoots (Study 17)
- managers in movie theaters (Study 18)

Some studies assessed a range of managers from the head person to first-level supervisor (Studies 1, 2, 3, 11, 13). For instance, in a newspaper firm, virtually all supervisory personnel were observed, from the publisher and executive editor, to the pressroom foreman and mailroom supervisor. Others (Studies 4, 5a, 5b, 6, 12, 14–16, 17, 18) looked at only one or two levels of management, for example, film directors and directors of photography.

In ongoing work environments and during competition

Some studies tapped leaders' behaviors as they occurred throughout the work day (Studies 1, 2, 3, 4, 5a, 5b, 11), while others were restricted to particular times, for example, during sailboat races (Studies 6, 14–16), meetings (Study 13), or film shoots (Study 17).

Spanning sectors and continents

Both the public (Studies 1b, 4, 5b, 6, 11, 13, 14–16) and private (Studies 1a, 2, 3, 5a, 12, 17, 18) sectors were represented. Managers from corporate (Studies 1a, 2, 3, 5a) as well as artistic (Studies 1b, 12, 17) communities were included. Leaders were observed on three continents: in Australia (Study 4), Finland (Studies 5a and 5b), and the United States, with five of the eleven studies in the Midwestern portion (Studies 1, 2, 3, 11, 13), six in the Northeastern section (Studies 6, 12, 14–16, 17), and one in the Southcentral portion (Study 18).

With one exception (Study 18), all of the supervisory personnel were observed using the Operant Supervisory Taxonomy and Index (OSTI). Although the definitions in the OSTI are sufficiently broad to allow managers to enact the categories in a variety of ways, we were still surprised to see how similarly leaders in four very different settings behaved when they interacted with their staffs. Despite the fact that the managers included Finnish construction supervisors (Study 5a), Finnish government managers (Study 5b), American theater directors (Study 12), and American sailboat skippers (Study 14), as Table 3.1 shows, the commonalities are striking.

Managers may phrase their questions differently. A Finnish construction supervisor asks: "Did you put those materials away?," while an American theater director inquires: "You're planning to use the wood stain you showed me?" But behind each question, the leader is trying to gather information about a follower's performance. When a sailboat skipper delivers a negative consequence in the heat of competition ("There's too much halyard. There's no air"), he lets his crew know something is amiss just as when the Finnish government manager lets his staff know about an error ("You made these minutes incorrectly").

Leaders pleased (or displeased) with performance are of kindred mind, despite differences in nationality and occupational group: A Finnish construction supervisor who has just inspected on site exclaims, "Great, you have done it so quickly." A jubilant American skipper says of his vessel, "Yes, yes, yes. It's a good day for Mercury." While these examples are drawn from only four settings, they illustrate how comparably leaders can express themselves even though they differ according to time pressure, occupation, nationality, and countless other factors.

Conducting replications: leaders of individuals (Studies 2, 3, and 4)[5]

While the studies as a group give a range of the diverse subjects and settings, let us concentrate on the seven studies assessing effectiveness. Of these, the initial three studies were done in an ongoing organization. As is typical of the vast majority of samples gained in field research, each was a sample of convenience.

Study 2 took place within two divisions of a large medical insurance firm, employing approximately 2,600 workers. The two divisions included 740 workers and 45 managers, from which the 24 managers in the study were selected. Managers in the two divisions were primarily concerned with the processing of claims and correspondence, and the reviewing of medical records; managers in selected departments dealt with audits, reimbursements, and sales.

Study 3 was conducted in a newspaper organization, employing approximately 250 persons. Thirty-three managers plus the publisher were observed. The managers were in six departments: advertising, business, circulation, personnel, production, and news. Three organizational levels were represented: department head (6); middle level manager (14) and, in the news department, editor (6); and first-line supervisor (3) and, in news, assistant editor (4). All were high school graduates with an average age of 39.1 years; 29 were male, 9 female.

Because of the small number of studies done and the variability of the findings in Studies 2 and 3 (and 6), Brewer and his associates (1994) conducted *Study 4* to examine "the generality of Komaki et al.'s ... model of supervision in a police force, an organization characterized by a rigid and formal chain of command" (p. 71). The study focused on one level of supervisor, the patrol sergeant, within a force of 4,000 officers in a major city with a population of one million in Australia. "The sergeant's main functions included deployment, supervision and training of subordinates, paperwork (crime reports, court briefs, etc.), office and cell duties, and community policing. ... Each sergeant supervised a stable team of officers" (p. 71). Teams typically included from five to seven officers. The city was organized into sixteen divisions. The twenty sergeants in the study were spread evenly across the sixteen divisions.

Monitoring and/or consequences distinguished between effective and marginal managers

In these three studies, effective managers either monitored significantly more often (Studies 2 and 4) or provided more consequences in general (Study 3) or more neutral consequences in particular (Study 4). Based on these findings, we concluded that our model's predictions were supported with leaders as varied as insurance managers (whose workers processed claims and performed audits), newspaper managers (who together with workers published a daily newspaper), and police sergeants in a quasi-military organization.

We had little evidence from these initial tests, however, that the model would work with leaders of groups. Each claims processor entered data from medical forms; few, if any, interactions with co-workers were necessary to complete the task successfully. The same was true for newspaper workers; with the exception of production workers, reporters could complete their assignments independently and advertising personnel could take orders from customers, again independently. Police officers went out on patrol by themselves or with a partner, not as a division team. Not surprisingly, virtually all of the interactions these workers had with their bosses were one-on-one.

Deliberately sampling for heterogeneity: leaders of teams doing interdependent tasks (Studies 6, 14, and 15)

Because the initial studies of our model were limited to leaders who worked primarily one-on-one with followers, doubts remained about the applicability of the model. We were curious: could our findings extend to tasks requiring coordination among team members for their completion? Would the model hold with leaders of groups? Maybe, with teams, leaders lose saliency as group norms or dynamics take on increasing importance.

Another issue regards the complexity of the task. Situations requiring the orchestration of team members are notoriously difficult to manage. In analyzing what made the difference between high-error and low-error crews flying B–747 jets, NASA researchers found that it was *not* a lack of technical knowledge and skill (Smith, 1979; Foushee, 1984). Instead, the majority of problems were related to "breakdowns in crew coordination" (Foushee, 1984, p. 889). Some of the more serious errors, for example, occurred when a cabin crew member repeatedly requested assistance from the cockpit crew at inopportune moments. Confirming the results of these studies is an analysis of jet transport accidents over an eight-year period in which breakdowns in crew interactions were judged to play a significant role in more than 60 of the accidents (Cooper, White, & Lauber, 1979). Perhaps the model cannot be used in situations with these intricacies.

Despite the fact that practitioners and academics agree about the importance of coordination (Blake, Mouton, & Allen, 1987; Mitchell, 1982), reviewer after reviewer bemoans the sparsity of studies. Hackman and Morris (1975) note that "although literally thousands of studies of group performance have been conducted..., we still know very little about why some groups are more effective than others. We know even less about what to do to improve the performance of a given group working on a specific task" (p. 2). Three years later, Hackman and Morris (1978) write that "there has hardly been a pouring forth of conceptual and empirical attacks on the group effectiveness problem" (p. 58). In 1984, following a review of military teams and related small-group research from 1955 to 1980, Dyer concludes that "despite all of the small-group research that has been conducted, one sometimes feels that, in fact, this is all we know: It's just teamwork" (p. 294). In 1986, Goodman, Ravlin, and Argote express chagrin about the "dearth of information about permanent groups in organizations" (p. 2), noting the number of studies to be "limited to an average of about twelve studies per year" (p. 22). In short, despite ready recognition of the importance of group performance, proven ways of improving it are lacking.

Distinctions have been made among interdependent tasks (March & Simon, 1958; McCann & Ferry, 1979; Shaw, 1973; Thompson, 1967; & Victor & Blackburn, 1987). Thompson (1967) identifies three levels of interdependence: pooled, sequential, and reciprocal. In pooling, relatively little coordination is involved other than the expectation that all components will follow standard routines. An example would be several snow removal plows, each plowing different sections of a main thoroughfare (Bass & Barrett, 1981). When sequentially interdependent, one component's activities must follow another's. Ground controllers are an example. As an airplane leaves one traffic space, control of the plane is transferred to another controller in charge of the space the aircraft is now entering. Reciprocal interdependence is considered the most difficult to coordinate because mutual adjustments must be maintained. A five-man basketball team or a sailboat racing team raising or lowering a particular sail are examples.

Unfortunately, researchers who emphasize tasks typically do not take the next step and identify what can be done to improve the execution of these tasks. Coming closest to combining all three elements are Hackman and Walton (1986) in their proposal for a theory of leadership on task-performing groups in organizations. While leaders are given specific recommendations, no distinction is made between interdependent and independent tasks.

The primary exception is that of McCann and Ferry (1979) who discuss the role of the leader in their closing paragraphs: "The fundamental task for unit managers is to: (a) assess their degree of interdependence with other units; (b) determine the management costs entailed; (c) share these perceptions with the other units to the degree possible; and (d) decide upon which joint coordinative behaviors to use" (p. 117). While McCann and Ferry (1979) mention the leader, the prescriptions are vague. What leaders should specifically do to "share these perceptions" of management costs is not identified. Nor is it mentioned what the "joint coordinative behaviors" are. In short, in the task, group, and leadership literatures, all three elements – prescriptive statements, team members, and interdependent tasks – are rarely combined.

Furthermore, the measurement of group effectiveness is raised as a critical issue. "Too often, findings must be qualified," according to Dyer (1984), "due to problems with the measurement of the dependent variable (e.g., unreliability, the lack of construct validity), the lack of measures for some variables, and/or errors in administration of measurement instruments" (p. 299). Goodman, Ravlin, and Argote (1986) question the way in which the dependent variable is defined, wondering whether it is possible to explain individual performance with the same model as one uses to explain group performance or member satisfaction. McGrath (1984) laments that "we have a powerful array of sophisticated tools for data processing and analysis. They are, if anything, too strong for the data we usually feed them. We need better data to put into them" (p. 365). He recommends "a better balance of data collection methods that do not rely entirely on self-reports of workers or of managers" (p. 365).

Hence, in Study 6 and then in Studies 14 and 15, we sought out leaders of groups, particularly those doing interdependent tasks.

Study 6 (Komaki, Desselles, & Bowman, 1989)

To see if the model could be applied with tasks requiring coordination among team members, we conducted Study 6. We extended our original hypothesis and posited that the quantity and quality of monitors and consequences would be important but that a particular aspect of performance, namely, team coordination, would be critical as well. Effective leaders would identify the critical points when team members needed to cooperate with one another.

Team coordination referred to the intersection of two or more team members' actions, where team members can include the leader as well as the subordinate. The intersections can include simultaneous and serial actions. For it to count as team coordination, leaders must refer to two or more members *and* their intersection. Leaders can monitor, referring to the team coordination aspects of the task (e.g., "Ready to put chute up *as soon as I round the mark?*"). Or they can monitor without reference to team coordination (e.g., "Ready to put chute up?"). Similarly, leaders can provide consequences or antecedents with and without reference to team coordination. Our rationale was that leaders who focus on these coordination points are more likely to have subordinates who correctly anticipate other team members' actions, synchronize their actions accordingly, and thus avoid unnecessary duplication, errors, and interference.

We first directed our efforts toward procuring a site that included leaders of groups doing interdependent tasks. Because of my participation in sailboat racing, I was aware of the many maneuvers involving precisely-timed orchestration among crew members. After a series of cold phone calls and meetings, I arranged a fleet racing competition – using a round-robin regatta format and involving a fleet of ten J-24 sailboats, nineteen skippers, thirty-six crew members, eleven observers, and four varsity coaches from an East Coast university.

The index of supervisory success was the Sailing Effectiveness Measure, identifying each skipper's win-loss record. To accentuate the coordination needed among team members, we set up the race course[8] so that it prolonged activities requiring interdependence: in this case, the raising and lowering of a specific type of sail.

Hence, by procuring a site which possessed characteristics across which we wanted to generalize, we were able to purposively sample for the heterogeneity we desired.

Winning sailboat skippers monitored and provided consequences

As predicted, series standings correlated significantly and negatively[9] with consequences, $r = -.47$, $p < .05$, and monitors, $r = -.51$, $p < .05$, during the races themselves.

Team coordination not related to series standings

Using the OSTTI with its sub-category of team coordination, we could test the extended hypothesis concerning team coordination. It was not supported. The frequency of team coordination statements by the skippers was not significantly related to race results, $r = .04$.

Among the reasons we conjectured for the lack of support for the extended hypothesis, including team coordination, was the leaders' behavior; skippers spent only a tiny portion of time (from 4 to 6 percent) talking about how the crew could coordinate with one another. Another problem was the measure of effectiveness. Series standings took into account the entire race, but the aspect of the race requiring the most teamwork (hoisting one of the sails) took less than 10 percent of the entire race; the effectiveness measure, while superb in some respects, may have been a relatively insensitive index of how well the crew cooperated with one another. Although including the concept of team coordination yielded no advantage for prediction in the present study, it highlighted the importance of directly addressing this neglected aspect of these challenging tasks.

Studies 14 and 15 (Komaki, Reynard, Lee, & Wallace, 1995; Reynard & Komaki, 1995)

Wishing to continue investigating what leaders should do to promote coordination among team members, Komaki, Reynard, Lee, and Wallace conducted Studies 14 and 15. Our goal for Study 14 was the same, that is, we wanted to see if we could extend the model to interdependent tasks. We also hypothesized in Study 15 that effective leaders would differ from lackluster ones in their timing, particularly in their delivery of AMC sequences.

We again directed our efforts to procuring an appropriate site, and made arrangements to collect data on leaders during sailboat races. This time, the boats were bigger (forty feet rather than twenty-four feet), there were more crew (eight to ten rather than three), and there were more leaders (two to three leaders rather than one) aboard each boat.

Another major difference was the videotaping of the crews, which enabled the Sailing Teamwork Effectiveness Measure (STEM). The STEM focused on that portion of the race – the hoisting of one of the sails, the spinnaker or chute – that required cooperation among team members.

Leaders whose teams raised sails fastest monitored the most

As we had found earlier, effective sailboat skippers – those whose crews raised the chute the fastest – monitored significantly more than their slower counterparts (Study 14), $r = -.33$, $p < .05$.

Team coordination had little, if any, impact

The time leaders spent making team coordination statements, while still accounting for a tiny proportion of the communications (not even 1 percent during the entire race), was not related to effectiveness, $r = -.04$.

Effective skippers provided quick AMC sequences

As hypothesized, the effective leaders delivered AMC sequences more quickly (Study 15), $r = .53$, $p < .001$. That is, the faster a skipper delivered a sequence consisting of an Antecedent, a Monitor, and then a Consequence, the more effective the team's performance.

Although the expanded version of the model was not supported, Studies 6, 14, and 15 indicated that leaders should monitor (Studies 6 and 14), provide consequences (Study 6), and deliver quick AMC sequences (Study 15). Together with the studies of the leaders of individuals, these findings in support of the model can be generalized across leaders of individuals and groups, as well as across tasks differing in their coordination requirements.

We encourage future researchers to continue investigating the critical issue of coordination, perhaps using other definitions and assessments of team coordination and effectiveness. One recent news article reinforces the point. It tells of a well known American consumer products company that failed to coordinate its efforts. Wishing to expand into southern China, the company built a factory and created market demand for the product, but forgot a key coordination point: how to get the goods from the factory they had built to the potential consumers they had created. As a spokesperson for the industry remarked, "if you don't connect the two ... it's all for naught" (Gargan, 1996, p. 45). Company officials, unable to figure out how to transport the goods, eventually had to "abandon most of the expansion, at a significant loss" (p. 45).

Along these same lines, one of the most highly regarded[10] general managers in Kotter's (1982) study, Richard Papolis, spent much of his time dealing with coordination issues. Richard was convinced that it is essential to keep warring factions talking.

> Many companies fail because they do not. Marketing, engineering, and production people often don't understand one another. It is not unlike the Jews and the Arabs. The key here is to build each group's esteem in the eyes of the other group. My role is to help make them interact with one another in a constructive way. The general manager's role is making sure that the dialogue happens. (p. 114)

In at least one-third of Richard's discussions, as shown in Table 6.3, these coordination issues were paramount. In one exchange, at the meeting of the officer's group, lasting about three hours, Richard "refereed an obvious fight between his marketing and manufacturing vice presidents" (p. 115). While it is difficult to say whether Richard would be successful without addressing these points of contention, we encourage future research on this critical issue of coordination.

Deliberately sampling for heterogeneity: leaders in cultures differing in reverence of silence (Study 5a and 5b)

Questions arose about an even larger aggregation, the culture in which leaders and followers reside or operate. Can any model be universally valid? Can our model assuming informal, day-to-day interactions among team members be successfully applied in cultures that revere reticence? Psychologists studying people in different cultures continually ask questions such as these (Triandis & Berry, 1980; Jahoda, 1980).

Some scholars contend that similar practices yield similar returns, whether the workplace be in the USA or Japan (e.g., Lincoln, 1989). As an example, operant conditioning principles have been successfully applied to facilitate work performance in countries including Mexico (Hermann, de Montes, Dominguez, Montes, & Hopkins, 1973), the former Soviet Union (Welsh, Luthans, & Sommer, 1993), Korea (Sommer, Bae, & Luthans, 1996), Israel (Elizur, 1987) and Finland (Nasanen & Saari, 1987).

At the same time, we as scientists reside in communities that seek out general truths. In response to our own "cultural" environment, we perhaps not surprisingly continue to search for similarities among human beings. In fact, a drama critic reviewed a recent group of plays centered on the struggles of African-, Hispanic-, and Asian-American families. He ended up arguing: "It's a bitter truth: Despite all the ferocious arguments they arouse these days, ethnic differences are superficial" (Feingold, 1996, p. 77).

On the other hand, others have argued that cultural borders make a difference (Brislin, Lonner, & Thorndike, 1973; Dawson, 1971; Kanter, 1991; Tainio & Santalainen, 1984; Triandis, Kurowski, & Gelfand, 1994).

In a seminal series of studies, Hofstede (1984) found the preferences and values of persons varied substantially from country to country. Managers in Japan and Korea, for example, place a much higher value on group efforts than those in the United States (Howard, Shudo, & Umeshima, 1983), although these values continue to change (Kim, Park, & Suzuki, 1990). Vivid contrasts have been found in the value different cultures place on power and masculinity (Erez, 1994).

Cross-cultural scholars insist that, whatever our predispositions about the universal nature of our theories, it is critical to test them (Jahoda, 1980; Triandis & Berry, 1980). Theories of leadership effectiveness, in particular, need cross-cultural testing (Bass, 1990). Theories are typically developed in a single country. For example, leader match (Fiedler, 1967), leader-member exchange (Graen & Schiemann, 1978), charismatic style (Bass, 1990; House, 1977; Tichy & Ulrich, 1984), the quality decision-making model (Vroom & Yetton, 1973), and the operant model of effective supervision were all developed in the United States; performance maintenance theory (Misumi & Peterson, 1985) was developed in Japan. The studies testing the model to date, while positive, have included primarily American citizens in the United States.[11] Testing allows us to see whether or not our theories are based on "ethnocentric constructions of reality" (Triandis & Berry, 1980, p. ix).

Another compelling reason for testing the model is our (culturally-based) assumption that "everyday, informal exchanges" take place among workers (Komaki, Zlotnick, & Jensen, 1986, p. 271) and that these give-and-take exchanges would be regarded positively or at least neutrally. In the Scandinavian countries (Finland, Denmark, Norway, Sweden), in some Asian countries (Japan, China), and in certain North American cultures (the Apaches, the Quakers), however, silence is highly valued (Kang & Pearce, 1983; Stedje, 1983; Tannen & Saville-Troike, 1985). Persons who take time before they speak are looked upon as more reflective and thoughtful than those who talk immediately. Quiet persons are viewed as wiser and more judicious than those who express themselves freely.

In Finland, the strong, silent individual is a customary and cherished stereotype. The Finns refer to themselves as "reserved" and "conservative in their general outlook" (Saarinen, 1987, p. 142). Scandinavian artists have been described as having made "privacy a haunting theme" (Lindwall & Olsen, 1983, p. 63) and as incorporating "silence" into their work, with the " 'not-words' seeming much more important than what is actually said with words" (Grinde, 1982, pp. 50–51). This attitude about silence is exemplified by an episode in an old Finnish movie (described by Lehtonen and Saja-vaara (1985)). The scene is:

> the common room in a traditional Finnish farmhouse. The farmer and his wife are carrying out their daily tasks in the room. A middle-aged man enters, takes off his hat and shakes the snow from the top of it, walks slowly across the room, and sits down on the bench that runs

along the wall. The man takes his pipe from his pocket, fills it very
slowly, sticks it into his mouth, and smokes the pipeful in silence. The
farmer and his wife go on doing their duties. Finally – (the farmer asks):
"Is it very far you come from?" (p. 193)

Such scenes are not uncommon even among loved ones. One Finnish author
predicted he might say " 'I love you' once in a lifetime" when perhaps his
wife of twenty years is "on her deathbed" (Knutas, 1993, p. 27).[12]

This Finnish tolerance for reticence has been empirically documented.
With a sample of 1,094 Finnish respondents, Sallinen-Kuparinen (1986)
found 31.5 percent would speak up only when they are asked a question,
and only 26.7 percent experienced anxiety when they remained silent while
interacting with others. In contrast, over 86 percent of an American sample
reported feeling uncomfortable when silences occurred in their day-to-day
interactions (Newman, 1982).

Because cultural differences in the value placed on silence may
lessen the usefulness of theories developed in a culture in which quick-witted,
freely expressive persons are seen as "savvy," we addressed two issues in
Studies 5a and 5b: (a) whether effective managers from a country such
as Finland that values reticence would spend more or less time monitoring
and providing consequences than their less effective counterparts, and
(b) whether Finnish subordinates would react positively or negatively to
managers who spent more time monitoring and providing consequences.
The model predicts that the effective managers would spend more time,
and the subordinates would respond more positively, whereas a culturally-
based view would predict less time and less positive attitudes.

To address these questions, two indigenous researchers, Marita Hyttinen
and Stina Immonen, obtained data in two Finnish sites, using the OSTI.
Hyttinen's sample (Study 5a) consisted of thirty-one construction managers
who were responsible for adherence to production guidelines and safety
rules in the building and restoring of private (hotels, homes) and public
(dormitories) buildings. The managers were located on sixteen building
sites from November 1989 to May 1990 in and around Tampere, Finland.
The managers were employed as supervisors or assistant supervisors in a
large construction company with projects abroad as well as in Finland.
With the exception of one woman assistant supervisor, the managers
were male.

Immonen (Study 5b) looked at sixteen government administrators who
were responsible for the timely and judicious collection of revenue. There
were eight departments, with one administrator and one assistant administrator per department. All worked in a single agency in Helsinki, Finland.
All administrators were male with a master's degree in law. All assistant
administrators were female; all were high school graduates, some were
college graduates.

Effective leaders monitored more and provided more consequences even in cultures where silence is valued

Supervisors rated highly by their work crews spent more time monitoring and providing consequences, $t = 1.9$, $p = .03$.

Finnish workers with the best attitudes had managers who monitored more and provided more consequences

Workers' attitudes in a government agency were more positive as their administrators gathered more information and provided more feedback about their performance, as shown in Table 4.10 (p. 120). Employees with the highest mental well-being worked in departments in which the administrators provided more monitors and consequences. The correlations ranged between .71 and .80. Workers who were the most satisfied with their job security were monitored more frequently, $r = .82$.

These findings parallel those obtained with samples of American managers in the field (Studies 2, 3, 6, 14, 15) as well as those in the laboratory (Study 10) and suggest that the US-developed model of effective supervision can be used successfully in a culture such as Finland in which reticence is revered. The implication is that within the boundaries expressed, the model's recommendations transcend different managers, varying aggregations of workers, tasks differing in their coordination requirements, and cultures varying in their penchant for silence. Perhaps, as Mintzberg (1973) suggests, whether the leader be a baseball coach in Botswana or a bishop in Belize, the manager must delegate the work and motivate subordinates to do the work. Such similarities, it appears, render these differences immaterial, and support a more universal view of effective supervisory behavior.

Future research

Many more investigations are needed to establish the generalizability of the model. One of the most frequently asked questions is whether the model works with chief executives, presidents, and vice presidents. To date, too few leaders at the highest organizational levels (in Studies 2, 3) have been assessed. While we have no reason to doubt that the model will hold, particularly in light of the descriptions of the general managers Tom Long and Richard Papolis (Kotter, 1982), it would be worthwhile to test this hypothesis systematically.

One particularly promising classification system for categorizing managers at different levels is described in a study by Blood, Graham, and Zedeck (1987). In this study, they developed a method of reliably classifying on a continuum jobs such as the following: Messenger, File Clerk, Driver, Cafeteria Cashier, Control Clerk, Social Security Tax Auditor, Chief PBX Operator, Claims Adjuster, Senior Auditor, Head Buyer, and Container Coordinator. To do this, they regressed job ratings of different dimensions against actual pay. Use of only the five most predictive scale scores produced a multiple correlation coefficient of 0.97. The five scales were: (1) object variety, (2) number of required interactions, (3) amount of required interactions, (4) directing the work of others, and (5) clarity of task structure. One could use dimensions such as the above to categorize the workers that the manager supervises. The higher the level of workers that the manager supervised, the higher the level of the manager. Although the study took place in a single organization, a world-wide shipping company, the results could be used across organizations, since the method is independent of the individual's title or pay. Using this classification system, one could test whether our model is indeed applicable to leaders at different levels.

Another intriguing research direction, stretching the model considerably, would be to see whether it would work as well in non-work settings. We would welcome a series of studies looking at the interactions between parents and children, husbands and wives, friends, and even colleagues. Our hypothesis is that those relationships marked by reciprocal monitor-own performance sequences, and even give-and-take exchanges, would be predictive of longer lasting and/or more salubrious interactions.

IN SUMMARY

In short, we have identified five limitations of our model: (a) the nature of the task, in this case, only execution-type tasks, (b) the maintenance stage of the motivational process, (c) the sufficiency of resources necessary to do the job, (d) the possession of the necessary knowledge, skills, and abilities on the part of the leaders, and (e) the possession of the necessary knowledge, skills, and abilities on the part of the followers. When, and *only* when, these conditions are in place, the recommendations of our model will hold.

Hence, it is not only important that leaders limit their use of the model to maintaining the performance of followers executing tasks. It is also critical that both leaders and followers possess the necessary knowledge, skills, and abilities, and that sufficient resources are available to do the job.

We end our discussion of the research on the model by sketching its sweep. Based on the variety of leaders, followers, and settings, ranging from the fever pitch of racing competition to the relative calm of an insurance company, including both one-on-one situations and tasks requiring the cooperation of team members, and spanning cultures where silence is ignored and where it is venerated, we can recognize the areas within which the model holds true. With a judicious awareness of both the boundaries and breadth of our model, we can see both its limitations and its broad reach as a means of helping to make workplaces better places.

7 Taking stock

This chapter summarizes our model's findings.

Initially, our model drew its inspiration from the theory of operant conditioning, with the leaders' behaviors and the interplay between leader and follower, for its part, enhancing effectiveness. Since then, the model has been shaped by a variety of literatures: I/O (for the idea of moderators), group, leadership, and interactional (for the process between leaders and followers), and cognitive and emotional (for reasons concerning why the model works). The results of eighteen studies, capsuled in Figure 4.1 (p.79) and Table 7.1, have also influenced it. Conducted by investigators on three continents, the studies range widely. After identifying ways of assessing leaders' behaviors and effectiveness, the initial field studies looked at the quantity and quality of the leaders' behaviors. In order to see if monitors and consequences distinguished between effective and less effective or lackluster leaders, researchers tracked leaders who differed in their success at mobilizing others. Some of the studies looked at leaders of individuals in the field (Studies 2, 3, 4, 18) and laboratory settings (Studies 8, 9, 10); others looked at leaders of teams (Studies 6, 14); and still others took place in a culture (e.g., Studies 5a and 5b in Finland) other than the model's country of origin, the United States. All these studies (with the exception of Study 18) collected information about leaders' behaviors, using the Operant Supervisory Taxonomy and Index (or one of its variants), and then summarized how much time each leader spent monitoring, for example.

Later studies went beyond these summary scores to scrutinize leaders' behaviors over time. One set of studies concentrated on the leaders themselves (Studies 15, 16). Study 15, for example, looked at leaders' speed in stringing together AMC sequences – first providing an Antecedent, followed by the next Monitor, and then the next Consequence. Another set of studies highlighted the often neglected follower (Studies 7, 13, 17, 18). We looked in Study 7, for instance, at what the follower did in the five-second interval immediately after the leader monitored, and, then at what the leader did in the next interval, then at what the follower did, and so on in a continuing stream.

Table 7.1 Capsule of eighteen studies in connection with the model

| Measuring leaders in field | Quantity and quality | | | | Behaviors of leaders | | Over time | | |
| | Behaviors of effective leaders | | | Strident notes | Effective | Lackluster | Lags/trends | Exchanges with follower (F) | |
	Of individuals	Of teams	In different culture					Facilitating	Dampening
BEHAVIORS 1 Psychometric properties of OSTI	2 M particularly via work sampling	6 M, C, and A	5a M and C	3 A as a suppressor variable	15 Quick AM and AMC sequences	15 Sluggish sequences, especially AM	7 M stimulated C, whereas A depressed C	7 Reciprocal interaction between leader and follower: M set stage for follower OP, which in turn, set stage for M	7 Follower inhibitor: *F less* likely to set stage for leader M
11 Criterion-related validity of in-basket	3 C including positive, negative, and neutral	14 M	5b M and C related to positive *F* attitudes	3 NC *negatively related*	15 More As during MC sequence	15 More As, Ws, NCs, and Ss during AM sequence	16 Over race course, A, M, and W peaked and faded depending on task requirements		
EFFECTIVENESS									
6 Outcome measure for sailing	4 M particularly self-report and neutral C			14 NC *negatively related* 5a S *negatively related*		16 More W approaching critical phase of task		13 M set stage for *F* OP	

12 Teamwork for theater production teams	18 M via work sampling related to F attitudes	5b S *negatively* related	17 over long project patterns differed by team except positive consequences decreased as project neared end
14–15 Teamwork and strategy for sailing	8 M and C as well as M alone	14 M *negatively* related to decision-making strategy	
17 Innovative ideas	9 M alone		
	10 M and C versus M and versus C		

Note: Numbers identify studies. OSTI = Operant Supervisory Taxonomy Index. M = Monitor, C = Consequence, A = Antecedent, NC = Not Communicating, S = Solitary, W = Work-related, OP = Own Performance. *F* = Follower. AMC = Antecedent–Monitor–Consequence sequence.

Many of the results were predicted by our model. We forecast, for example, those about monitoring (M) and consequences (C) which are the cornerstones of the model. Some results, however, were not foreseen. We did not predict the surprising findings in Studies 3, 5a, and 5b, and 14 and 15 about antecedents (A), not communicating (NC), and solitary (S), for instance. Nor did we anticipate that these same behaviors would be placed prior to the monitor, in an AM sequence, by the lackluster leaders. As often happens, however, the unanticipated findings provoked some of the most intriguing explorations – in this case, illuminating the actions of the lackluster leaders.

Given what we have learned so far, we would like now, at last, to pose an answer to the initial question asked by coffee farmer Isak Dinesen, at the beginning of the book.

WHAT DO EFFECTIVE LEADERS REALLY DO?

Substance and style of the behaviors

Effective leaders monitor

Effective leaders – on the right in Table 7.2 – find out how their subordinates are doing. They stroll, peruse, and mingle with their staff. In the midst of these ongoing activities, they look and inquire. They do not assume that all is going well. They monitor, to see and hear for themselves.

In five of six studies conducted in the field using the OSTI measure (Studies 2, 4, 5a, and 5b, 6, 14), managers who were successful in motivating others spent more time monitoring than their lackluster counterparts.

Particularly via work sampling

Effective leaders use a particular type of monitoring: sampling the work. They watch workers in action, and scan the work itself. Insurance managers (in Study 2) went to the rooms where operators keyboarded data from claim forms; sometimes the managers merely watched, and sometimes they picked up and perused the forms. Workers in movie theaters reported that their managers (in Study 18) watched them as they worked, sometimes seeing if they were working efficiently, and sometimes examining the work they completed.

Even when work sampling was difficult to do, our results showed that effective managers managed to find a way. To sample police on patrol, for example, sergeants (in Study 4) would have had to literally locate the officers, get in a vehicle and track them down. Instead, effective leaders in this setting used another method of monitoring: self-report. When officers came into the station, the more effective sergeants asked how it had gone on patrol. Our point is that effective leaders do not leave observation to chance. They find or make the time to gather information about their followers' performance.

Effective leaders provide consequences

The second thing that effective leaders do is let followers know how well or how poorly they are doing. They provide consequences. And they do this more often than their less effective counterparts.

Consequences, we found, separated the effective and lackluster managers in four of six studies done in the field (Studies 3, 4, 5a and 5b, 6).

All kinds including positive, negative, and neutral

Consequences are not restricted to those that are positive. Effective leaders provide all kinds. The construction supervisors (in Study 5a) rated favorably by their building crews provided positive, negative, and neutral consequences. Sometimes they merely described what someone had done: "He made a call yesterday for those materials" (a neutral consequence). They also did not shy away from providing negative consequences: "Oh, no! All the wrong tiles. You ought to take the blue ones to this room." Effective supervisors also let their crews know when they approved: "You have done good work; no signs of errors." Or, they might comment to a co-worker, "He has worked with care; all the tiles are straight."

Effective leaders do not rely on either monitors or consequences alone

Neither monitors nor consequences alone, however, is sufficient for effective supervision of others, as two laboratory Studies (8 and 10) showed. Managers who provided only consequences, even primarily neutral and positive ones, had significant declines in workers' performance. When managers gave only monitors, performance did not differ significantly from when they provided both monitors and consequences, but followers' attitudes suffered. Followers who were only monitored made many more complaints about their bosses, and had far fewer good things to say about them. Since both satisfactory performance and positive attitudes are critical to a truly effective manager, both monitors and consequences are necessary.

Lackluster leaders are more laconic

What about the lackluster leaders? Do they differ only in degree (how much time they spent) from the behavior of more successful managers? As it happens, lackluster leaders (on the left hand side of Table 7.2) do spend less time monitoring and providing consequences than their more effective counterparts. But they differ in kind (what they did in lieu of these behaviors) as well, as shown in the bottom portion of the chart.

Table 7.2 Differences charted between lackluster and effective leaders in quantity and quality of their behaviors

Lackluster leaders		Effective leaders
	Gather information about performance **MONITOR**	
Less often ↓		More often ↑ Via work sampling
	and Evaluate or indicate knowledge of performance **CONSEQUENCE**	
Less often ↓		More often ↑ Providing all kinds, not predominantly negative
	Remain silent during work-related conversation, for example **NOT COMMUNICATING**	
More often ↑		Less often ↓
	Work alone, not interacting, in privacy of office, for example **SOLITARY**	
More often ↑		Less often ↓

Note: Refer to studies 2, 3, 4, 5a, 5b, 6, 8, 9, 10, and 14

Lackluster leaders spend more time than effective leaders not communicating. These lackluster leaders are more likely to be passive participants, not taking an active role in shaping the conversation or steering it toward performance-related topics. We found this tendency in two studies (3 and 14). Lackluster skippers at the helm of forty-foot sailboats spent more time remaining silent while crew members around them talked about the location of the mark and the other boats. Marginally effective managers (in Study 3) remained on the periphery while assistant editors at the newspaper talked about the latest news at the courthouse.

Lackluster leaders are more solitary

Lackluster leaders also spend more time by themselves. We found this to be the case in both Finnish studies (Studies 5a and 5b). Lackluster government managers spent more time in their offices, rarely coming out to talk with workers. A similar pattern, although only approaching statistical significance, surfaced again on Finnish construction sites. Supervisors who were not as effective spent more time in their offices or walking from place to place than at the places where crews were working.

Contrasting effective and lackluster leaders in action

Comparing the way in which three supervisors in a packaging plant handled an equipment breakdown provides illustrative examples (Gellerman, 1976). One of the supervisors, Charlie, we discussed in Chapter 3; his counterparts, Lonnie and Dave, are also responsible for a multi-shift operation in which high-speed machinery sends ingredients, and eventually ingredient-filled packs, down tubes.

When Charlie had a breakdown on his shift, as shown in Table 3.2b (p.46), he called maintenance and then immediately turned his attention to his employees, reassuring the somewhat uncertain operator, who had reluctantly thrown the emergency switch (a consequence (C)) (Gellerman, 1976). As Charlie showed the young man from the labor pool how to hand-feed the machine, he checked to make sure that the young man was properly timing his delivery of ingredients into the hopper (a monitor (M)) and let him know how he was performing (C).

In contrast, when Lonnie had breakdowns during his shift, he abandoned his employees, choosing to stay at the problem site, even though there was not much he could do; the labor contract stipulated that only a union maintenance man would work on the machines. Lonnie, however, insisted on remaining in the area, sometimes making comments (work-related (W)), which were usually ignored. Lonnie had had "grievances filed against him for such prohibited acts as tapping an out-of-line part with a hammer" (p. 94). When the interviewer, Gellerman (1976), asked Lonnie:

> if resuming his patrols as soon as he knew the maintenance man was on the job might not have been better than remaining on the scene during the entire repair, he replied that the best way to make sure the machine was repaired as quickly as possible was to stay with the maintenance man, guaranteeing that he would not slow down or take it easy. (pp. 94–95)

Given that Lonnie did not quickly resume his patrols, he probably had less time to monitor particularly via work sampling.

Lackluster leaders also provide fewer consequences of all sorts. Dave, who usually spent time interacting with his employees when the lines broke down, was nowhere to be seen once the machines were repaired and the line resumed running. " 'When we're running,' Dave said, 'I just leave them alone. . . . I've got a different job now. . . . Now I have to start checking all the little things to make sure we don't start sliding backwards' " (Gellerman, 1976, p. 97). In this case, he was referring not to his people but to the checks he would have to make of the equipment to catch trouble before something got out of hand. For his people, it was as though he subscribed to the philosophy that "no news is good news."

While Dave did not provide many consequences when things went well, Lonnie did not provide consequences when problems occurred. He noticed an employee, whose machine had jammed, reaching into the loading trough to pull out and discard packages that were stuck there. This procedure had been the subject of a recent series of meetings between supervisors and operators. Even though the procedure was both inefficient and unsafe, Lonnie did and said nothing. When asked if he was going to stop the employee, Lonnie said no, "'because the jam was nearly cleared already'" (Gellerman, 1976, p. 94). Later, Lonnie elaborated, saying that he had not wanted to discourage the efforts of the employee, who had been trying to get production started again, even if the procedure was not prescribed. The second reason he gave was that "the employee would only have resented it if he had been corrected, and would have found some way to 'get even', probably at the expense of productivity" (p. 94).

Both Dave and Lonnie exemplify what lackluster leaders do. When progress or good news occurs, they rarely provide positive or neutral consequences either directly or indirectly. Even when problems occur, they ignore them, failing to provide negative consequences. Hence, it is not surprising that Lonnie is "not highly rated by management, and that his department's productivity record tends to be poor" (Gellerman, 1976, p.95). Dave is not evaluated as poorly, but his "actual production record seldom matches that of a smoother running shift" (p. 97).

On the other hand, effective supervisors like Charlie not only make their standards clear, but they regularly gather information. Charlie, aware that it can be boring when everything is running smoothly and the only sounds are the hum of the machines, routinely checks how workers are doing during brief "visits" to each work station, and provides consequences in a natural way on an everyday basis. When progress or good news occurs, he finds occasion to provide positive and neutral consequences: " 'Five hundred thirty-seven cases' ", said supervisor Charlie when workers arrived the day after a successful shift. Then he would "grin and thrust out his hand for a quick congratulatory shake, and move on" (Gellerman, 1976, p. 90).

When problems occur, these exemplary managers go right to the source. On the spot, they warn errant workers, providing negative consequences directly rather than indirectly: " 'I know you'd rather watch what those maintenance boys are doing' ", supervisor Charlie said to the young man from the labor pool. Through even the briefest of contacts, an effective manager can maintain easy, positive relationships, bantering back and forth. With one operator, a lady considerably older than Charlie, he had a standing joke:

> She "wouldn't permit him" to inspect more than one pack at a time; otherwise she threatened to "slap his hand." Naturally he pretended to grab at a second pack and she pretended to slap, then they both giggled and he said that he was really only making sure that she was still on the ball. (pp. 90–91)

Given such exchanges, it is not surprising that Charlie is highly rated by his superiors[1] and liked by employees with his "shift's productivity among the highest in the factory" (p. 93).

In summary, as Table 7.2 (p.186) shows, effective leaders monitor, particularly via work sampling, and they provide all kinds of consequences, not predominantly negatives ones. Lackluster leaders, on the other hand, spend more time either not communicating or solitary.

Pacing of leaders' behaviors over time

Leaders also differ in the timing or pacing with which they deliver certain behaviors.

Effective leaders give quick AMC and AM sequences

Effective leaders deliver AMC sequences quickly, while lackluster leaders are more sluggish in providing them. Thus the critical dimension, as shown in Table 7.3, is the time it takes.

The same holds true for the AM sequence. The AMC sequence can be divided into two parts: the interval that occurs before the monitor, which we refer to as the AM sequence, and the one that occurs after the monitor, the MC sequence. Effective leaders (in Study 15) monitored more quickly once they had given an antecedent. Lackluster leaders, on the other hand, took much longer before they monitored.

Effective leaders give more leisurely MC sequences

The same does not hold true during the MC sequence. Effective leaders (in Study 15) took more time than their lackluster counterparts before they gave a consequence.

Seeing pacing in action

To illustrate how leaders actually operate, we can return to two sets of leaders (in Study 15) during a sailboat race. As shown in Tables 3.3 (p.55)

Table 7.3 Study 15: Differences charted between lackluster and effective leaders in pacing of antecedent–monitor–consequence (AMC) sequences

Lackluster leaders	Effective leaders

First Antecedent, followed by next Monitor, followed by next Consequence
AMC SEQUENCE

Note: A = Antecedent, M = Monitor, C = Consequence

and 3.4 (p.59), the effective leaders (on the left) had a series of quick AMC sequences, two lasting only ten seconds and one taking place in seventy-five seconds.

In contrast, the lackluster leaders (on the right) were much slower. After giving an antecedent, the lackluster leaders gave more orders (A), looked out over the water (S), and discussed race tactics (W), followed by a series of negative consequences. The tactician continued to look out over the water (S). And the swirl of unmonitored behaviors continued. Finally, after four and a half minutes, one of the leaders finally monitored and then quickly delivered a negative consequence.

Table 7.4 Study 17: transcript of film crew B during a shoot

Time	Speaker	Statement/action
		(Preparing to film a shot)
6:02.45	D	Guys, are we running? (M)
	DP	No, not yet. I will check it first. (OP)
6:03.00	D	(Letting crew know he wants to monitor) **Can I just look at it before we go?** (A)[a]
	DP	Yes. (OP)
	D	(Looks through the camera). (M)[b]
.15	D	(Repositioning camera) **That's how I want it.** (Shows to DP). (C)[c]
	DP	(Looking at Director). (NC)
.30	D	Okay? (W)
	DP	Straight and centered. (W)
	D	Yes, that is for her; straight and centered. (W)
	DP	Yes, okay. (W)
.45	D	We can do more than one take. (W)
	DP	**Okay. Let's go!** (A)[a]
	D	And action! (A)
	DP	(To crew) Camera is rolling. (A)
	D	**(Watches actors and other crew members)** (M)[b]
6:04.00	D	Cut! (A)
	D	**That was lovely for me!** (C)[c]
	D	Can we do one more for safety? (A)
	DP	Okay. Sure. (W)
.15	D	Beautiful! (C)
	D	We'll do it again. (A)
	D	Can I see it one more time? (A)[d]
.30	DP	I'm sorry, we didn't focus yet. (OP)
	D	Okay. (C)
	D	Nothing, but that was beautiful. (C)

Note: D = Director, DP = Director of photography
a Marker Antecedent in Antecedent–Monitor–Consequence (AMC) sequence
b Marker Monitor in AMC sequence
c Marker Consequence in AMC sequence
d Note here that the Director intended to monitor

Another set of leaders, on a film crew (in Study 17), are shown in Table 7.4 as they are preparing for a shot.[2] During the 6:03.00 interval, the director (D) gives an antecedent, telling the crew he wants to see the shot in the camera, and he monitors, looking through the camera to see how the director of photography (DP) has positioned the camera. During the next interval (in this case, broken into fifteen-second intervals), the director repositions the camera, motions to the DP, and delivers a benign but negative consequence. As shown, this AMC sequence took place within thirty seconds.

The next AMC sequence begins with the next antecedent of the DP[3] during the 6:03.45 interval. Once the camera begins to roll, the director attempts to gather information (M), watching the actors and other crew members. In the next interval, the director exclaims: "That was lovely for me!" (C), concluding another thirty-second AMC sequence.

Placement of leaders' behaviors over time

Where behaviors occur within a sequence – their placement – makes a difference as well. Differences in placement, we found, separated effective from lackluster teams of skippers (in Study 15).

During MC sequence, effective leaders spend more time:

Providing antecedents

During the MC sequence, effective leaders give more antecedents than during the AM sequence. This difference in placement can be seen in the chart on the right in Table 7.5. The effective leader, after monitoring, spends more intervals – in this case, three – in contrast to providing none before monitoring.

Table 7.5 Study 15: differences charted between lackluster and effective leaders in placement of antecedents

Lackluster leaders	Effective leaders
Convey expectations of performance (e.g., give orders, reminders, cues) ANTECEDENTS	
More antecedents BEFORE monitoring	More antecedents AFTER monitoring

```
      00   10   20   30   40   50   00   10              00   10   20   30   40   50   00   10
  A   |-●--o--o-----------------------o---------------    A   |-●-------o-----o------------------------o---
  M   |--------------------------------------●------       M   |---●------------------------------------------
```

Note: A = Antecedent, M = Monitor

During AM sequence, lackluster leaders spend more time:

Providing antecedents

The opposite is true for the lackluster leaders. As can be seen in the chart on the left in Table 7.5, the lackluster leader spends more intervals giving antecedents – in this case, three – before monitoring.

Solitary

During the AM sequence, a similar pattern holds for the behaviors of solitary, not communicating, and work-related, as shown in Table 7.6. Lackluster leaders are more likely to wander away from the group, perhaps turning away from the group to finish their own work or even retreating to the privacy of their offices.

Table 7.6 Study 15: differences charted between lackluster and effective leaders in quantity of solitary, not communicating, and work-related during AM sequence

---

Lackluster leaders   *Effective leaders*

During AM sequence:

```
    00  10  20  30  40  50  00  10          00  10  20  30  40  50  00  10
A |-●--o--o-------------------------o--------------|    A |-●--------o----o-------|--------●-----------o---|
M |-------------------------------------------●------|    M |----●-----------------------------|-----------●--------|
C |---------------------------------------------●|    C |----------------------●|-----------------------●|
```

Work alone, not interacting, withdrawing from followers, for example
SOLITARY

MORE likely to seek out solitude   LESS likely to seek out solitude

```
s |---------------------------------o--o---------|    s |--------------------|-------------------|
```

Remain silent during work-related conversation, for example
NOT COMMUNICATING

MORE likely to attend to others talking   LESS likely to attend to others
about work details   talking about work details

```
NC |----------o--o----o-----o---------------------|    NC |--------------------|-o--o----------------|
```

Talk about work details rather than focusing on what needs to be done
WORK-RELATED

MORE likely to dwell on work details   LESS likely to dwell on work details

```
W |----------------o----o-----o----------------|    W |----------------------|---------o-----------|
```

Note: AM sequence = period from first Antecedent to next Monitor. A = Antecedent, M = Monitor, C = Consequence, W = Work-related, S = Solitary, NC = Not communicating.

Laconic

During the AM sequence, lackluster leaders also spend more time being uncommunicative or laconic. They remain on the periphery of the group, only passively participating as the group talks about work-related topics.

In work-related discussions

The same is true for work-related discussions during the AM sequence. After giving an antecedent, lackluster leaders are more likely to shift their attention from conveying their expectations about performance to discussing work details.

These differences are graphically illustrated in Tables 3.3 (p.55) and 3.4 (p.59), corresponding to the actual placement of leaders' behaviors during races. One can see how many more intervals the lackluster leaders spent during the AM sequence giving antecedents, being solitary, or spending time on work related details (for 6, 15, and 6 intervals, respectively, of 53 intervals).

In short, effective leaders are much quicker AMCers, while lackluster leaders are much more sluggish or "SLAW-like," according to their profiles discussed below.

PROFILES OF EFFECTIVE AND LACKLUSTER LEADERS

One of the highlights of our research so far has been to pinpoint the action patterns not only of effective leaders, but those of lackluster leaders as well. What separates the effective leaders from the lackluster in successfully mobilizing their staffs day after day, month after month? Lackluster leaders may be just as intelligent and motivated, but somehow they fall short. The difference is not any single behavior or any particular time period. Rather, it is a combination of actions involving both pacing and placement. To highlight these complex patterns, we describe two profiles, a quick AMC profile for the effective leaders and a SLAW profile for the lackluster leaders.

As shown in Table 7.7, the quick AMC profile characterizes effective managers. These managers provide rapid sequences in which they first deliver an antecedent, follow quickly with a monitor, and then, after more discussion about performance, deliver a consequence.

In contrast, the profile for lackluster managers reflects sluggish AMC sequences in which it takes much longer to monitor. We use the acronym SLAW for these leaders, referring to the four behaviors they display before finally monitoring (as shown in Table 7.7): Solitary, Laconic or uncommunicative in conversation, what we refer to as not-communicating; delivery of Antecedents; or talk about the details of the Work.

Table 7.7 Study 14: profiles of lackluster and effective leaders

SLAW profile	Profiles	Quick AMC profile
	AMC sequences	
Sluggish	and	Fast
	Before monitoring:	
	Work alone, not interacting, in privacy of office, for example	
	SOLITARY	
More often ↑		Less often ↓
	Not communicating, e.g., remain silent during work-related conversation	
	LACONIC	
More often ↑		Less often ↓
	Convey expectations of performance	
	ANTECEDENTS	
More often ↑		Less often ↓
	Discuss details of work but not performance	
	WORK-RELATED	
More often ↑		Less often ↓

Exchanges with followers

Effective leaders set stage for performance-based, give-and-take exchanges

Effective leaders establish a special relationship with their followers. Beginning by monitoring (M) performance, as shown in Table 7.8, they stimulate their followers to talk about themselves. Once the followers begin to talk about how they are performing (own performance (OP)), they, in turn, set the stage for leaders to respond. Leaders typically follow by providing consequences (C) or continuing to monitor (M). Followers, in turn, are stimulated to talk more about their own performance (OP), and this fruitful cycle continues.

This ongoing give-and-take exchange focused on performance can be seen in Table 7.9 in a series of conversations among film crew members during days two, three, and four of a seven-day shoot. On day two, with the camera about to roll, the director asks the director of photography (DP) if he is ready (M). After the DP replies (OP), the director provides a positive consequence.

The next day, a similar Monitor–Own performance–Consequence sequence occurs. This time, the director is walking around the set (M) in the vicinity of the DP, who is setting up the camera for the next shot. As often happens when leaders monitor via work sampling, the DP approaches the director and begins talking about what he is going to do (OP), which the director acknowledges (C).

Table 7.8 Studies 7 and 17: differences charted between lackluster and effective leaders in interactions with followers when leaders monitor

Lackluster leaders	Effective leaders

Monitor LESS often | Monitor MORE often

```
    00  10  20  30  40  50  00  10          00  10  20  30  40  50  00  10
M   ------o---------------------------    M   ------o---------------------------
```

In turn, their followers:

Talk LESS about their own performance | Talk MORE about their own performance

```
     00  10  20  30  40  50  00  10          00  10  20  30  40  50  00  10
F OP ----------o-----------------------o----   F OP ----------o--o-----------------o----o-
```

Leaders then:

Provide FEWER consequences | Are stimulated to provide MORE consequences

```
    00  10  20  30  40  50  00  10          00  10  20  30  40  50  00  10
C   -------------------------o-----------    C   ----------------o------------------o-------
```

and FEWER monitors | and MORE monitors

```
    00  10  20  30  40  50  00  10          00  10  20  30  40  50  00  10
M   ------o----------------------------    M   ------o--------------o----------------o-
```

Later, their followers:

Talk LESS about their own performance, thus, cutting short the dialogue. | Are stimulated to talk MORE about their own performance, continuing reciprocal interactions.

```
     00  10  20  30  40  50  00  10          00  10  20  30  40  50  00  10
F OP ----------o-----------------------o-   F OP ----------o--o-----------------o----o-
```

Note: M = Monitor, *F* OP = Follower Own Performance, C = Consequence

Ten or so minutes later, the director is again monitoring via work sampling, watching crew members and actors, when the DP asks, "Can I do this?" (OP). The director, after hearing the DP's ideas, delivers another positive consequence.

Effective leaders stimulate followers to talk about their own performance

Followers' talking about their own performance plays a pivotal role, as illustrated in an exchange on day four between the director and the person responsible for sound (S). Under increasing pressure, the director monitors. Not receiving an answer, the director expresses his displeasure: "Where is sound?" (C) and, "C'mon, we're doing a close-up of this line" (C). The sound person acknowledges the director's frustration, apologizing: "Okay, I didn't know that, I'm sorry" (OP). The director starts to ignore the apology, but then, realizing what went wrong, he graciously acknowledges: "Sorry, we should have told you" (OP). These thirty seconds of dialogue, containing

Table 7.9 Study 17: transcript of film crew A during a shoot

Time	Speaker	Statement/action
		Day two of seven
		(With the camera about to roll, director [D] asks director of photography [DP])
6:11.00	D	**You ready?** (M)
	DP	*Yes.* (OP)
		(Camera rolls. Shot completed.)
	D	Brilliant! (C)

Time	Speaker	Statement/action
		Day three
		(Between shots)
1:10.45	D	(**Walking around the set**) (M)
1:11.00	D	(**Continues monitoring**, watching DP who is setting the camera up for the next shot) (M)
	DP	(Approaches director) *I'm going to do a little dolly shot in here* (OP)
	D	Okay. Okay. (C)
		(About 10 minutes later)
1:22.00	D	(**Watching crew members and actors**) (M)
	D	(Then explains to actors what they should be doing) (A)
	DP	(DP who has been arranging the camera, asks) *Can I do this?* They [referring to actors] will stand, not like that but like this and then we'll see them being there? (OP)
	D	Yeah, yeah, that's a good idea! Yeah. (C)
		(Another 10 minutes later)
1:33.00	D	(**Watching crew setting up next shot**) (M)
		(Crew member [A] walks up)
	A	Are we going to need a dresser set? (W)
	D	Yeah.
	A	Okay.
.15	A	*We are just setting this up. Okay, let me go and get who it is going to be...* (OP)
		What is this? What is the next one? (W)
	D	This is scene G... (W)
	A	GB? (W)
	D	GA. (W)
	A	GA, okay. (W)
		I'll find out who is in it. (OP)
	D	Okay. (C)
		It's Pam, Andy, Eksteen. (W)
.30	A	Eksteen...we need. (W)
	D	And we may get them in the background. (W)
	A	Okay, that's fine! *I'm going to bring people on to the dresser set.* (OP)
	D	Okay. (C)

Day four
(Under pressure, D wants to get the shot done as quickly as possible)

3:41.45	D	Okay? **Is everyone ready**? (M)
	DP	*Hmn.* (OP)
	D	**Sound**? (M)
		Hey, where is sound? (C)
	S	(The person responsible for sound [S] returns hurriedly to the set) *Yes, the sound is ready*! (OP)
	D	(Annoyed) C'mon, we're doing a close up of this line. (C)
	S	*Okay.* (OP)
.00	S	*I didn't know that, I'm sorry.* (OP)
	D	(Pause) *Sorry, we should have told you.* (OP)
	D	**Are you guys ready for this**? (M)
	S	*Yes.* (OP)

(Five minutes later, D is talking to the assistant director [AD] who is checking the day's schedule)

3:47.00	D	Oh god, I think I'm going to faint soon, Bob. (OP)
.15	D	I feel so much time pressure for this. (OP)
	D	How far are we behind? (OP)
	AD	I don't know. I'm checking. (OP)
	D	Totally screwed, but we are not totally behind right? (OP)
.30	AD	Seven hours. (C)
	D	Ha? (W)
	AD	Seven hours. (C)
	D	Oh, my god! (OP)
	AD	I was thinking about the other shots. (W)
	D	Yep, yep. I should have finished all these shots. (OP)
.45	AD	Yeah. (W)
	D	All these shots, my god! (OP)
	AD	*Hey, (if I) do this*... (OP)
	D	What? (W)
	AD	(Studying schedule)...*I'll reorganize this whole thing.* (OP)
	D	All right. (C)

(Almost five minutes later)

3:51.45	DP	(Joining group) *So, tell me, how does it look for today*? (OP)
	AD	Well today, you still have this huge chunk of stuff. (W)
.00	D	How many shots is this? (W)
	AD	But you know, tomorrow, you guys will be covering quite well. But, this is good, this is one shot and you are getting rid of that one. We can push one shot over there. (W)
	DP	Hmn, hmn. (W)
	D	Yeah, yeah. (W)
.15	AD	So, do this one and we'll be all right. (W)
	D	Hmn. (W)
	AD	This will give us.... If you do E and F after this, that is Mr. Eksteen over the shoulder. (W)
	D	Right, right. We should do that. (A)
		(Five minutes later, still discussing scheduling)
6:28.15	D	**Is that scheduled**? (M)
	AD	(Looking at schedule) *No, I mean yes, in a way that is the last shot of the night.* (OP)

Table 7.9 Continued

Time	Speaker	Statement/action
.30	D	Uhh ... (C)
6:28.45	AD	*What we are trying right now is 50/G.* (OP)
	D	Which is 50/G? (W)
	AD	50/G is him going to projector. (W)
		(A few minutes later, returning to scheduling)
6:30.00	DP	*How much more do we need to do?* (OP)
	AD	*We have three shots I think.* (OP)
	DP	*Three shots for today?* (OP)
	D	*Yeah.* (OP)
	DP	*That's all?* (OP)
	AD	*Well, we have another shot that I'm going to add.* (OP)
	DP	Ha? (W)
.15	AD	*We have another shot that I'm going to add, because that's all you know.* (OP)
	DP	All right, if we can do it, that's great! (C)
	D	(Listening the whole time, D nods almost imperceptively)
.30	DP	*If we can stay here twelve hours and a half.* (OP)
	D	(Nods again, smiles) We're okay. (C)
	DP	*And we have three more shots to do and we still have another thirteen hours then we can complete.* (OP)
	A	(Crew member approaches) *How are we doing?* (OP)
	D	Okay. (C)
.45		(DP and AD exit, another fellow crew member, B, crouches next to D)
	B	*So, now we're catching up right?* (OP)
	D	(D pulls his chair towards B, grasps B's shoulder) Thank you, my friend. (C)
	B	(Clasping D's hand) You're welcome, my friend. You're welcome. (W)
	D	(In earnest) What a crew I have man! (C)
.00	D	Really the best crew I have ever ... ever in this world! (C)
	B	We have to stick together man. (W)
	D	It's great! (C)

Note: D = Director, DP = Director of Photography, S = person responsible for sound, A = crew member, AD = Assistant Director, B = crew member

two own-performance statements, speak volumes. Both parties got the conflict out into the open. The director expressed his annoyance. The sound person acknowledged the director's irritation, yet stood her ground and explained what had occurred. The director heard her explanation and indicated what could be done to prevent the same problem from recurring. With both parties willing to listen and to discuss their own performance, they could and did solve the problem.

In essence, effective leaders provide a milieu that promotes discussion of performance.

These exchanges are strikingly different from those of the training director and his boss discussed in Chapter 1. Recall the extended fuming of the training director as he remembered how his boss stormed out of the room and exclaimed, "I wouldn't pay $500.00 for that piece of crap!" and then how, the next day, his boss shoved a piece of paper across his desk and hurried away with virtually no comment. Imagine what a series of thirty-second conversations like the one above might have done for their obviously blocked relationship.

The importance of these back-and-forth discussions can also be seen in an extended series of conversations between members of the film crew, on day four, beginning at 3:47.00. The director admits to feeling the time pressure and feeling faint. Both he and the DP constantly ask, "How far are we behind?" (OP) and "How much more do we need to do?" (OP). As the assistant director (AD) pores over the schedule, he eventually comes up with a plan (OP). The conversation continues with discussion of what is now scheduled, and how much more needs to be done. Hearing about the adding of another shot, the DP concludes: "All right, if we can do it, that's great!" (C). Listening intently, the director nods almost imperceptibly as the DP offers to extend their already long days of shooting: "If we can stay here twelve hours and a half" (OP). The director nods again, and then, with a smile creeping up, finishes the DP's sentence: "We're okay" (C). A fellow crew member, Bernini, sits down near the director and asks, "So, now we're catching up right?" (OP). The director pulls his chair towards him, grasping his shoulder, and says: "Thank you, my friend" (C). In turn, Bernini, clasping the director's hand, replies: "You're welcome, my friend. You're welcome" (W). The director suddenly blurts out, "What a crew I have, man! Really the best crew I have ever . . . ever in this world!" (C).

At this point, it is only speculation as to what role the previous dialogue, interspersed with talk of the crew's own performance, played. Perhaps the crew's interest in how they were doing, their willingness to put in another grueling thirteen-hour day, was influenced by the previous interactions. This fertile performance-related dialogue suggests the power of what can happen when parties care about the outcome and keep listening and working together to achieve it.

In contrast

Lackluster leaders avoid interactions with followers

In contrast to the effective leaders, lackluster leaders display a wholly different pattern of interactions, as shown in Table 7.10. Sometimes the patterns are very sparse and include a minimum of discussion, as the leader decides to spend his time solitary.

Supervisor Lonnie would often choose to spend time away from his employees during breakdowns, choosing instead to "hover around the site of a breakdown while risking loss of control of the rest of his line" (p. 95). In fact, there is "a high stool near his desk at one end of the line. The line was

Table 7.10   Studies 7 and 14: differences charted between lackluster and effective leaders in interactions with followers when leaders dwell on work

Lackluster leaders	Effective leaders
During AM sequence:	
MORE likely to dwell on work details than employees and their performance.	LESS likely to dwell on work details after providing antecedent
W ----------------o-----o----o-----------------	W ----------------------------------o-----------
Following example, their followers:	
MORE likely to talk about work details	LESS likely to talk about work details
F W -------------------o-----o-------------------	F W --------------------------------o--------------
Leaders, in turn:	
MORE likely to pay attention to others talking about work details, prolonging these work-related discussions	LESS likely to become distracted by others talking about work, cutting short these work-related discussions
NC -------------o--o----o----o-----------------	NC -------------------------o--o----------------

Note: AM sequence = period from first Antecedent to next Monitor, W = Work-related, F = Follower, NC = Not Communicating, M = Monitor, OP = Own Performance

so long that the only way to see all of it at once would have been to perch on that stool" (pp. 93–94). But Lonnie reported that "he sat there so seldom that his people were surprised when he did" (p. 94).

Lackluster leaders set stage for discussions of work details

Some lackluster leaders do interact with followers, but their exchanges focus on the work rather than on performance. Supervisor Dave, for example, when he had breakdowns, stayed with his employees, but paid attention to the work. As his employees "busied themselves with cleaning and bringing in supplies ... [he spent time] offering encouragement by rolling a stack of containers or picking up debris" (NC or S) (p. 96). He had a fairly lengthy conversation with one operator, who talked about her problem getting along with one of her helpers. This was not the first time, as Dave remarked to Gellerman. " 'That's always just below the surface with her,' he explained. 'Just takes a day like this, and it all boils over. I had to hear her out, and then I jollied her along like I always do' " (p. 96). Gellerman even asked Dave why he did not consider transferring one of the two women and thus ending the problem. Dave answered, " 'I could, but then I'd have to transfer anyone else who got sore at somebody, and there'd be no end to it' " (p. 96). Given the willingness of the supervisor to continue discussing the topic, however, we can see how the spiral of follower-work-related and supervisor-not-communicating, as shown on Table 7.10, would probably continue unabated. Once lackluster leaders deliver an antecedent, they are more apt to get wrapped up in the minutiae of work detail. Following their example, as their followers continue talking about work details, and the cycle continues.

We can also see how supervisors exhibiting some of the SLAW behaviors – in this case, being laconic and talking about the work – can be less effective than their quick AMC counterparts who elicit more back-and-forth discussions related to what each is going to do to get the task done.

IN SUMMARY

To sum it up, lackluster managers fitting the SLAW profile are sluggish in completing AMC sequences. Instead of monitoring quickly, these managers provide more instructions (A) after the marker antecedent, or they get distracted: they get involved talking about work minutiae (W) or paying attention to others doing the same (NC), or they leave the scene to work on their own tasks (S).

The final set of "musical scores" in Table 7.11 summarizes what effective leaders do. The actions are dynamic. Pacing makes a difference. The effective leaders are quick to deliver AMC sequences. Once they provide an antecedent, they rapidly follow through with a monitor. Unlike SLAW-like leaders who leave the scene or get immersed in work details, effective leaders do not get distracted from the issue of performance at hand. Instead they seek out followers. They express interest in what they are doing. They make themselves accessible, and followers, in turn, approach them.

Table 7.11 Summary of differences charted between lackluster and effective leaders and their followers

Lackluster leaders	*Effective leaders*

Leaders more likely:

```
       00   10   20   30   40   50   00   10           00   10   20   30   40   50   00   10
A   |-•--o--o---------------------o---------------|   A   |-•---------o-----o------|-------•------------o---|
M   |------------------------------------•------|   M   |---•--------------------|--------------•-------|
C   |------------------------------------------•|   C   |--------------------•|---------------------•|

W   |---------------o-----o----o----------------|   W   |-----------------------|--------------o------|
NC  |---------o--o-----o----o----------------|   NC  |-----------------------|-o--o--------------|
S   |------------------------------o-o-------|   S   |-----------------------|--------------------|
```

While followers more likely:

```
F OP |-------------------------------------o--|   F OP |-------o-----o-----o---|----------------o------|
F W  |----------o--o-----o----o---------------|   F W  |-----------------------|-o--o----------------|
```

Note: Refer to studies 2, 3, 4, 5a, 5b, 6, 7, 8, 9, 12, 13, 14, 15, and 17. A = Antecedent, M = Monitor, C = Consequence, W = Work-related, NC = Not communicating, S = Solitary, F Follower, OP = Own Performance

These leaders' interactions with followers are therefore more frequent, and yield more productive relationships. Effective leaders steer conversations toward performance; as they interact, they let followers know, in a comfortable way, how they are doing. The result is an ongoing back-and-forth exchange between leader and follower, in which the follower's performance is always clearly in focus.

By viewing what effective leaders do as a musical score – an interactive flow between players – we can see that the relevant actions take considerably longer than a few seconds or even a few minutes. As with the seamless stream of a melody, the behaviors of effective leaders and their followers are essentially continuous, occurring every day, in a give-and-take exchange in which everyone is heard.

8 Implications for future theory, research, and practice

Having established how our model works, we arrive at the crucial question for real-world application: is the model relevant for the year 2000 and beyond? With telecommunications frequently substituting for human interaction, is the model even necessary? Will it work with hard-nosed venture capitalists as well as free-spirit coffee farmers? The answers are yes, yes, and yes.

Venture capitalist Arthur Rock (1987), for example, is always on the lookout for business plans in which to invest. He writes in the *Harvard Business Review* about how he judges which entrepreneurs will succeed and which will fail. What does he look for? *Not* "the largest untapped market or the highest projected returns or the cleverest business strategy" (p. 67). "Good ideas and good products are a dime a dozen." What he seeks, instead, are good people. He searches for character, grit, and, in particular, honesty "about how well – or how badly – things are going" (p. 64).

Rock recounts a specific case. An executive in the computer industry wanted so desperately to succeed that he simply took his marketing people's word for it when they told him how much they could sell. And he believed his engineers' glowing promises of when the computer would be ready for market. Of course, the computer was late. The executive was stuck with a huge sales staff. When the computer was finally ready, he could not meet the over optimistic sales forecasts.

Rock cites another example, a company president, also from the computer industry,[1] who heard only what he wanted to hear. The executive thought that everything was rosy until, one day, he was faced with an order that he couldn't fill. His software division manager finally admitted, " 'We've been making a lot of mistakes we haven't told you about. We're at least a year behind' "(p. 65).[2]

The striking fact is that such awful miscommunications and misunderstandings happen every day in both the private and public sectors. Sometimes even the most basic elements are not in place. When Ramon C.

Cortines took office as New York City Schools Chancellor, for instance, he was heralded on the *New York Times* editorial page as having an "absolute commitment to excellence in education" (Herbert, 1994). Why? Because he found out things that even the school board president did not know. On one unannounced visit, he found "the children were orderly, but that class had not one thing to do with science, and there was no sign that science had gone on there previously" (Dillon, 1994, p. B3). In another classroom, he found a teacher so flustered that she did not know how to supervise her two teacher aides. In one school library, "the only reading material he found . . . was a 1982 *Time* magazine." Upon hearing this dismal news, Carol Gresser, the board president exclaimed: " 'Is it any wonder that our students are not learning?' " (p. B3).

Sometimes we need look no further than the headlines to see such failures of management. One catastrophic example, chronicled in the business pages of the *New York Times*, involved the financial trading firm Kidder, Peabody & Company. Problems in the firm's internal auditing system created a huge, and unnoticed, discrepancy between transactions recorded as trades (and hence as profits) and trades that were actually consummated. Once the error (to the tune of an estimated $348 million) was exposed and one bond trader was brought up on fraud charges, defenders within the company claimed that supervisors couldn't be blamed for relying upon the flawed audit system (Nasar, 1994, p. D14). But others in the industry disagreed. One analyst asked pointedly, "Even though you didn't have line responsibility for audit and control, don't you have responsibility for independently verifying what's going on?" (p. D14). The case has already had one lasting result for Kidder: the false hyper-inflation of profits for the year ended up with the takeover of the firm by Paine Webber.

All of this suggests that the constant need to solicit information, to monitor and to listen, will be with us for some time – certainly well into the next century. Whether it is textbooks in classrooms, production schedules, or trading practices, managers will need to know what is actually going on in the workplace, and to use this knowledge effectively. This is why our model exists.

RESEARCH DIRECTIONS ABOUT LEADERS AND THEIR SUPERVISORY BEHAVIORS

Quick AMC and SLAW profiles

Despite the potential usefulness of our model in the future, more work needs to be done to validate the quick AMC and the SLAW profiles. We encourage researchers to identify leaders fitting one of these multi-dimensional profiles, and assess their actual effectiveness, as we have started to do in field tests of the model.

What accounts for the SLAW profile?

Another promising research direction is to identify why the placement before monitoring of these aforementioned four behaviors – Solitary, Laconic (not communicating), Antecedents, and Work-related – seems to be at odds with effectiveness.

One hypothesis is that leaders fitting the SLAW profile simply spend less time doing other more worthwhile activities such as monitoring. They therefore nip fewer problems in the bud and provide fewer consequences, reducing the very fuel that maintains performance. In partial support of this idea, Brewer, Wilson, and Beck (1994), in Study 4, report that "supervisors who spent more time engaged in solitary activities spent less time in interactions with subordinates, with this reflected in reduced time providing antecedents ($r = - .35$), monitoring ($r = - .49$), engaged in work-related discussions ($r = - .80$) and talking about their own performance ($r = - .68$)" (p. 75).

While solitary, leaders are often outright absent from the work scene, having left or not yet arrived. A recent example occurred behind the scenes at the Long Island Railroad. The *New York Times* headline read: "Inquiry finds errors, not snow, stopped railroad" (Wald, 1994, p. A1). The errors included a variety of management foul-ups, including the absence of two top officials. After a twelve-inch snowfall, workers scheduled to begin clearing switches at 4 a.m. either did not show up or delayed their work until 8 a.m. "The railroad advised riders to take the subway to Jamaica, where buses would be waiting, but no one at the railroad thought to order the buses" (p. B4). Further, one vice president, "who could have taken charge early and prevented catastrophe" (p. B4), continued with meetings on a topic unrelated to the storm in another city. The railroad's top executive elected not to come to work, staying at home in Virginia. Such nonchalance, once made public, fanned the wrath of 100,000 riders who had been stranded on cold platforms. While the same problems might have occurred had the top officials been on the scene, it will still be interesting to continue to study what happens, particularly in crisis situations, when leaders are simply not present.

An interesting light is shed by Brewer, Wilson, and Beck (1994). Curious as to what police sergeants did during their solitary activities, they divided the category of solitary into the subcategories: (a) driving patrol cars, (b) doing paperwork at the station, and (c) other, including walking around and checking equipment. While they did not find that solitary in general correlated either positively or negatively with effectiveness, they did find some intriguing patterns worth further investigation. The more effective sergeants were those who "spent less time in their cars on patrol and more time at their desk doing paperwork" (p. 76). They speculate that:

> Supervisors who spent more time at their desk had many opportunities (compared with those on the road) to solicit reports from their

subordinates and to provide contingent consequences when subordinates returned to the station (e.g., to make out a report, to question/arrest an offender, to have a meal break), and this perhaps provides part of the explanation for the relationships between these sub-categories of solitary activity and team performance. (p.76)

Another, not necessarily incompatible, hypothesis is that the SLAW behaviors themselves set into motion a spiral of actions and attitudes on the part of workers. With our categories of Work-related and Not communicating, the leader is present, either discussing work-related matters or remaining in a group in which others discuss these matters. In both cases, however, neither the leader nor the followers focus on performance. An example is provided in Table 5.1, in which two followers try to get the leader, Dr Roy, to address a performance-related issue. Dr Roy deflects their concerns by stating that it is not a problem, and repeatedly brings the conversation back to talking about the work. With bosses dwelling on the work, all but the most stalwart followers are likely to eventually follow and turn away from conversations about performance. Komaki and Citera (1990) found, in Study 7, that managers were less likely to monitor when their subordinates were engaged in work-related discussions. This example illustrates how workers can influence their leaders' subsequent interactions, and how their work-related conversations can essentially inhibit more productive discussions about performance.

Antecedents, on the other hand, concern performance. Why are they associated with lackluster leaders? An illustrative example is provided in Tables 3.3 and 3.4, in which the lackluster skippers in Study 15 provided antecedent after antecedent before they finally monitored.[3] One hypothesis is that antecedents given before monitoring are simply not as well received by followers prior to monitoring as they are after monitoring. Perhaps they are less tailored to the situation at hand than those given after monitoring. Another possibility is that if a welter of instructions are given in a short space of time, some of the instructions may seem incompatible with each other, in which case bewilderment might ensue (A. Robertson, personal communication, March 21, 1997). Another idea concerns the actions of the leaders themselves. The giving of antecedents, we found in Study 7, dampened further meaningful discussions about performance; managers were almost three times less likely to provide a consequence after providing an antecedent than after displaying any other behavior. Perhaps they are simply more redundant and managers giving antecedents simply develop a repetitive momentum of their own (B. A. Jacobs, personal communication, May 13, 1996).

Further research is needed to ferret out the reasons for the deleterious impact of the placement of solitary, laconic behaviors, antecedents and work-related statements before monitoring.

Why are quick AMC sequences associated with effective leadership?

Another recommended line of research is to find out why, as revealed by our research, quick AMC sequences characterize effective leaders.

Sheer frequency?

One possibility is the frequency of antecedents, monitors, and consequences within a given period of time. The evidence from six field tests of our model suggests that the overall amount of time spent monitoring and providing consequences makes a difference. But the correlation between antecedents and effectiveness has been essentially zero in five of six tests of the model. So frequency *per se*, at least for antecedents, is probably not the sole determining variable.

Is it the order?

Results of Study 15 suggest that order is important. Our findings show that effective managers provide rapid sequences in which they first deliver an antecedent, follow quickly with a monitor, and then, after more discussion about performance, deliver a consequence. Furthermore, when comparing AMC and AC sequences, we found the pacing of the former, but not the latter, to be significantly related to effectiveness. Effective leaders delivered faster AMC sequences but not necessarily faster AC sequences.

Perhaps density and a lack of distractions

Another, not necessarily incompatible, possibility is that the concentration or density of the behaviors makes a difference. The trio of behaviors occurring within a relatively short period of time may be significant. A colleague once predicted that it takes three articles published in the same journal on the same topic before one makes a discernible difference (F. Fiedler, personal communication, 1983). Perhaps, as well, it takes a full AMC sequence, expeditiously delivered, to make a noticeable difference.

Further research about the timing, order, and density of AMC sequences is highly recommended.

What about the substance of AMC sequences?

One of the most frequently asked questions about our model concerns the actual content of the exchanges. No doubt, it matters *what* is monitored and whether managers should provide consequences about the process or about the outcomes of performance. Unfortunately, little research has been conducted to answer these vital questions.

Process/outcome

Some management scholars have made the distinction between behavior and results, and have taken stands as to which should be emphasized. Gilbert (1978), for instance, argues for results. He suggests five criteria for measuring worker performance: (a) the measure should be an accomplishment; (b) those responsible should have primary control; (c) it should be a true overall objective rather than a subgoal; (d) it should not conflict with other goals; and (e) it should be quantifiable. Gilbert assumes that accomplishments can be quantified and that the results can be measured in such a way as to reflect workers' behaviors. He makes a strong case for emphasizing results rather than behaviors.

Daniels (1989) takes a more middle-ground position, arguing that both behaviors and results should be assessed. He suggests that results be measured first, and then behaviors. But he identifies five conditions under which it is critical that behaviors be assessed: (a) when performers are far short of the ultimate objective or result, (b) when the ties between the result and the facilitating behaviors are not obvious, (c) when the result, no matter how well-executed in the interim, is long delayed, (d) when the relevant behaviors are socially sensitive, and most importantly in our view, (e) when the results are beyond a person's control, and no quantity or quality of behaviors can guarantee a specific result.

Locke and Latham (1990) go a step further, suggesting that content should depend on the characteristics of the task. With simpler tasks, they propose that performance is affected "relatively directly by activating one or more of three automatized, universal task strategies or plans...and one or more automatized task-specific plans" (p. 293). With more complex tasks, they say, "universal plans and simple task-specific plans become progressively less adequate by themselves..., while problem solving and the development of task-specific plans become progressively more important" (p. 293).

Critical aspects

We suggest in another context[4] that leaders should focus on target behaviors that are critical for the successful completion of the task (Komaki, in press; Komaki & Reynard, in press). By critical, we mean those aspects of performance that are integral to the result; when these behaviors are omitted, the task is severely impeded. For instance, a manufacturing supervisor concerned about preventive maintenance (PM) of heavy equipment would be encouraged to focus on those behaviors that are integral to getting the task done. Analysis of PM practices in the Marine Corps showed that two behaviors (detecting incipient deficiencies and following through with appropriate actions) were critical. Hence, supervisors in this situation were advised to concentrate on these behaviors rather than other seemingly related behaviors (cleanliness of the shop floor and the number of workers working productively).

Performance/work-related

One explanation, which we have posed and found partial support for, regards the distinction made in the OSTI between work-related and performance-related conversations.[5] We have found, in Study 7, that followers of leaders who monitored more spent more time talking about their own performance and the leaders spent more time providing consequences. Moreover, in Study 16, there was a tendency for effective skippers to keep their conversations focused on performance just before critical labor-intensive periods of the race, whereas lackluster skippers were more likely to discuss work-related matters.

What we know about these various sub-categories, however, pales in comparison with what we need to know. We do not know, for instance, if a leader provides AMC sequences for subtask 1 before moving on to carry out the same sequence for subtask 2. Many subtasks are involved in completing a task. In putting on a play, for example, the producer has to be concerned with finding funds, performance space, a press agent, casting and so on. Leaders might provide AMC sequences for overall tasks before moving on to discuss the subtasks. Effective leaders we have seen, however, deliver a much more complicated sequence. The director delivers an antecedent about getting a press agent (a task that takes an extended time to accomplish). Immediately after, she might ask if the stage manager had any luck getting the keys to the rehearsal space (M) to which the stage manager might say "no" but he did track down the actor for the lead to which the director would exclaim: "Oh, great" (C).

Again, to further our knowledge and to provide a basis for hypotheses, we recommend further descriptive studies, looking at a variety of substance sub-categories: process and outcome, degree of critical importance, performance- and work-related, as well as task and subtask. Once we have an idea of how to define these sub-categories (not an easy task, we suspect), we could obtain data on their frequency in the field and then look to see if any of these sub-categories differentiated between effective and lackluster leaders.

Another potentially fertile direction would be to look at how the content of the interaction changes over the course of time. Perhaps a pattern exists in which more time is initially spent on non-work-related matters, then eventually more time is spent on work-related issues, and only later is much time devoted to performance-related issues.

By tracing the evolution of conversations between bosses and workers, we can better understand how effective leaders interact and what contributes to the efficacy of the AMC sequence. Such descriptive studies would shed light on where managers should focus their efforts in supervising within today's modern, multi-layer organizations. Identifying content is particularly

critical. In days past, it might have sufficed to manage by walking around
and perusing what workers were visibly doing. Today, however, particularly
with service-industry workers whose product is ephemeral, and knowledge
workers whose progress is often hidden behind computer screens, it is not
so easy. Doing these studies will help us to enter the next century more
productively.

Leaders' predisposing experiences and personality characteristics

Another recommended line of inquiry would be to see if leaders with the
quick AMC or the SLAW profile are more likely to have certain personality
traits or life experiences than their counterparts.

Persons who are *curious* about the world rather than self-absorbed, we
predict, will be more likely to fit the quick AMC profile. One example of a
highly inquisitive person, at least by his own self-report, is Bill Gates, Chief
Executive of Microsoft (Seabrook, 1994). He recalls watching a snowstorm,
at the age of 10, and wondering what the deepest snowfall ever was. Even
now, he describes himself scrutinizing a baseball game, asking himself,
"Who are these guys? Who are the good ones? How much are they paid?
How are the other teams compared to this one? How have the rules changed?
How do these guys compare to the guys twenty years ago? It just gets so
interesting. I know if I let myself go to ten games I'd be addicted" (Seabrook,
1994, p. 61). We expect that persons like Bill Gates would ask these questions about their followers' (and competitors') performance.

Having a *scientific bent* might also characterize those who are quick
AMCers.[6] Michael Schulhof, formerly a physicist and in 1992 the vice-
chairman of Sony USA and president of Sony Software, still describes
himself as a scientist. He would like to see more business people develop a
mastery of the fundamentals. "People in business tend to be impatient," he
says. "The scientists I worked with were anxious to see results. But they
realized that you had to build the foundation before you could put on the
roof" (p. 138). Such people, he says, took the time to find out what had
been tried before jumping to new conclusions. Perhaps this penchant to
learn fully about problems propels people to be quick AMCers. A related
leaning of scientists is to disavow theory as gospel. In fact, Schulhof contends, "that is the big difference between business graduates and science
graduates. The business graduates accept theory as gospel. The science
graduates accept theory as the starting point for experimentation" (p.
138). This suggests that needing to know takes precedence over telling
others what to do. Such a characteristic might forecast who would be
most likely to be a quick or a sluggish AMCer.

What Hackman and Walton (1986) refer to as *courage* might separate the
effective and lackluster leaders as well. This is a term not found in many
scholarly discussions of leadership. In describing the traits of the best
leaders, they point to those leaders willing to take risks, or to even incur

the wrath of the group, in order to correct dysfunctions and maintain certain standards. Perhaps this spirit helps explain why persons such as Helen Caldicott, who was the driving force behind Physicians for Social Responsibility in the 1970s and early 1980s, continue to campaign against nuclear weapons. Despite the fact that Dr Caldicott sacrificed her practice as a pediatrician and later her marriage of twenty-six years, she still contends that she would do it again. As she describes it: "'I couldn't *not* have done it. It's almost the blueprint I was born with. I could feel the heat of the bombs'" (Herring, 1996, p. C10). Internal heat such as this may propel people such as Helen Caldicott to be quick AMCers.

Certain life experiences, we expect, would also lend themselves to a quick AMC rather than a SLAW profile. Individuals who *suffered as a result of a lack of monitoring* might be more aware of its deleterious impact. For instance, the leader's own potential may have been previously overlooked by significant others (parents, teachers, coaches, or bosses) who jumped to conclusions without adequately monitoring. Or the talk may have been more pernicious. Van Maanen and Kunda (1989) describe a manager talking to his staff about a peer:

He's dead. He can't be highly successful anymore. We'll help him out but keep our distance . . . If he goes down, he might drag us down too. He's got no credibility anymore. A lot of unspoken stuff around him . . . I heard that the strategy is to make him such a bastard that everything goes around him. (p. 75)

A person whose reputation has been damaged by such loose talk may be more likely than others to become a quick AMCer. Additionally, negative experiences caused by a leader's own failure to monitor may predispose a person to monitor. One stage director tried a laissez-faire approach to rehearsals, leaving the monitoring (and consequences) up to others, and then had a disastrous run. He swore that he would never again fail to monitor.

Influence of outside factors

Another promising line of research is to identify the circumstances and conditions under which leaders are most likely to act in accordance with the model.

We have found managers more apt to provide monitors and consequences depending upon one or more of six conditions: (a) whose performance is involved: a superior, subordinate, peer, or outsider; (b) how the manager's performance is linked to the performance in question: closely or distantly related; (c) the quality of the person's performance: good, fair, or poor, (d) whether some outside evaluation has been expressed about the person's contribution: it can be explicit, embedded, or nonexistent, (e) the credibility of the source of information: believable or biased, and (f) the source's or messenger's method of delivery: with the messenger dispassionately presenting his or her case, being emotionally upset about what has occurred, or even blaming the manager.

We derived these factors inductively from analyzing responses on the OSIBA[7] as respondents put themselves in the position of a magazine publisher. These respondents, we found, would more often provide positive consequences when their subordinate's performance was involved, when it was evaluated as good, when someone else had explicitly identified the person as doing a good job, when the information came from a credible source, and when it was dispassionately delivered. Managers would be most likely to monitor when a believable source calmly requested help about a problem directly affecting the manager.

We also noticed some provocative combinations. Some respondents would recognize even the slightest improvement when the performer was either not saying very much or self-effacing, but would quickly provide harsh consequences when faced with poor performance and an "attitude." Others would avoid dealing directly with performance altogether even when provoked by a crisis, preferring to let subordinates fight it out among themselves. Another group of respondents, when faced with emotional displays, some of which were aimed at them, would consistently react to the display of emotion rather than to the underlying performance issues.

Bolstering our knowledge about the conditions enhancing or inhibiting the likelihood of quick AMC sequences would enable us to develop ways of creating situations to promote these types of interaction.

Relationship between monitoring and consequences

Compensatory model?

While we have found that managers who supervise others effectively have faster AMC sequences and higher quantities of monitoring and consequences, we do not know whether or not a trade-off exists between monitors and consequences. Can an abundance of consequences compensate for relatively few monitors? Or is the weakest link in the chain – the minimum percent of monitors or consequences – the best indication of the effectiveness of the manager? Is the time spent monitoring enhanced by the time spent providing consequences, thus producing a synergistic result greater than either behavior separately? In Studies 2, 3, 4, 5a, 5b, and 6, scores on monitors and consequences have not been aggregated in such a way that we can look at the relationship between the two. Hence, we have only an incomplete ordering of managers' supervisory behaviors, which is insufficient to answer the question of a compensatory relationship.

One way to get a complete ordering is to have an aggregation rule that mathematically specifies the relationship between the behaviors. Among the possible aggregation rules would be: (a) to add the monitor and consequence scores; (b) to multiply the scores; (c) to take the minimum score; or (d) to

Table 8.1 Illustrations of four aggregation rules using former New York Mayors

Aggregation rule	Jimmy Walker M C Score	Abe Beame M C Score	Ed Koch M C Score	Fiorello La Guardia M C Score
Add	$1 + 2 = 3$	$6 + 2 = 8$	$1 + 9 = 10$	$4 + 5 = 9$
Multiply	$1 \times 2 = 2$	$6 \times 2 = 12$	$1 \times 9 = 9$	$4 \times 5 = 20$
Minimum	1	2	1	4
Maximum	2	6	9	5

Note: M = Monitor, C = Consequence. Assume means and standard deviations are the same for monitors and consequences

take the maximum score. Table 8.1 illustrates how each of these rules would apply to monitor and consequence scores of some past mayors of New York City. If we wished to capture the supervisory behavior of former Mayor Jimmy Walker in a single score, we could combine his scores, using different aggregation rules. Walker, conjectured to spend 1 percent of his time monitoring and 2 percent providing consequences, would have a score of 3 percent with the "add" rule, 2 percent with the "multiply" rule, 1 percent with the "minimum rule," and 2 percent with the "maximum" rule. We could then generate comparable information by fitting a Constant Elasticity of Substitution (CES) function (Arrow, Chenery, Minhas, & Solow, 1961) to the data. Fitting a function in this way is common in economics. It assumes a large number of leaders (e.g., at least two hundred mayors), and requires substantial computer time. This maximum-likelihood search would tell us which aggregation rule comes closest to describing effective managers.

Taking each of the rules in turn:

(a) If we found that the *add* rule came closest, we would conclude that a *compensatory* relationship exists in which one behavior of the leader can make up for the other. Having many consequences could compensate for relatively few monitors and/or many monitors could make up for relatively few consequences.

(b) If we found that the *multiplication* rule provided the best fit, we would have evidence that monitors and consequences interact with one another to produce a *synergistic* reaction: some modicum of monitoring makes additional consequences more effective, and vice versa.

(c) If the *maximum* score turned out to be best, we would infer that the more monitoring or consequences, the better. This would be incompatible then with the idea that above a certain limit for monitors and consequences, supervisory effectiveness declines.

(d) If the *minimum* score proved best, this would fall in line with the old saying that a chain is only as strong as its weakest link. In this case, the lowest score on either monitoring or consequences would be the best indication of the behavior of the manager.

Probing the relationship between monitors and consequences in this way would enable us to see whether the relationship between monitoring and consequences is compensatory, with a surplus of one making up for a lack of the other. It would also show whether the minimum score best describes the supervisory behavior of a given leader, or whether the best indicator falls somewhere in the middle, suggesting a synergistic relationship.[8]

Questions about quantity and quality of monitors and consequences

Different methods of monitoring

Why is work sampling superior?

Although we found in Studies 2 and 17 that one method of monitoring, work sampling, made a substantial difference, we still do not know why it is so effective.[9] Does it have to do with the flow of information to the boss? Do subordinates respond better when they know that the information has been collected first-hand?

We suggest that the *directness* of work sampling leads to more accurate appraisals and consequences, and hence to better supervision. Several filters exist with the other methods of monitoring. With monitoring via secondary source, its first filter occurs when the manager obtains information from someone other than the person who did the work. The second filter occurs when the manager hears an explanation of what was done. A similar problem exists with monitoring via self-report. In both cases, the quality of information obtained depends heavily on the person doing the reporting. Some may accentuate the positive and play down the negative; others may do the opposite. In contrast, by directly observing employees at work, leaders probably obtain a clearer picture of what followers have done.

Another reason for the superiority of work sampling may be the *enhanced communication* that occurs between follower and leader. When the film directors in Table 7.9 mingled with the crew on the set and sampled the work, crew members would often stroll up and begin reporting on what they were doing.

A subtle difference exists between monitoring via work sampling and self-report. When a manager asks: "How's it going?," the question demands an answer. The worker cannot refuse. In contrast, sampling the work lets the worker know the manager is interested, but it does not require that the worker say anything if he does not wish to. When the worker initiates discussions of his own performance with the manager, the exchange is more likely to be responsive to the follower's needs rather than the manager's.

One manager, in fact, after hearing about our model, actually shifted from monitoring via self-report to work sampling. When she sat down with her subordinate, an analyst, to see what he was really doing, she was startled to notice that he was struggling with extremely messy data. She then realized that this was the main reason for the analyst's ineffective work. Once the data were rectified, the analyst's performance and morale improved. By simply sampling his work, the manager was able to solve the problem; her old method of monitoring via self-report had produced awkward exchanges with which the subordinate was clearly uncomfortable.

We highly recommend further research looking at the differences between the different methods of monitoring.

Are monitors via work sampling and self-report compensatory?

One question that is sometimes raised is whether or not managers can make up for a lack of work sampling by relying on self-report. We think not, given the two benefits of monitoring via work sampling discussed above. Further research should be done, however, to see if the two result in different levels and types of communication.

When should self-report be used?

The fact that we make no specific predictions about using self-report does not mean that it should be avoided. In fact, our results show that all managers, from the most effective to the least, do some monitoring via self-report.[10]

Perhaps different methods of monitoring are appropriate at different times. When, for example, the follower already talks freely about his performance, monitoring via self-report is probably unnecessary. But when the manager monitors via work sampling and the follower does not voluntarily disclose what he is doing, the manager might try to figure out when would be the best time simply to ask.

There is probably a good reason for combining self-report with work sampling. The two, we predict, provide a richer, fuller picture than either alone. Followers can provide their perspective, explaining, as the sound person did to the director in Table 7.9 (p. 196).

It is also possible that self-report serves a function beyond the collection of information. Perhaps, for example, managers who sample work without also asking subordinates how their work is progressing are perceived to be sending a message of mistrust.

While most of the research to date has been done looking at work sampling (in Studies 8 and 9), few investigators have tried to verify the reasons for using one type of monitoring rather than another.[11] Future research is needed.

Subtleties among positive, negative, and neutral consequences

A topic of intense interest is that of leaders approving or disapproving what followers do. While the studies connected with the model showed that effective leaders used a combination of positive, negative, and neutral consequences, neither shunning nor favoring one type of feedback over another, much research remains to be done.

Do negative consequences typically delivered in work settings have deleterious side-effects?

Opinions about the use of negative consequences are diverse, with relatively few studies to back up the various claims (Arvey & Jones, 1985). The answer to the question about the unfavorable effects of negative consequences is mixed. Operant researchers, for instance, actively discourage punishment and recommend using it only as a last resort (Kazdin, 1989; Miller, 1997). This is based primarily on laboratory research conducted with infrahuman subjects, using a highly intense punishment procedure, in this case, electrical shock (Azrin & Holz, 1966; Hutchinson, 1977). Not surprisingly, the side effects were sometimes severe. Among them were: (a) emotional reactions which were temporarily disruptive and counterproductive to further learning; (b) escape from and/or avoidance of the situation and the agent delivering the punishment; and (c) attempts to actually physically attack the agent responsible for the punishment.

When the consequences are considerably milder, as they are in most work settings, they are not necessarily to be shunned. Cherrington, Reitz, and Scott (1971) found that college students, acting as subjects, who received more typical negative consequences (more in line with the way in which we have defined them) for low performance, generally had higher levels of performance. Similarly, O'Reilly and Weitz (1980), in a study of 140 managers, found that employees performed better for supervisors who used sanctions more quickly.

A more recent study, again with college students, corroborated this. Schnake (1986) found that groups which observed a co-worker receiving a cut in pay for low productivity produced significantly more than either the control group or the groups that observed a co-worker receiving a threat of a pay cut. He concluded that "punishment may be used effectively in organizations" (p. 344).

In Baron's (1988) topical research, he compared constructive and destructive criticism and found the results varied depending on the type of criticism delivered. Subjects reported feeling significantly angrier and more tense after receiving destructive rather than constructive criticism. Destructive criticism also resulted in subjects' setting lower goals and reporting lower self-efficacy. In contrast, constructive criticism did not have any of these undesirable results, leading Baron to conclude that it is not the delivery of negative feedback, *per se*, that produces such effects, but the manner in which such information is conveyed.

In fact, at the time we were conducting work on the model, Baron's office was right next door. Our discussion of our results spurred him to examine the data sheets we used. Looking at the verbatim comments, Baron found few, if any, instances of anything approaching the destructive criticism he had described in his research (R. Baron, personal communication, 1987). Instead, the consequences we classified as negative were uniformly mild and benign, and rarely made reference to anything personal. For example, the insurance managers in Study 2 made such statements as:

- "Hmm, I dunno about that."
- "Let's try this and see how it works."

These statements parallel those we have heard in many other settings:

- (Bank manager to assistant): "Thanks, but I really needed those figures yesterday."
- (Supervisor Charlie to his workers about the previous day's production): "It wasn't too bad, but we can do better."
- (Helmsman to crew after directing them to square back the pole): "Square back the pole more." (Table 3.3, P.55, at 6:02.20)

From our observations, most negative consequences, at least those delivered by working adults, are relatively impersonal and typically tame. While some negative consequences are, no doubt, harsh, a blanket veto against negative consequences as a group seems unnecessary and unjustified based on evidence of deleterious side effects experienced at work.

They may, in fact, be beneficial particularly when they are accompanied by positive and neutral consequences. The idea of a combination of both positive and negative is based on extensive research in the area of learning (Logan & Wagner, 1965). When leaders provide primarily positive consequences, subordinates may know what behaviors are desired but not necessarily which ones are not desired. By providing negative consequences as well, managers can help subordinates to zero in on acceptable conduct. Subordinates learn from both. In keeping with the learning literature, we contend that a combination of positive and negative consequences will have a more positive impact on subordinate performance and attitudes than the use of either alone.

Are positive consequences problematic?

The case for using positive consequences seems to be fairly straightforward,[12] with solid agreement about its beneficial impact and numerous studies to back up this claim from I/O (e.g., Bass, 1981; Campbell, Dunnette, Lawler, & Weick 1970; Ilgen, Fisher, & Taylor, 1979) and operant psychologists (e.g., Hopkins & Sears, 1982; Komaki, Coombs, & Schepman, 1991).

We would caution, however, that the exclusive use of either positive or negative consequences will have a negative impact on subordinate performance and attitudes. Relying exclusively on positive consequences, for example, creates a credibility problem for a boss. Subordinates may begin to question the adequacy of the manager's supervisory skills. The subordinate may wonder, "Does she really know what I'm doing? Does she have what it takes to make the necessary corrections?" The opposite would also hold true. When bosses only find fault, subordinates may become discouraged and wonder if the boss will ever notice what is going well. Relying exclusively on negative consequences can harm morale.

Why neutral consequences may be more palatable

It was interesting to note the relatively high use of neutral consequences in the Australian police force (Study 4) and the US ROTC units (Study 12). In these settings, more than half of the consequences were neutral. The police sergeants, for example, mainly used one of three types:

> simple messages of encouragement (e.g., "Yep. That's all right", "Another one!"), direct instructional feedback (e.g., "You need a statement from the driver to complete that report") or indirect instructional information via discussion of other officers' performance (e.g., "He's then required to log-in with the on-duty sergeant").
>
> (Brewer, Wilson, & Beck, 1994, p. 75)

One reason for the widespread use of neutral consequences may be their relative unobtrusiveness and the fact that they are not overtly evaluative.

Given the controversial nature of negative consequences, and the model's new subcategory of neutral consequences, we highly recommend further research.

Role of indirect consequences

Another intriguing topic, yet to be explored, is that of feedback delivered not to the workers themselves but to another worker when the person discussed is not present. These indirect consequences were singled out in the OSTI because we thought they played a special, albeit unspecified, role in the supervisory process. To our surprise, as shown in Table 4.4 (p. 99), they constitute a sizable portion of overall consequences, ranging from one-half to two-thirds of the total.

As opposed to direct consequences, which are delivered to a person straightaway and operate in an easily observable fashion, the exact way in which indirect consequences work has yet to be identified. One possibility is that they act as vicarious reinforcers or punishers (Bandura, 1986). When the worker performs as he learns is desired, he is vicariously reinforced. In the same way, when he transgresses, he is vicariously punished. In this sense, indirect consequences, we predict, contribute to motivation. Evidence exists to suggest this might be the case. Schnake (1986), in the experiment referred to earlier, found that groups which observed a co-worker receiving a cut in pay for low productivity produced significantly more than either the control group or the groups that observed a co-worker receiving a threat of a pay cut. It is possible that the indirect consequence – how the boss evaluates others – serves as a cue as to how the boss might evaluate the subordinate himself.

Who uses indirect consequences?

It would be instructive to assess whether indirect consequences are used more often by certain types of leaders. Evans, a leadership researcher (personal communication, 1989), has suggested that charismatic leaders might be more likely to use positive, indirect consequences in their speeches than less charismatic leaders.

Are direct and indirect consequences compensatory?

Another provocative question arises regarding whether indirect consequences can be substituted for direct ones. While indirect consequences can be beneficial, there are probably risks in assuming that they can substitute or compensate for direct ones.

One of the problems is in their transmission. A direct consequence makes itself known, one might say, directly. But with an indirect consequence, the intended recipient may or may not ever hear of it. One study on how information filtered through a manufacturing facility is pertinent here (Davis, 1968). When middle-level managers were specifically asked to forward information down through three levels of the chain of command, information concerning preparation for a layoff was effectively communicated. On the other hand, information dealing with the opening of a new entrance to the management parking lot was only sporadically transmitted. In both cases, managers were specifically asked to pass along the information. Given that no such requests would be made concerning an indirect consequence, and given the sporadic rate of transmission when these managers were specifically requested to do so, we propose that the transmission rate for indirect consequences would be less than optimal.

Moreover, managers who do not discuss their evaluations directly with their staffs risk the possibility that these evaluations may be intentionally or unintentionally distorted. The greater the distortion, the greater the opportunity for misunderstanding.

For these reasons, indirect and direct consequences are not thought to be compensatory. Managers who use them interchangeably are not likely to be effective in maintaining the motivation of their subordinates.

Finding an optimum combination of consequences

In the final analysis, we think that any one subcategory of consequences, whether it be the sign (positive, neutral, or negative), or the delivery (indirect or direct), the style – (sincere or insincere), or the content (process or outcome), falls woefully short of describing what effective leaders really do. For instance, the need to transmit consequences directly differs depending on their sign. When supervisor Charlie, for instance, bragged that his people went " 'right back into production without waiting to be told' " (Gellerman, 1976, p. 93), it is probably not as critical that he transmit this positive consequence directly as it is to transmit bad news. The chief executive officer of the Bank of America talks about the dangers of hearsay (Clausen, 1980). He recounts a conversation about a person in another part of the state: " 'Do you know him?' " " 'No,' " the respondent answers, " 'but I hear he's no good.' " The person being referred to may not know what is being said nor may he have an opportunity to defend himself. Furthermore, discussing a subject's shortcomings with other parties is counter to the strong ethic that exists regarding the "saving of face." In fact, we predict that marginally effective managers are more likely than effective managers to deliver consequences that are both negative and indirect. While indirect consequences probably possess special communication value, sole reliance on them is not recommended. Along the same lines, managers are not encouraged to rely on passing along negative consequences indirectly.

Another factor in delivering consequences is context. We would predict that the process of giving feedback is an ongoing, cascading one in which it may be necessary to hear how one is doing in different ways at different times and perhaps even from different individuals. Another related hypothesis is that the credibility and motivation of the source as well as the needs, background, and prior experience of the follower makes a substantial difference in how the feedback is received by the candidate and whether it facilitates performance improvements.

To round out this much needed picture, we recommend what we refer to as a within-subject extreme consequences study. To do this study, we would need an accessible setting such as doctoral examinations with the candidate and her committee members or critiques of readings with the playwright and her audience members. In each case, the proceedings are more or less open to the public, the candidate (or playwright) has produced an extensive body of work, and the committee members (or audience) make known their judgments about the quality of the work.

The evaluatee would rank the consequences given along a continuum from helpful to harmful. Then comparisons would be made of the distinguishing characteristics of the feedback falling into one extreme or the other. Assuming that the evaluatee's assessments might change over time, his opinion could be solicited shortly after the critique and after a delay. Among the comments that are ultimately seen as the most helpful may be those that are negative but at the same time responsive to the needs, background, and prior experience of the evaluatee. Descriptive research along these lines would help us to glimpse how these many elements are woven together.

Parametric issues

Another set of questions involves the intriguing but none the less thorny question of how to determine the optimal range of behaviors or sequences in the model. How much time, at minimum, must managers devote to monitoring and providing consequences? How many AMC sequences are enough? How much time is too much?

These questions cannot be answered simply. Some studies have been cited as evidence that more is, indeed, better (e.g., Anderson, Kulhavy, & Andre, 1971; Cook, 1968; Hundal, 1969; Ivancevich, Donnelly, & Lyon, 1970). In general, tests of our model have shown that the more monitors and consequences, the better. But the highs and lows of monitors and consequences differ from setting to setting, as shown in Table 4.4 (p. 99). The amount of time spent by effective managers monitoring varied from a low of 2.9 (in Study 2's insurance firm) to 11.5 percent (in Study 5a's construction site). Even if providing positive consequences is beneficial, it may be possible to have too much of a good thing. If the "typical" effective manager spends approximately 5 percent of her time providing positive and neutral consequences, would the effect of a three-fold increase, to 15 percent, be excessive? Possibly.

Positing an optimal range

Similar concerns were raised in a seminal article by Hebb (1955). He, too, questioned whether or not a variable, in this case, arousal, may have a different impact, depending upon its level on the continuum. For example, mild arousal may result in increasing alertness, interest, and positive emotion, while arousal at its highest level may result in conflicting responses. With the continuum ranging from "absent" to "strong," Hebb identified mild levels of arousal as "an optimal level of arousal for effective behavior" (p. 250).

This optimal level is depicted in Figure 8.1, showing a curvilinear relationship between the dependent variable and the different levels of arousal. Performance increases as arousal increases. This does not continue indefinitely, however. At some point, increases in arousal show no commensurate increase in performance, and past a certain range, increases in arousal lead to declines in performance. The now-classic inverted U-shaped curve graphically illustrates the point that there exists a level of arousal at which performance is optimal. Arousal levels above and below this point are reconsidered "sub-optimal" because they are associated with poorer performance.

We draw an analogy between Hebb's work and our model. An optimal range may exist within which supervisory effectiveness is greatest and beyond which supervisory effectiveness declines. By "optimal," we mean defining values that fall within the limits associated with highest supervisory effectiveness. This requires that upper and lower limits be located. Practically, one would like to be able to specify the minimum and maximum

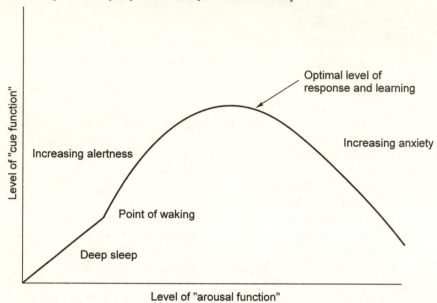

Figure 8.1 Level of arousal: inverted U-shaped curve, depicting optimal and sub-optimal levels of arousal
Source: Hebb (1955, p. 250). Copyright © 1955 by the American Psychological Association. Adapted with permission.

amount of time managers should spend monitoring, providing consequences, and giving AMC sequences, in order to be most effective.

This exploration of an optimal range could potentially contribute to the development of operant conditioning theory. By assessing the upper and lower limits, one moves in a direction beyond merely identifying what works to doing more parametric analyses (Baer, Wolf, & Risley, 1968).

Determining the optimal range

To do this, we would first establish the unit of measurement, in this case, an index of relative frequency, such as standard deviation units (or standard scores). For example, a theater manager who monitors 11.3 percent of the time would obtain a standard score of .5, while a bank manager who monitors 4.3 percent of the time would also obtain a standard score of .5.

To identify the optimal range, we recommend examining extreme cases or "outliers." By definition, outliers are isolated cases that fall outside the range of most observations. The assumption is that these individuals are functioning beyond the limits of the optimal range, provided that anomalies in data collection and retrieval are ruled out as possible causes.

To establish upper and lower limits, a minimum of twenty managers per organization in a minimum of twenty organizations should be observed, and the distribution of their scores examined. Outliers are identified within each organization and for monitors and consequences separately. Once this has been done, the standard scores of these outlying managers are used to set the upper and lower limits within the organization. These standard scores are then averaged across all organizations, separately for the upper and lower limits. The result is four average standard scores: two identifying the upper and lower limits for monitors and two identifying the upper and lower limits for consequences.

To identify whether or not managers who are effective fall within acceptable limits, we would: (a) identify effective managers and (b) assess the level of monitoring and consequences (or durations of AMC sequences) for each manager. Once all of this information is collected, managers exhibiting acceptable levels are compared with (a) those exhibiting insufficient levels of either and (b) managers exhibiting excessive levels of either. If the group exhibiting acceptable levels contains a greater number of effective managers than does the group exhibiting insufficient or excessive levels of monitoring and consequences, then one could say that the optimal range has been established.[13, 14]

In short, departing from the conventional line of thinking that "more of a good thing is better," we recommend a concept of optimal range, which is defined by an upper and a lower limit for each relevant behavior.

INTERACTIONS BETWEEN LEADERS AND FOLLOWERS

Our research has just begun to explore the interaction patterns between leaders and followers. To find out what well functioning pairs do, and how to develop synergistic relationships in which people virtually finish each other's sentences, we need more descriptive and prescriptive research like that of longitudinal ethnographic researchers (Barley, 1990) and marketing research firms (Gladwell, 1996). The latter firms train cameras on customers in stores such as Nordstrom and K-mart and employ trackers with clipboards to see what the customers who buy actually do. "Reel upon reel of grainy entryway video" shows "customers striding in the door, downshifting, refocusing, and then, again and again, making that little half turn" (p. 66). From these data, market researchers make recommendations for everything from store layout to merchandise display.

Focus on the follower

One highly recommended direction is to emphasize the follower. Just as we have focused on effective leaders, we can raise questions about effective followers. Do successful followers do something different in kind or in degree from less successful ones? Unfortunately, few guidelines of this nature exist other than some of the work on organizational citizenship

(Bateman & Organ, 1983; Smith, Organ, & Near, 1983) and leader–member exchange theory (Graen & Uhl-Bien, 1995). While some, such as Graen and Uhl-Bien (1995), recommend ambitious multi-level and multi-domain research programs, they do not tell followers what they can do to enhance their position in the organization.

As the model's results (e.g., Study 7) highlighted followers, my co-researcher Mitzi Apter-Desselles and I became more and more intrigued. We developed a model of follower success in which we distinguish between what is required – doing the prescribed aspects of the job – and what is discretionary – going "above and beyond the call of duty." *Discretionary* behaviors differ from required ones in that they are: (a) discontinuous, e.g., actually volunteering for a less desirable assignment differs qualitatively from accepting a less desirable assignment, (b) proactive, e.g., taking action before problems arise requires an individual to be proactive rather than merely react to problems, (c) constructive, e.g., attempting to correct a nonstandard condition contributes to the effective functioning of the organization, and (d) optional, e.g., persuading peers to endorse a boss's unpopular decisions cannot be required or prescribed in advance.

We spotlighted these discretionary behaviors because we agreed with researchers and practitioners alike that there is more to doing well on the job than just doing the job well (Borman, Pulakos, & Motowidlo, 1986; Katz & Kahn, 1978; Lufthansa German Airlines, 1987; Wakabayashi & Graen, 1984). In fact, these subtle behaviors may explain a phenomenon which occurs in many organizations: seemingly qualified individuals are often passed over at promotion time or let go when companies cut back. One example occurred in the Toronto branch of a brokerage firm when a boss, Charlie Allen, had to lay off one of three currency traders (Uchitelle & Kleinfield, 1996):

> The consensus choice happened to be a woman who was indisputably the top performer, but had the weakest political bonds. "I knew that she was the best in the department," [Charlie] said. "But she had not networked. And I had to inform her that she was terminated. And she looked at me with tears in her eyes and said, 'But Charlie, you know better.' I will never forget what she said and how she looked that day," he reports sadly. (p. 29)

She was fired not because she was not doing her job well, but because of a lack of these discretionary behaviors that go beyond doing what is required. Thus, being capable alone may not guarantee upward mobility; doing both the required *and* the discretionary may be necessary.

Although we may have uncovered a side to success that has been ignored by traditional predictors, more research needs to be done. To test these hypotheses, we propose doing an extreme groups approach, comparing the top and bottom groups. Assuming that the top followers exhibit more of these discretionary behaviors than the bottom followers, we should then be able to conduct an experiment to see if we can enhance these discretionary behaviors. The treatment might consist of a behavioral self-management program (Watson & Tharp, 1996) in which trainees would identify desired behaviors, self-monitor their own performance, and then select and arrange consequences contingent on their desired behaviors.

Identifying own performance discussions

Another related research direction is to track the followers' "own performance" discussions. Among the intriguing questions to be answered are: (a) When do such exchanges take place? Are they more likely to occur one-on-one or in a group? Do they happen more often face-to-face or at a distance (via telephone or electronic mail)? Do they take place in the process of a task or at its completion? (b) Who initiates the discussion? Is it the follower or the leader? (c) Is there a connection between who initiates the discussion and when it take place? (d) How do leaders and followers react? Answers to each of these questions would shed light on the interaction process and lead to further hypotheses.

Based on the results so far, we pose several hypotheses. We predict that productive pairs will be more likely to have a balance of give-and-take in their interactions. In Study 17, for example, neither the director nor the director of photography consistently dominated the conversation. This balance is particularly important to ensure that the follower, who is in a less powerful position, can and will speak up.

Another hypothesis, based on Studies 7 and 15, is that AMC sequences within successful pairs will be quicker, with the leader interspersing monitors and neutral and positive consequences throughout the conversation. Correspondingly, we predict, there will be more discussion of the subordinate's own performance.

Third, we predict that such pairs will pick up more on subtle cues and react appropriately, with each party in the exchange responding to the other. The follower might require only the slightest hint to begin talking about his own performance. This is important because the monitoring done by managers is sometimes veiled. Goltz (1993) has found that leaders who monitored sometimes asked straightforward questions (e.g., "Did you get your reports from Debbie?") and sometimes did not. At times, she reports that managers periodically monitored by "starting a statement which the subordinate was expected to complete, such as 'And the Taekwondo people...'" (Goltz, 1993, p. 183). Or workers may voluntarily leave samples of their work for the leader to peruse with the new leader taking the new information into account and acting appropriately (Hackman & Walton, 1986).

Effective leaders, we predict, will be more responsive to followers as well. For instance, they might wait until followers approach them rather than interrupting their flow of work. This effective manager might also make sure that she zeroed in on things that were under the subordinate's influence. For example, an effective manager might monitor how carefully a lab technician measured the concentration of unknown fluids rather than monitoring only the reliability of the technician's results, since these may vary because the concentration of the fluid is unstable over time.

Lastly, we predict that successful pairs will deal with conflicts constructively when they happen. We assume some conflict to be inevitable, with each pair having at least some occasions in which they differ. Denying conflict does not mean that it does not exist. In fact, open admissions of conflict might be a healthy sign. The end result may be that the pair can better negotiate differences.

For instance, the follower, after being criticized, might reply, as in Table 7.9 (p.196): "I didn't know that, I'm sorry" to which the leader, realizing that the sound person had not been warned, offered, "Sorry, we should have told you." In this case, neither party avoided the conflict. The leader delivered a negative consequence, the follower acknowledged the leader's concern, and the leader, now seeing things from the follower's point of view, saw how he could rectify the situation the next time.

This ability, even with a small incident such as the above exchange, would more explicitly amplify what McCall and Lombardo (1983) learned when contrasting executives who do well with those who derail or are stopped abruptly in their career progression. They found that the executives in both groups were very similar in many ways. They were "incredibly bright, identified early, [had] outstanding track records, had a few flaws, [were] ambitious, and [had] made many sacrifices" (p. 9). What separated them, however, were their people skills. Four of the five differences involved how well they treated others. Those who succeeded "maintained composure under stress, handled mistakes with poise and grace, focused on problems and solved them, [and] got along with all kinds of people – were outspoken but not offensive" (p. 9).

Tracing developmental patterns

It would also be instructive to see if and how successful relationships evolve over time. One possibility is that such relationships succeed from the beginning, with each party accurately and sensitively reflecting the other.

A not necessarily incompatible hypothesis is that a learning process takes place. Perhaps, as the parties go through stages in their relationship, their interactions get better and better: the good relationships get better, progressing through different stages, and the poor ones do as well. Graen and Uhl-Bien (1995) outline four phases to describe how relationships with leaders progress to maturity: (a) a "stranger" phase, in which "followers behave only as required and do only their prescribed job," (b) an "acquaintance" stage, in which "not all exchanges are contractual," (c) a third stage (unnamed), between the second and fourth, and (d) a "mature partnership" in which the "individuals can count on each other for loyalty and support ...[and]...the exchanges are not only behavioral but also emotional" (p. 230).

To shed light on this developmental process, we recommend a longitudinal study in which leaders and followers would be observed at different stages: (a) during their initial set of interactions (e.g., their first performance-related discussion), (b) as the follower is still learning the job (e.g., after the first week), (c) after the follower has been on the job for a month, and (d) at monthly intervals thereafter. The design would make use of a within-subject comparison, with each follower serving as his own control. To see if changes occur over time, we would contrast their interactions during the different phases.

Another possibility, gleaned from real life and portrayals on the stage, is that the relationship does not evolve gradually over time, but only when conflicts occur *and* only when future steps are taken to avoid the conflict. Given a misunderstanding, one or both parties learns what to do the next time. Perhaps the leader learns to monitor more often so that she can spot problems before a crisis occurs, or she discovers that she needs to solicit discussions of the follower's own performance even if the follower does not volunteer himself. She might find out that she has to provide timely negative consequences so as to prevent problems from continuing. Or perhaps the follower learns to clarify – in essence, to monitor – what the leader wants, or he learns that he needs to initiate conversations about his own performance even if the leader does not specifically request it.

We encourage future researchers to conduct descriptive and prescriptive studies. Whatever the results of these studies, they will have implications for our model as well as for improving the ways in which leaders are selected, trained, appraised, and motivated. Conducting prescriptive research studies will enable us, for example, to document what kinds of AMC sequences should be delivered and whether these interactions can be learned. They will also show which aspects of subordinate performance should be highlighted in the subordinate's formal performance review. At the same time, they will make managers answerable, in their own reviews, for critical aspects of their performance.

PUTTING THE PREMISE INTO PRACTICE

Our model sounds promising. But can it be used right now? What, if anything, does it offer to help today's leaders carry out their organizational missions?

Whether at the apex of technology or on a traditional coffee farm, getting things done day after day and year after year is a complex undertaking. It requires at least three things. First, one must have policies and plans that are well thought out and consistent with one's mission. Second, one must have adequate resources to do the job: the space, the time, the equipment, and most importantly of all, people with the knowledge, skills, and abilities needed to succeed. Last, one must have leaders who provide suitable supervision. As Arthur Rock (1987), the venture capitalist, says, "A great idea won't make it without great management" (p. 66).

Unfortunately, in the sometimes harried quest to achieve the mission, we often overlook management. We find the resources, we develop the vision, we put the policies into place. But, although effective supervision is a key element of success, it is frequently where we fall short. As Rock (1987) says, "Strategy is easy, but tactics are hard" (p. 63).

Sometimes management problems are merely inconvenient, as in the case of the stranded Long Island commuters. Sometimes they are extremely costly, as in the cases of the computer company's mishandled launch of a new product and the New York trading firm's auditing catastrophe. Sometimes, however, they can make a life and death difference.

A dramatic example is a case involving New York City's Child Welfare Administration. The 1995 beating death of six-year-old Elisa Izquierdo drew an outpouring of sorrow and rage and, soon thereafter, a probe of the organization itself. The ensuing revelations were mortifying. As one newspaper headline put it, "She suffered in plain sight but alarms were ignored" (Bernstein & Bruni, 1995, p. A1). By one account, there were seven clear warnings that, if heeded by the appropriate personnel, would have saved the girl's life:

> The Child Welfare Administration rejected, ignored or appeared to have ineptly investigated at least seven formal reports of the girl's possible abuse or neglect. And the pattern of error, omission, and illegality reflected in the handling of her case was the same documented in other child fatalities reviewed by the state. (p. Al)

A school official, for example, phoned to register her concerns after noticing Elisa's scratches, bruises, and signs of emotional distress. As it happened, the family had a lengthy history of documented problems; child protection workers had, at one point, removed all of the children from the household until the mother entered a cocaine treatment program. But because the agency had lost all of these files (they still have not been found), the caseworker who visited the home after the latest complaint knew nothing of this history. He found a clean, well-kept home, and concluded that nothing was wrong.

The mistakes continued. Symptoms of abuse, ranging from a bruised hand, lost hair, and withdrawn behavior, to a sudden appearing limp, were reported to the agency and ignored. It appeared that the "official who rejected her report never checked that file, never added the school's observations to it, and never relayed them to Elisa's city caseworker" (p. L22). Concerned social workers from a nonprofit group called the agency. An emergency room physician called. Nothing was done. Months later, Elisa was beaten to death in the family's apartment and her mother charged with (and later convicted of) murder.

The investigation revealed a tragic circus of bureaucratic bungling, and Mayor Rudolph W. Giuliani's political response was swift. He quickly announced a reversal in the city's child welfare philosophy, from that of favoring keeping families intact to one geared toward "criminal justice and the protection of children" (Firestone, 1996, p. B4). He also pulled the troubled agency out of the welfare bureaucracy, and appointed a close friend of his, with a reputation for social advocacy, as its new director. Both steps were widely hailed, even by political opponents. Plans were announced to raise the qualifications and salaries for caseworkers. The agency's new head, a foster child himself, was called "an advocate with a heart" who had "the toughness to say the abuse of children won't be tolerated" (Myers, 1996, p. B4).

In this case as in many others, however, faith was placed entirely in a change of policies and administrators. Even if the new director, Mr Nicholas Scoppetta, could set a new tone and garner more resources from having an "ear" to the Mayor, and even if the policy change was exactly what was needed, it was only part of the solution. As one skeptic cautioned, "this agency has been run very, very poorly for two years." Truly reversing that trend would require permanently altering the day-to-day behavior of hundreds of staffers: taking phone calls properly, judiciously opening cases, fastidiously keeping and retrieving records, and conscientiously tracking the status of children in fluctuating, sometimes treacherous, environments. A true change in effectiveness requires not just that the policies (e.g., higher caseworker standards) and the people (e.g., the new director) be in place, but the day-by-day management skills as well.

Given what we have learned about the management process, we would make three recommendations, not only for New York's crippled agency, but for any organization. The first is to *train* existing supervisory personnel in need of instruction. The second is to use our model's profiles in the *selecting and hiring* of personnel. The third is to instill the basic ideas of the model at all levels of the organization by *appraising and motivating* personnel with these findings in mind. What follows is a more detailed discussion of how to carry out these recommendations in an organization.

Recommendations for training leaders

Managerial personnel need to know – or to learn – how to supervise effectively. What is entailed? Four steps are recommended (Anderson & Faust, 1973). First, the training objectives – what managers should do to effectively supervise others – are identified. The next step is to assess the skills that trainees possess prior to training. This evaluation of their strengths and deficiencies can be used to help tailor instruction. During the training itself, trainees should have ample time to practice and to receive feedback. Last, but not least, the training should be evaluated and then, based on the results, revised so each succeeding class profits from the lessons learned.

Identifying training objectives

If we had to identify only two objectives, we would encourage those who aspire to heighten their leadership talent to sustain a *dialogue* about the followers' own performance, and then, based on what they find, to take appropriate action and provide relevant consequences. To ensure the dialogue gets started, leaders should take an *inquiry mode*, monitoring performance particularly using work sampling.

Assessing trainees' entering behavior

Prior to training, the behavior of all supervisory personnel should be assessed to see where they stand relative to the objectives. To assess the monitoring skills of the child welfare caseworkers' supervisors, for example, we would see whether and how they obtained information about their caseworkers – by looking at the supervisors' written records about each caseworker and by interviewing caseworkers themselves. Such an assessment prevents unneeded training and helps tailor the instruction to areas in need of emphasis.

Providing training

Depending on where trainees stand relative to this two-pronged behavioral approach, they would either practice having performance-related dialogues or learn different ways of monitoring or both. For example, with managers who already exhibit proficiency in maintaining a dialogue about performance once it gets started, but who have trouble getting the follower to discuss his or her own performance, the instruction would be tailored to create settings known to be conducive to subordinates' discussing their own performance. In some cases, we have found that seeing employees at work unleashes a raft of questions from subordinates. In other cases, we have found that it is a matter of timing. Some followers are much less likely to discuss what they have done if they are in the middle of doing it; after they have completed a portion of the task, however, they might be quite willing and even eager to discuss it. Sometimes followers are more likely to discuss their own performance after the manager takes the time to sample pertinent records or talk to educational or medical personnel related to the cases the case workers are handling. Training can help leaders to make this sometimes subtle assessment, and to practice initiating the dialogue.

On the other hand, for managers who have trouble sustaining a discussion about performance, we would arrange practice in this aspect as well. One tactic, based on our research findings, is to focus on performance and not get distracted by other work-related matters, however tempting it may be to stray into minutiae. Another tactic is to simply listen. When award-winning playwright August Wilson first started writing plays, he was given this advice when he became stymied trying to get dialogue going between his characters: "Just start listening" (Weber, 1996, p. H11).

Whatever the discrepancies between the entering behaviors and the behavioral objectives, trainees would be given time to practice in a variety of situations with different followers, so that trainees master both monitoring and sustaining dialogue in a variety of settings with different subordinates.

Evaluating training effectiveness

The final step is systematically to evaluate the extent to which the trainees master the objectives. Ideally, these behaviors should be assessed immediately after training as well as periodically on the job. These findings would also make a valuable contribution to the management development and training literature. In Goldstein's (1980) review of the training literature, he bemoans the "sad state" (p. 254) of the field. He describes how much material concerning management behavior is "dominated by low utility anecdotal presentations" (p. 254). Four years later, in a review of the training literature, Wexley (1984) notes how he intended to have a section on management development but finally eliminated it because "so little research has been conducted on this topic" (p. 521). Latham's (1988) review includes a section on leadership training, but he laments "the lack of attention to theory and the lack of research influencing practice" (p. 545). By systematically evaluating the effectiveness of training, we can see whether it is possible to groom managers to supervise others more effectively.

To the extent that the particular behaviors of sustaining a performance-related dialogue have been documented as being associated with effectiveness, thus providing a target for which individuals can aim, and to the extent that leaders can learn how to carry out these sometimes complex and dynamic behaviors, then the development of an effective management style ought to be amenable to training.

Recommendations for selecting leaders effective in supervising others

A longer-term strategy is to incorporate the findings of our model about the quick and SLAW profiles into the selection of new supervisors and managers.

Who should be hired? The obvious answer is the "best" person. But how do we decide? In the classic selection process, four steps are necessary. The first step is to define success and to collect data on the individual's supervisory success on the job, referred to as the *criterion*.[15] The next step is to identify the *predictors*, the salient characteristics of individuals that are hypothesized to be related to job success. The third step, referred to as the *validation process*, is to assess the relationship between the predictors and the criterion. Once we establish that the purported "predictors" actually predict job success, we can use them as the basis for decisions about who to hire. The fourth step is to use the proven predictors in selecting persons for supervisory positions.

Even though most selection systems attempt to capture an individual's managerial potential in the broadest, most complete manner possible, and even though the topic of leadership is prominent, the heart and soul of supervision – the influence process between manager and subordinate – often receives little or no attention. The traditional predictors include cognitive abilities, interests, personality variables, previous experience, and technical expertise (Campbell, Dunnette, Lawler, & Weick, 1970). One key managerial function, supervising others, is often omitted. A case in point is the assessment center developed by American Telephone and Telegraph (AT&T) in the 1960s (Bray, Campbell, & Grant, 1974; Bray & Grant, 1966) to tap, among other dimensions, leadership. Despite their inclusion of a number of exercises designed as tapping leadership, it is not uncommon for no one to be named a leader. Instead, exercises are typically referred to as "leaderless," placing the individual among his or her peers. Success is achieved by influencing colleagues. Although the ability to influence peers is an important aspect of leadership, it is not the same as, nor a substitute for, getting work done through subordinates.

New predictors of managerial success

Our recommendation is to select among candidates using a new set of predictors that tests of the model have documented as being predictive of effectiveness in supervising others – the amount of time spent providing monitors and consequences, the pacing of AMC sequences, and placement of SLAW behaviors.

To obtain information on these predictors, we recommend the observational instrument, the OSTI, or the in-basket assessment, the OSIBA. Another possibility is to develop a standardized assessment-center-like exercise in which candidates have an opportunity to demonstrate their prowess at supervising others. Like the OSIBA, this new exercise would be a simulation, albeit with different conditions. In this case, each candidate would be the designated leader, with directly-reporting subordinates. The subordinates would be the same for all of the candidates, and would be trained in their roles to react similarly across conditions and candidates. When a candidate monitored, for example, the subordinate would produce the same materials with the same mistakes. Each leader would be responsible for accomplishing the same task under the same set of conditions. The point of the exercise would be to assess the quick AMC and SLAW profiles. Thus, this exercise would incorporate many of the strengths of an assessment center: a standardized testing situation and the realism that comes from having subordinates assigned to help carry out a task.

Validating new predictors

To demonstrate the difference it might make to base decisions about whom to hire solely on the findings of the model, we provide an extreme groups illustration. We used the twenty-eight leaders[16] in Studies 14 and 15 as the potential hires or "candidates". We contrasted those candidates in the top third of the group in terms of their predictor(s) scores with those in the bottom third. Comparing these extreme groups, we identified differences in their criterion scores. The criterion was a clear-cut outcome, the Sailing Teamwork Effectiveness Measure (STEM), indicating the number of seconds it takes to hoist a particular type of sail.[17] For the predictors, we used: the amount of time spent providing monitors and consequences, the pacing of AMC and MC sequences, and/or the placement of SLAW behaviors.[18] To assign candidates to the extreme groups, everyone was rank-ordered by predictor score (e.g., predictor 1 in Table 8.2). Those candidates in the top

Table 8.2 Study 15: identifying candidates in the top and bottom groups

Candidates using predictor 1	Predictor 1 scores	Candidates using predictor 2	Predictor 2 scores	Candidates using predictors 1 and 2
		Top group		
A	22.04	Y	4.00	
B	22.02	C	4.50	C
C	20.98	H	6.86	H
D	19.70	D	7.33	D
E	18.72	R	8.17 →	
F	18.46	B	8.50	B
G	17.91	K	9.80	
H	16.79	F	10.00	F
I	16.33	P	11.00	
J	16.18	J	12.00	
K	15.53	Q	12.25	
L	14.41	A	13.67	
M	13.91	M	13.67	
N	13.44	O	15.00	
O	12.08	AA	15.00	
P	11.16	N	16.00	
Q	10.96	Z	16.67	
R	9.45	S	18.75	
S	8.45	E	20.00	
		Bottom group		
T	8.00	L	21.33	
U	7.22	G	22.00	
V	4.69	I	26.00	
W	4.57	BB	28.00	BB
X	3.58	X	28.50 →	X
Y	3.57	T	36.50	T
Z	3.35	W	41.00	W
AA	3.12	U	55.00	U
BB	1.00	V	70.00	V

Note: Predictor 1 scores refer to each candidate's score on one of the predictors (e.g. percentage of time spent monitoring), and predictor 2 scores to the scores on another predictor (e.g. pacing of AMC sequences). Leaders chosen using predictors 1 and 2 scored in the top third for predictors 1 *and* 2. Alphabetical (A through BB) = leaders = individual candidates.

Table 8.3 Study 15: comparing criterion scores using different predictors in selecting among candidates

| Predictors[a] | | Mean criterion score by group | | | |
		Top	Bottom	t	p
One predictor	*Percentage of time spent* Monitors	44.2 [9][b]	73.2 [9]	−1.36	.19
	Pacing AMC sequence[c]	42.1 [9]	67.6 [9]	−1.17	.26
	MC sequence[d]	39.6 [9]	81.1 [9]	−2.13	.05
Two predictors	*Pacing and placement during AM sequence*[e] AMC[c] and Antecedents	50.9 [7]	97.0 [5]	−1.80	.10
	AMC[c] and Solitary	37.7 [6]	102.0 [5]	−2.35	.04
	MC[d] and Solitary	38.3 [4]	130.5 [4]	−4.01	.007
	MC[d] and Work-related	18.0 [2]	134.7 [3]	−3.40	.04

Note: Criterion = Sailing Teamwork Effectiveness Measure = number of seconds to hoist particular type of sail, chute (M = 54.9). Predictions: percentage of time spent = number of intervals/total number of intervals. Monitors = gathering information about performance. Pacing = speed in seconds with which sequence given. AMC sequence = delivering first Antecedent (giving an order), followed by next Monitor, followed by next Consequence (providing feedback). MC sequence = delivering first Monitor, followed by next Consequence. Placement = where behavior such as Antecedent occurred, in this case, during AM sequence. Refer to Table 8.2 to see how individual leaders were placed in the top and bottom groups.
[a] Unless noted otherwise, more is better.
[b] The numbers in brackets indicate the number of leaders included in the group.
[c] In this case, quicker is better.
[d] Slower is better.
[e] For placement, fewer intervals are better

third (n = 9) for a single predictor were in the top group and those in the bottom third (n = 9) in the bottom group.

Using monitoring alone as the predictor, as seen in Table 8.3, the nine candidates in the top group averaged 44.2 seconds on the criterion in contrast to 73.2 seconds for the nine in the bottom group. Although these scores were below and above the STEM mean of 54.9 seconds, the scores for the two groups were not significantly different from one another. The findings were similar, using the AMC sequences as the predictor.

Using the pacing of MC sequences[19] as the predictor, however, we found that the top group, consisting of those with the slowest MC sequences, averaged 35.6 seconds and the bottom group 81.1 seconds, with the two groups differing significantly from one another, $t = -2.13$, $p = .05$.

Next, we used two predictors: the pacing, and the placement of behaviors within the AMC sequence. Those leaders in the top third of the first *and* second predictors were in the top group; an analogous procedure was used in constituting the bottom group. Smaller group sizes resulted, as shown in Tables 8.2 and 8.3. For one pair of predictors (AMC pacing and placement of antecedents during the AM sequence), the top and bottom groups consisted of seven and five leaders, respectively. For another set of predictors (MC pacing and the placement of work related during the AM sequence), there were only two and three leaders, respectively, in the top and bottom groups.

Using the combination of predictors resulted, again, in criterion scores that differed significantly from one another. The most dramatic difference was in the case of the MC pacing and the placement of work-related behavior during the AM sequence. With these two predictors, the spread between the two groups became much more pronounced with the two skippers in the top group averaging 18.0 seconds and the three leaders in the bottom group averaging 134.7 seconds, $t = -3.40$, $p = .04$.

The advantage of using the combination of pacing and placement predictors is that the former reflects what effective leaders do, whereas the latter is associated with lackluster leaders. Effective leaders are those who quickly pace their antecedents, monitors, and consequences while paradoxically providing consequences after they monitor at a more leisurely pace. Lackluster leaders, on the other hand, will display the SLAW behaviors. Hence, candidates are sorted by how well they meet the standards of effective leaders *and* on how well they avoid the pitfalls of lackluster leaders. Those candidates ranked as delivering the quickest AMC sequences, the most leisurely MC sequences, and spending the least number of intervals acting like a SLAW leader (being solitary, laconic, or delivering antecedents and discussing the work) are those predicted to be the best at motivating their subordinates.

Hence, we recommend one of three sets of predictors in the following order – the amount of time spent providing monitors and consequences, the pacing of AMC sequences, and the combination of the pacing of AMC sequences and placement of SLAW behaviors.

As can be seen, one could use these sets of predictors to enhance significantly decision-making about supervisors and managers. If this method were used in the Child Welfare Agency mentioned earlier, for example, the candidates chosen would be likelier to inquire and less likely to engage in non-performance-related discussions, thus enhancing the supervisory process and adhering more closely to the mandate of the agency: looking out for the welfare of children.

Maintaining organization-wide performance

To ensure that all of the gains continue and that behaviors taught during training are in fact reinforced after training, it is important to see that superiors sample the work to assess how followers are doing, follow up by letting subordinates know how well they are performing, quickly pace their AMC sequences, and watch the placement of the SLAW behaviors.

To assure full cooperation, it is essential to instill the message in every part of the organization. Senior staff, led by Mr Scoppetta himself, should provide quick AMC sequences to the followers, the caseworkers, and their supervisors. They should do the same for the policy makers and those responsible for providing resources, as well.

It is critical to listen and to keep dialogues focused on performance. With child welfare caseworkers, for example, supervisors should find out whether caseworkers continue to make judicious decisions about whether or not to remove children from parents who often seem to be doing their best under miserable circumstances. At the same time, supervisors should continually recognize performance in the face of tremendous odds – struggling with "children who don't want to be separated even from parents who beat or rape them" and "making calls to neighborhoods so dangerous and buildings so desolate that caseworkers openly carry switchblades" (Harrison, 1996).

With all parties, performance achievements as well as deficiencies should be pinpointed. The ultimate goal is to set up a system that reveals, on an ongoing basis, how the agency is doing, both when it is doing well at saving children's lives and when it is not. These consequences, particularly positive and neutral ones, will help to ensure that our workplaces are indeed better places to work.

IN SUMMARY

At the beginning of this book, we discussed the composer Morton Feldman, and how essential he felt it was to listen; he saw himself as a servant to music, declaring, " 'I owe my life to these sounds' " (Zimmerman, 1976, pp. 12–13). He and composer Christian Wolff still talk nostalgically about the idyllic week they spent with John Cage and Earle Brown, where " 'we began to listen, we began to listen ... for the first time' " to the intervals between sounds as well as the sounds themselves (Zimmerman, 1976, p. 6). We would do well to heed his advice. If we had to sum up all that we have learned in the past decade, we would encourage those who aspire to heighten their leadership talent to lead by listening.

This refrain is beginning to reverberate from a variety of quarters. Mobil Oil took out a quarter-page advertisement ("Caught in the Web," 1995, p. A31), urging their customers to keep talking with them. In the ad copy, discussing the impact of the World Wide Web, Mobil emphasizes that communication is no longer one-way; it is interactive and responsive.

Realizing that they are "a company with strong opinions, a powerful brand name and extensive global operations," they are aware that they elicit strong reactions. Whether the result is bouquets or brickbats, they enjoin their readers, customers, shareholders and partners: "let's keep talking."

The Speaker of the House of Representatives of the United States, Newt Gingrich, does this as well. Despite his incendiary public persona, he is regarded as a skillful executive behind the scenes, "extraordinarily deft at brokering disputes, building consensus and keeping his fragile coalition together" (DeParle, 1996, p. 48). President Clinton acknowledged how Gingrich had kept the House freshmen united during a particularly tight budget discussion: " 'He's held them together pretty well, on a course that I have often disagreed with. . . . You must give him credit for that' " (DeParle, 1996, p. 36). How does Gingrich do it? He listens. In the back rooms, he's known as "the best listener in America." Among his fellow Republicans, Gingrich typically plays a conciliatory role, keeping warring factions at the table. Stories of Gingrich as a "resident House therapist are legion" (DeParle, 1996, p. 48). In disputes, he gets each side to acknowledge the concerns of the other, as when some freshmen wanted a "quick execution of the National Endowment for the Arts . . . [while] moderates wanted a period of transition to private financing." Why does he do this? " 'I don't do it because I like it,' Gingrich says, 'I do it because it works' " (DeParle, 1996, p. 48).

And when it works, it really works. A food critic, Ruth Reichl (1996), for example, has singled out a New York City restaurant, the Gotham Bar and Grill, for the highest rating: four stars. She is particularly fond of their extraordinary waiters, who, she says, tune into:

> almost imperceptible vibrations. Give the waiter the slightest hint that you are interested and he will describe the food in loving detail. Indicate that you are not and your order will be taken without a word. . . . I've had fast meals when I was in a hurry, slow ones when I was not. The result is that each meal has left me remarkably well cared for. (p. C26)

For his part, composer Christian Wolff talks about the sensitive interpersonal exchange that takes place in making music. His music has been likened to "a kind of social situation you find in streets" (Zimmerman, 1976, p. 26). While he knows that much of classical music-making has to do with the individual's relationship with the score, he also perceives how individuals relate to one another. " 'Most of my scores,' he says, 'have to do with groups of people. . . . and . . . how the individuals relate to each other as they play' " (Zimmerman, 1976, p. 25). Sometimes their exchanges are predictable: " 'one person plays a sound, and then another person has to play a sound which has to follow directly on the first person's sound' " (Zimmerman, 1976 p. 26). The most memorable interactions, however, are unpredictable, in which:

> the duration of the player one's sound is indefinite. He can play as long or as short a time as he wants. And player two simply has to, as soon as

player one starts to play, he knows that any minute, any second now, any fraction of a second, he's going to play. But he doesn't know quite when. And the rhythm produced by the situation is like no other rhythm. (p. 26)

If we can attain that rhythm, that reactive quality of dialogue between leaders and followers in organizations, we can expect to see more missions completed, more missing files found (or never lost), more coffee plants well tended. While our operant model of effective supervision has only begun to realize the potential of these powerful exchanges between leaders and followers, in these rhythms can be found the heart of leadership. This, we believe, is how skippers and their crews move in harmony to hoist sails and ultimately win races, and how film personnel interact as creative partners who can practically finish one another's sentences. This, we submit, is the way we all want for management to work.

Notes

PREFACE

1 While we recognize that not all managers are leaders, nor all leaders managers, the terms "leaders", "managers" and "bosses" will be used interchangeably here to reflect common usage.

1 BACKGROUND

1 Quoted from Sayles (1979) in the introduction of his leadership book.

2 INTRODUCING THE MODEL

1 Army trainees could accrue "tokens" to be traded in for privileges such as time off.
2 The first antecedent in the sequence, referred to as the marker antecedent, is represented as ●, whereas subsequent antecedents are represented as ○.
3 Considerably expanded definitions of both monitors and consequences are presented in Ch. 3, as well as real-life examples of AMC sequences. Ch. 4 goes further, discussing the evidence about the relationship between effectiveness and supervisory behaviors and sequences.
4 Ch. 4 discusses the precedents for this dual emphasis, and also how supervisory effectiveness has been operationally defined. The measures have included evaluations of teams coordinating with one another to produce an outcome and an observational assessment of workers' attitudes about their boss.
5 Ch. 5 illuminates our treatment of the interaction process, and presents findings highlighting the influence of the follower in the process.
6 Ch. 6 describes the breadth of the model. It discusses the rationales for the moderators, some of which stem from the work of others and some of which originate in our findings that for certain tasks the model can even be counterproductive.

3 DEFINING AND MEASURING WHAT LEADERS DO

1 Except for the fact that we today view loaded terms such as "primitive" with skepticism.
2 Because observers needed to remain unobtrusive, they had problems getting close enough to identify the content of records leaders were consulting. Hence, we eventually omitted archival records as a subcategory in the OSTI.
3 The fact that a subordinate may or may not be aware of the occurrence of monitoring, however, has implications for the way in which it should be measured.

If subordinates do not always know when monitoring occurs, they can not accurately report on its frequency. As a result, assessing the level of monitoring, based solely on the reports of subordinates, would not be appropriate.

4 Yes. Yes.
5 Yes.
6 Young man.
7 Yes. Described in 12 in Table 3.2b. With the young man. Yes. Yes.
8 Consequence. No. Yes. Yes.
9 Yes. Because of the definition of performance: young man is responsible and Charlie is taking corrective action. Yes. Disapproval. Yes. Negative.
10 Yes. No.
11 Described in 7, 11, and 12 in Table 3.2b. No.
12 No. Described in 6 in Table 3.2b. No.
13 Yes. Yes. Using the scope (identified in 3 in Table 3.2b) and visual inspection (2).
14 In 13 in Table 3.2b. His unwillingness to shut down the line. He admitted he probably could have prevented it.
15 No. Because one of his employee's performance was not involved. Charlie (and ultimately maintenance) was responsible for the operation of the equipment.
16 No. The same rationale as in 15; neither the young man nor the operator is responsible for the operation of the hand-feeder, hence, he is not monitoring their performance.
17 Work sampling.
18 Yes. Crew member's. Yes. An order had just been given, so the crew member, by inference, is responsible.
19 Yes. Yes. Directly. Negative. Yes. Neutral. No. No. Negative. Because the leader indicated the crew member needed to make a further adjustment to the sail.
20 Leader is gathering information about performance. Yes. Self-report.
21 Consequence. Because it indicates knowledge of performance. Yes. Negative, direct.
22 No. The call to maintenance.
23 Yes. No. Yes. Yes. Yes. "Either you call or you're not gonna work here." The same way.
24 Monitor. Via work-sampling.
25 Consequence. Positive, indirect.
26 Monitor. Monitor. Both were gathering information about performance.
27 3 and 6 in Table 3.6b. Both are self-report monitors.
28 Yes. 5 in Table 3.6b. Negative.
29 Consequence. Yes. He already knew because he talked about the letter in 10 in Table 3.6b.
30 Neutral because the evaluation is not clear. Indirect because Bert was not present.
31 Refer to Chapters 4 and 8.
32 Due to substantial reliability problems, with reliability score percentages hovering in the 60s, no subcategories at present satisfactorily distinguish among the clarity of antecedents (Komaki et al.,1986).
33 Refer to the definition of performance earlier in the chapter.
34 The number of intervals observed per observation, with few exceptions, was 30.
35 The category (and subcategory) agreement scores are identical to the overall scores except that the denominator is the number of intervals in which a given category (or subcategory) occurred.
36 Cohen's (1960) kappa statistic is another method sometimes used. It assesses the proportion of joint agreements about the occurrence or nonoccurrence of a target behavior after the proportion of agreements due to chance have been excluded.
37 Because of the low base rate of the categories of interest (with monitors, and consequences occurring as little as two percent of the time), this results in a very

strict definition of reliability for the categories and sub-categories. For further information, refer to Komaki, Zlotnick, and Jensen (1986).

38 Discussed in Ch. 6.

4 RESEARCH ON THE MODEL: BEHAVIORS AND EFFECTIVENESS OF LEADERS

1 A study is defined as a set or sets of data collected and reported upon by a common set of authors. Some "studies" (e.g., Studies 1a and 1b) include data on the same variable (OSTI) in more than one setting (theater and bank) with a common set of authors, and some "studies" (Studies 5a and 5b) include data on different variables (performance ratings and worker attitudes) in more than one setting (construction and government) with a common set of authors. Other "studies" (e.g., Studies 13, 14, and 15) were part of a larger research program and shared the same subjects and setting but had different variables and authors.

2 For a capsule of the major findings, refer to Table 7.1.

3 For more information on how the ratings and rankings were used to place the managers in two extreme groups, refer to Komaki (1986).

4 These ratings by subordinates were independent of the measure of leaders' behavior obtained by our observers. A lack of such independence between criterion and predictor variables has been a common complaint of ratings when the same individuals make both ratings (Bass, 1990). In the Ohio State studies, in some of the transformational/charismatic studies, and in Study 17, the same group of employees was the source of information for both the predictors and criterion. In Study 17, employees identified their attitudes towards their supervisor on an employee survey, as well as estimating the frequency of their supervisors' behavior. Critics have questioned whether relationships in the data were simply the result of both ratings being made by the same individuals, hence, raising the question of using alternative measures.

5 Racing experts did not judge weather conditions to be a significant factor.

6 We multiplied here (rather than, say, added) because of our belief in what is termed a non-compensatory model. That is, we assumed that each aspect was critical and that one score should not compensate for another. By multiplying, we prevented high scores (say, 90 percent) in execution and vision from compensating for a lower score (say, 60 percent) for group morale. Refer to Ch. 8 for discussion of aggregation issues.

7 As we did in Study 15.

8 Another study, with parallel results, was also done with a subset of the construction managers (Mattila, Hyttinen, & Rantanen, 1994). It is not reported here as a separate study. Readers are highly recommended, however, to peruse the study, which uses an innovative effectiveness measure for evaluating how managers stay within budget.

9 We assumed monitors × consequences was a complementary rather than a compensatory index, as with TTEM, discussed earlier. For more on this distinction, refer as well to Ch. 8.

10 Despite the surplus of significant associations with the attitudinal and well-being measures, it was interesting to note that none of the behaviors correlated with workers' satisfaction with their supervision, at least as operationally defined on the Job Diagnostic Survey.

11 Skippers who accrued the *smallest* number of points, coming in first, second, or third rather than eighth, ninth, or tenth in the series, were considered more effective, hence, the correlation coefficient was negative.

12 The correlation was negative because the most effective leaders were those with the *fastest* times.
13 The lackluster leaders were those with the slowest chute hoisting times, hence, the correlation was positive.
14 In Study 4, in which another method of monitoring, self-report, was associated with effectiveness, "a strong, informal organizational constraint" (Brewer, Wilson, & Beck, 1994, p. 74) was reported for sampling the work. In fact, checking first-hand required the sergeant's supervisor to leave the premises and seek out police officers on patrol. Not surprisingly, "less than 5 percent of all monitoring actually involved direct observation of subordinates' patrol performance" (p. 74).
15 The same argument is not as plausible for monitors. Leaders might provide more positive and/or neutral consequences for better performing teams, but they would not necessarily scrutinize smoothly operating crews more than poorly operating ones.
16 Discussed in Ch. 6.
17 For the second hypothesis about the perceived importance of the task, refer to Ch. 5.
18 For the second hypothesis about the evaluation concerns of the persons being monitored, refer to Ch. 5.
19 Each of these statements was carefully scripted, paralleling remarks we had heard managers make in actual work settings. This was also true of responses to subordinates' (inevitable) questions. In answer to the question, "Should I do it this way?," the manager would try to use the answer as a springboard for the experimental manipulation. In the consequences-only condition, the manager would say: "Expect you're doing that"; in the monitors-only condition, she would ask, "Have you been doing that?"
20 Data were aggregated in Studies 1 to 5 over twenty observations, yielding a single summary score (e.g., number of of intervals manager monitored/number of total intervals = percent of time spent monitoring). In the laboratory studies, the focus was not on when the supervisory behaviors were delivered, but rather on what behaviors were delivered.
21 And uncannily presaging the inner workings of IBM's Deep Blue supercomputer that played successfully against the world chess champion, Garry Kasparov (McFadden, 1997). In designing Deep Blue, the developers had to program it to assess the status of the board as well as to predict as many as eight and nine moves ahead.
22 For the second hypothesis about antecedents, refer to the next section; for the third prediction about team coordination, refer to Ch. 6.
23 With a mean AMC duration of 53 seconds versus 143.2 seconds for all leaders.
24 With a mean AMC duration of 275 seconds versus 143.2 seconds for all leaders.
25 Because of interrater reliability problems, this subcategory was not included on all studies.
26 In which one or more categories occurred during that interval.
27 Because of double-coding (in which the coders identified all the categories that occurred), the sum of the rates can be greater than 1.0.
28 Preliminary examination of skippers in the bottom one-third (those obtaining the slowest hoist scores) show that the bottom group spent more time on work-related discussion just as they approached the upwind mark rounding. Instead of attending to the crew's performance as the skippers in the top group, these lackluster skippers continued to dwell on work details (e.g., the mark, the other boats) as opposed to performance (e.g., how the team should hoist the chute).

5 RESEARCH ON THE MODEL: WHY THE MODEL WORKS

1 Refer to Ch. 4 for the results regarding the impact of monitoring alone on performance.

2 Refer to Ch. 4 for test of another hypothesis.

3 Detailed in Ch. 3 and distinguished in the OSTI from *nonwork-related*, which does not deal with the work. *Work-related* concerns the work but not performance, and *performance-related* can involve the leader herself (own performance) or deal with others (e.g., when the leader provides antecedents, monitors, and consequences to others).

4 Refer to Tables 5.4 and 7.9.

5 It is interesting to compare the first four intervals of Table 5.2 with the last five. In the fifth interval (20), the manager talks about the work and then, in the next three intervals, provides a set of antecedents that is followed by the subordinate talking about the work. Given this pattern, one might speculate what would occur after the subordinate discussed the work-related topic of the manager's schedule.

6 Brewer, Sochia, and Potter (1996) show that males are more likely than females to provide specific negative feedback, suggesting that the gender of the sender may play a role.

7 This may have occurred because a group rather than a pair was interacting. The exchanges were sometimes fast and furious, with people often talking simultaneously.

8 The lag sequential analyses also indicated that leaders' monitoring of performance during group meetings set into motion positive, negative and neutral reports by subordinates about their own performances, but primarily negative reports of their reportees' performance.

9 Evidence from Study 15 bears this out as well. Instead of focusing on the crew's performance, these ineffective leaders would get distracted and talk about what strategies to take at the next mark.

10 Refer to Innovative Ideas Measure in Ch. 4.

11 Our plan is to add more pairs, and to design a measure to assess crew effectiveness.

12 For an extended exchange on another film shoot, refer to Table 7.9.

13 In later formulations, operant researchers refer to "establishing operations" in which an event "A" serves to establish another event "B" as an effective form of reinforcement (Keller & Schoenfeld, 1950; Millenson, 1967). For instance, event A might be the manager monitoring, while event B is her delivery of a neutral consequence. Regrettably, research is scant on how this dynamic works. More studies are needed to determine if evidence exists to support this explanation.

14 Discussed earlier in Ch. 4, along with Study 10.

15 As well as some predispositions and experiences on the part of one of the authors.

16 Intriguingly, little commensurate research has been done on the positive emotions of ecstasy and elation.

17 Like Masson and McCarthy (1995), we disagree.

18 Our emotional responses to receiving antecedents, acting on them in good faith and then being denied our just due are not limited to work settings. We can see the effect with anyone who delivers an antecedent, whether a parent, lover, teacher, friend, co-worker, or subordinate. Antecedents, indicating "I want you to do something for me," trigger a chain of expectations and subsequent affective reactions about how a person "should" be treated after doing what has been requested.

19 Some evidence exists for this in Study 5b. Managers whose workers were the least satisfied with their job security monitored the least often, $r = .82$ to $.87$.

6   RESEARCH ON THE MODEL: BOUNDARIES AND BREADTH OF THE MODEL

1 The inclusion of moderators in operant-inspired models such as ours is a rarity. Individual differences such as workers' knowledge, skills, and abilities are seldom a topic of discussion (Kazdin, 1989; Miller, 1997; Sulzer-Azaroff & Mayer, 1991). The context in which operant conditioners typically operate helps explain this omission. Rarely have hospital and school administrators been able to afford the luxury of rejecting or selecting program participants, based on demographic characteristics. Instead, they must work within the system, ensuring that reinforcement programs will work with proper attention to the correct contingencies.
2 Or in the case of execution-type tasks, the proportion of the task considered execution; in the case of the maintenance stage, the proportion of the stage considered maintenance.
3 Fortunately, some progress has been made. Study 7 identified circumstances under which managers are most and least likely to provide monitors and consequences.
4 Other classification systems have been used by developmental psychologists. They distinguish among theories depending on their functional area or facet of development. Theories by Freud (1960) and Erikson (1963), for example, are subsumed under the personality development category, Piaget's theory (1977) under cognitive, Shirley's (1931) under motor, and Gibson's (1984) under perceptual. The assumption is that some theories are more useful than other theories in explaining different functional areas of the developmental process. Piaget's (1977) ideas about the attainment of the formal operational stage help to explain children's cognitive development, whereas these ideas would be less useful in explaining motor development.
5 Originally presented in Ch. 4, as were Study 6, 5a, 5b.
6 Refer to Figure 4.2 for sailboat racing course.
7 The correlation between the SEM and the STEM was not significant, suggesting that the two were not tapping overlapping constructs, $r = .17$, $p = .40$. Further details are in Ch. 4.
8 Windward, leeward, twice around.
9 Correlation was negative because effective leaders were those with the smallest (lowest) number of points in the series or the fastest (lowest) chute-hoisting times.
10 Both "hard" and "soft" measures were used. The former included financial indices. The latter included ratings from peers, superiors, and subordinates as well as sources in the investment community.
11 The exception is Study 4, conducted in Australia.
12 One of the Finnish co-investigators agreed, spontaneously noting: "If then . . . ."

7   TAKING STOCK

1 Forestalling objections that both supervisory methods and employee qualifications are important components, Gellerman (1976) counters that ". . . supervisors less effective than [Charlie], working on the same shift and with essentially the same level of experience among their workers, cannot match [Charlie's] sustained productive output, while more skilled supervisors than [Lonnie], also in the same shift and with the same caliber of employees, consistently out-produce him" (p. 95).
2 Compare with exchanges of another film crew in Table 5.5.
3 Both the director and DP are assumed to be leaders here, with their comments being treated as interchangeable; when one leader gives an antecedent and the

other leader gives the monitor and consequence, it is still considered an AMC sequence. This interchangeability is in line with the way in which we calculated AMC sequences with the leaders aboard the boats in Table 3.3.

8 IMPLICATIONS FOR FUTURE THEORY, RESEARCH, AND PRACTICE

1 Rock has provided venture capital to help finance companies such as Fairchild, Teledyne, Intel, and Apple. He estimates that in the past thirty years, he has looked at roughly three hundred business plans a year. Of those, he may invest in one or two annually.

2 Rock contends that it was not a lack of expertise on the part of the president; given his technical background; he should have known.

3 Described in Ch. 7 and illustrated in Table 7.7 Study 3, described in Ch. 4, in which antecedents were found to fit the pattern of classic suppressor variable also provides another intriguing perspective.

4 That of measuring performance in motivational programs.

5 Where performance = the percentage of time spent on antecedents, monitors, consequences, and own performance.

6 Although some would disagree, having identified leadership as "antithetical to scholarship" (Lee, 1996).

7 As described in Ch. 3.

8 Assuming that information on AMC sequences or other comparable information were not available.

9 Other evidence exists as well. One work sample measure was developed, for maintenance mechanics, in which mechanics performed one of four tasks (e.g., disassembling and repairing a gearbox) (Campion, 1972). The investigators found that in contrast to the paper-and-pencil tests, the only predictor of supervisory evaluations of job success was performance on the work sample measure.

10 Table 4.4 shows that as many as two-thirds of the monitors delivered by effective managers are via self-report.

11 Some researchers (e.g., Aiello & Svec, 1993) have studied electronic monitoring. But their definition of monitoring does not coincide with our definition, which assumes that an *individual* collects the information.

12 Although some writers (Farson, 1987) have expressed quite vehement reactions to being praised, harking back to childhood when one's parent used the "sandwich" approach in which a few words of praise inevitably led to a scolding.

13 Or one could use another test, and see whether or not all of the managers who are marginally effective are in the insufficient and the excessive groups. The next step would be to identify whether or not the relationships between supervisory effectiveness and monitoring and consequences are curvilinear. While a discussion of advanced curve fitting is beyond the scope of this book, mathematical operations such as fitting a non-linear function such as a quadratic (Cohen & Cohen, 1975) could be used.

14 This method is purely probabilistic; it assumes a given percentage of managers in every organization fall outside the acceptable range. But this assumption may not be tenable in every organization. One could argue that successful firms would be less likely to have ineffective managers than would troubled organizations. Another potential problem is that the range of time managers spend may be tightly clustered around the mean in some organizations.

15 We have done this for select groups, as discussed in Ch. 4.

16 Actually, groups of leaders consisting of at least two, a helmsman and a tactician and/or crew boss.

17 Refer to Chapter 4 for discussion of the STEM.
18 Correlations of these predictors with the criterion are shown in Tables 4.8, 4.10, and 4.11.
19 Though the correlation between the criterion and the MC sequence was − .35, it was not significant, as shown on Table 4.10.

References

Adams, J. S. (1965). Inequity in social exchange. In L. Berkowitz (Ed.), *Advances in experimental social psychology* (Vol. 2, pp. 267–299). New York: Academic Press.

Aiello, J. R. and Svec, C. M. (1993). Computer monitoring of work performance: Extending the social facilitation framework to electronic presence. *Journal of Applied Psychology, 23*, 537–548.

Amabile, T. M. (1988). A model of creativity and innovation in organizations. In B. M. Staw and L. L. Cummings (Eds.), *Research in Organizational Behavior, 10*, 169–211.

Anderson, R. C. and Faust, G. W. (1973). *Educational psychology*. New York: Dodd, Mead, & Co.

Anderson, N. and King, N. (1993). Innovation in organizations. In C.L. Cooper and I.T. Robertson (Eds.), *International Review of Industrial and Organizational Psychology, 8*, 1–34.

Anderson, R. C., Kulhavy, R. W. and Andre, T. (1971). Feedback procedures in programmed instruction. *Journal of Educational Psychology, 62*, 148–156.

Andrasik, F. (1979). Organizational behavior modification in business settings: A methodological and content review. *Journal of Organizational Behavior Management, 2*, 85–102.

Argyris, C. (1973). *Intervention theory and method*. Reading, MA: Addison-Wesley.

Aristotle (1952). Politics, Book V, Chapter 9, Verse 33 (B. Jowett, trans.). In R. M. Hutchins (Ed.), *Great books of the Western world*. Chicago: Encyclopedia Britannica. (Original work "published" about 350 BC).

Arnett, J. (1969). *Feedback and human behavior*. Baltimore, MD: Penguin.

Arrow, K., Chenery, H. B., Minhas, B. and Solow, R. M. (1961). Capital-labor substitution and economic efficiency. *The Review of Economics and Statistics, 43*, 225–247.

Arvey, R. D. and Jones, A. P. (1985). The use of discipline in organizational settings: A framework for future research. *Research in Organizational Behavior, 5*, 367–408.

Ayllon, T. and Azrin, N. (1968). *The token economy: A motivational system for therapy and rehabilitation*. New York: Appleton-Century-Crofts.

Azrin, N. H. and Holz, W. C. (1966). Punishment. In W. K. Honig (Ed.), *Operant behavior: Areas of research and application* (pp. 380–447). New York: Appleton-Century-Crofts.

Azrin, N. H., Hutchinson, R. R. and Hake, D. F. (1966). Extinction-induced aggression. *Journal of Experimental Analysis of Behavior, 9*, 191–204.

Babb, H. W. and Kopp, D. G. (1978). Applications of behavior modification in organizations: A review and a critique. *Academy of Management Review, 3*, 281–292.

Baer, D. M., Wolf, M. M. and Risley, T. R. (1968). Some current dimensions of applied behavior analysis. *Journal of Applied Behavior Analysis, 1*, 91–97.

Bakeman, R. and Dabbs, R. M., Jr. (1976). Social interaction observed: Some approaches to the analysis of behavior streams. *Personality and Social Psychology Bulletin, 2,* 335–345.

Baker, D. P. and Salas, E. (1992). Principles for measuring teamwork skills. *Human Factors, 34,* 469–475.

Baldwin, T. T. and Padgett, M. Y. (1993). Management development: A review and commentary. In C. L. Cooper and I. T. Robertson (Eds.), *International review of industrial/organizational psychology* (Vol. 8, pp. 35–85). New York: Wiley.

Bandura, A. (1986). *Social foundations of thought and action: A social cognitive theory.* Englewood Cliffs, NJ: Prentice Hall.

Barley, S. R. (1990). Images of imaging: Notes on doing longitudinal field work. Special Issue: for studying processes of organizational change. *Organization Science, 1,* 220–247.

Baron, R. A. (1988). Negative effects of destructive criticism: Impact on conflict, self-efficacy, and task performance. *Journal of Applied Psychology, 73,* 200–206.

Barron, F. (1955). The disposition toward originality. *Journal of Abnormal and Social Psychology, 51,* 478–485.

Bartow, A. (1988). *The director's voice* [Interviews with A. Brown, pp. 20–35, Z. Fichhandler, pp. 105–127, M. W. Mason, pp. 194–211, L. Richards, pp. 255–268, P. Sellers, pp. 269–285, and A. Serban, pp. 286–299]. New York: Theatre Communications Group.

Bass, B. M. (1981). *Stogdill's handbook of leadership.* New York: Free Press.

Bass, B. M. (1985, Winter). Leadership: Good, better, best. *Organizational Dynamics, 13,* 26–40.

Bass, B. M. (1990). *Handbook of leadership: A survey of theory and research.* New York: Free Press.

Bass, B. M. and Barrett, G. V. (1981). *People, work and organizations* (2nd edn). Boston: Allyn & Bacon.

Bateman, T. S. and Organ, D. W. (1983). Job satisfaction and the good soldier: The relationship between affect and employee "citizenship." *Academy of Management Journal, 26,* 587–595.

Becker, W. C. (1974). Teaching concepts and operations, or how to make kids smart. In R. Ulrich, T. Stachnik and J. Mabry, *Control of human behavior* (Vol. 3). Glenview, IL: Scott, Foresman.

Becker, W. C., Madsen, C. H., Jr., Arnold, C. R. and Thomas, D. R. (1967). The contingent use of teacher attention and praise in reducing classroom behavior problems. *The Journal of Special Education, 1,* 286–307.

Beer, S. (1959). *Cybernetics and management.* New York: Wiley.

Bennis, W. G. (1959). Leadership theory and administrative behavior: The problem of authority. *Administrative Science Quarterly, 4,* 259–260.

Bernard, H. R., Killworth, P. D. and Sailer, L. (1979/80). Informant accuracy in social network data IV: A comparison of clique-level structure in behavioral and cognitive network data. *Social Network, 2,* 191–218.

Bernardin, H. J. and Beatty, R. W. (1984). *Performance appraisal: Assessing human behavior at work.* Boston: Kent Publishing.

Bernstein, N. and Bruni, F. (1995, December 24). She suffered in plain sight but alarms were ignored. *New York Times,* pp. 1, 22.

Bettenhausen, K. L. (1991). Five years of groups research: What we have learned and what needs to be addressed. *Journal of Management, 17,* 345–381.

Binning, J. F. and Barrett, G. V. (1989). Validity of personnel decisions: A conceptual analysis of the inferential and evidential bases. *Journal of Applied Psychology, 74,* 478–494.

Blake, R. R., Mouton, J. S. and Allen, R. L. (1987). *Spectacular teamwork: How to develop the leadership skills for team success.* New York: Wiley.

Blanchard, K. H. and Johnson, S. (1982). *The one minute manager*. New York: Morrow.

Block, R. A. (Ed.). (1990). *Cognitive models of psychological time*. Hillsdale, NJ: Lawrence Erlbaum.

Blood, M. R., Graham, W. K. and Zedeck, S. (1987). Resolving compensation disputes with three-party job evaluation. *Applied Psychology: An International Review, 36*, 41–46.

Blum, M. L. and Naylor, J. C. (1968). *Industrial psychology* (rev. edn). New York: Harper & Row.

Borman, W. C. (1978). Exploring upper limits of reliability and validity in job performance ratings. *Journal of Applied Psychology, 63*, 135–144.

Borman, W. C. (1983). Implications of personality theory and research for the rating of work performance in organizations. In F. Landy, S. Zedeck and J. Cleveland (Eds.), *Performance measurement and theory* (pp. 127–165). Hillsdale, NJ: Lawrence Erlbaum.

Borman, W. C. (1991). Job behavior, performance, and effectiveness. In M. D. Dunnette and L. M. Hough (Eds.). *Handbook of industrial and organizational psychology*, *Vol.2* (2nd edn, pp. 271–326). Palo Alto, CA: Consulting Psychologists Press.

Borman, W. C., Pulakos, E. D. and Motowidlo, S. J. (1986, August). *Toward a general model of soldier effectiveness: Focusing on the common elements of performance*. Paper presented at the annual meeting of the American Psychological Association, Washington, DC.

Braukmann, C. J., Kirigin, K. A. and Wolf, M. M. (1976, September). *Achievement place: The researchers' perspective*. Paper presented at the meeting of the American Psychological Association, Washington, DC.

Bray, D. W., Campbell, R. J. and Grant, D. L. (1974). *Formative years in business: A long-term AT&T study of managerial lives*. New York: Wiley.

Bray, D.W. and Grant, D.L. (1966). The assessment center in the measurement of potential for business management, *Psychological Monographs, 80*, 17.

Brewer, N. (1995). The effects of monitoring individual and group performance on the distribution of effort across tasks. *Journal of Applied Social Psychology, 25*, 760–777.

Brewer, N., Sochia, L. and Potter, R. (1996). Gender differences in supervisors' use of performance feedback. *Journal of Applied Social Psychology, 26*, 786–803.

Brewer, N., Wilson, C. and Beck, K. (1994). Supervisory behaviour and team performance amongst police patrol sergeants. *Journal of Occupational and Organizational Psychology, 67*, 69–78.

Brislin, R. W., Lonner, W. J. and Thorndike, R. M. (1973). *Cross-cultural research methods*. New York: Wiley.

Burke, M. J. and Day, R. R. (1986). A cumulative study of the effectiveness of management training. *Journal of Applied Psychology, 71*, 232–245.

Burns, J. M. (1984). *The power to lead*. New York: Simon & Schuster.

Burns, T. (1954). The directions of activity and communication in a departmental executive group: A quantitative study in a British engineering factory with a self-recording technique. *Human Relations, 1*, 73–97.

Burns, T. (1957). Management in action. *Operational Research Quarterly, 8*, 45–60.

Burt, W. H. (1957). *Mammals of the Great Lakes region*. Ann Arbor: University of Michigan.

Campbell, J. P. (1971). Personnel training and development. *Annual Review of Psychology, 22*, 565–602.

Campbell, J. P. (1977). The cutting edge of leadership: An overview. In J. G. Hunt, and L. L. Larson (Eds.), *Leadership: The cutting edge* (pp. 221–234). Carbondale: Southern Illinois University Press.

Campbell, J. P., Dunnette, M. D., Arvey, R. D. and Hellervik, L. V. (1973). The development and evaluation of behaviorally based rating scales. *Journal of Applied Psychology, 57*, 15–22.

Campbell, J. A., Dunnette, M. D., Lawler, E. E., III and Weick, K. E. (1970). *Managerial behavior, performance, and effectiveness*. New York: McGraw-Hill.

Campion, J. (1972). Work sampling for personnel selection. *Journal of Applied Psychology, 56*, 40–44.

Campion, M. A., Medsker, G. J. and Higgs, A. C. (1993, Winter). Relations between work group characteristics and effectiveness: Implications for designing effective groups. *Personnel Psychology, 46*, 823–850.

Carey, M. (1985). *How workers get their training* (US Bureau of Labor Statistics Bull. No. 2226). Washington, DC: US Government Printing Office.

Carr, I. (1992). *Keith Jarrett: The man and his music*. New York: Da Capo Press.

Cascio, W. F. (1987). *Applied psychology in personnel management* (3rd edn). Englewood Cliffs, NJ: Prentice-Hall.

Castellan, N. J. (1979). The analysis of behavior sequences. In R. B. Cairns (Ed.), *The analysis of social interactions: Methods, issues, and illustrations* (pp. 81–116). Hillsdale, NJ: Erlbaum Associates.

Cherrington, D. J., Reitz, H. J. and Scott, W. E., Jr. (1971). Effects of contingent and noncontingent reward on the relationship between satisfaction and task performance. *Journal of Applied Psychology, 55*, 531–536.

Clausen, A. W. (1980). Listening and responding to employees' concerns; interview by D. W. Ewing and P. M. Banks. *Harvard Business Review, 58*, 101–114.

Coates, T. J. and Thoresen, C. E. (1978). Using generalizability theory in behavioral observation. *Behavior Theory, 9*, 605–613.

Cobb, J. A. and Ray, R. S. (1976). The classroom behavior observation code. In E. J. Mash and L. G. Terdal (Eds.), *Behavior therapy assessment* (pp. 286–294). New York: Springer.

Coch, L. and French, J. R. P., Jr. (1948). Overcoming resistance to change. *Human Relations, 1*, 512–532.

Cofer, C. N. and Appley, M. H. (1968). *Motivation: Theory and research*. New York: Wiley.

Cohen, J. (1960). A coefficient of agreement for nominal scales. *Educational and Psychological Measurement, 20*, 37–46.

Cohen, J. and Cohen, P. (1975). *Applied multiple regression*. New York: Wiley.

Conger, J. C. and Farrell, A. D. (1981). Behavioral components of heterosocial skills. *Behavior Theory, 12*, 41–55.

Conger, A. J. and Jackson, D. N. (1972). Suppressor variables, prediction, and the interpretation of psychological relationships. *Educational and Psychological Measurement, 32*, 579–599.

Conner, D. and Levitt, M. (1992). *Sail like a champion*. New York: St Martin's Press.

Cook, D. M. (1968). The impact on managers of frequency of feedback. *Academy of Management Journal, 11*, 263–277.

Cook, T. D. and Campbell, D. T. (1979). *Quasi-experimentation: Design and analysis issues for field settings*. Boston, MA: Houghton Mifflin.

Cooper, G. E., White, M. D. and Lauber, J. K. (Eds.). (1979, June). *Resource management on the flight deck* (NASA Report No. CP- 2120). Moffett Field, CA: NASA-Ames Research Center. (NTIS No. N80- 22283)

Covey, S. R. (1989). *The seven habits of highly effective people*. New York: Fireside.

Cowan, G. S., Conger, J. C. and Conger, A. J. (1989). Social competency and social perceptivity in self and others. *Journal of Psychopathology and Behavior Assessment, 11*, 129–142.

Cronbach, L. J., Gleser, G. C., Nanda, H. and Rajarathnam, N. (1972). *The dependability of behavioral measures*. New York: Wiley.

Dabbs, R. M., Jr. (1983). Fourier analysis and the rhythm of conversation. Educational Research Information Clearinghouse (ERIC) Document no. ED 222 959.

Daniels, A. C. (1989). *Performance management: Improving quality productivity through positive reinforcement* (3rd edn). Tucker, GA: Performance Management.

Daniels, A. C. (1994). *Bringing out the best in people*. New York: McGraw–Hill.

Dansereau, F., Jr., Graen, G. and Haga, J. (1975). A vertical dyad linkage approach to leadership within formal organizations: A longitudinal investigation of the role making process. *Organizational Behavior and Human Performance, 13*, 46–78.

Darwin, C. R. (1872). *The expression of the emotions in man and animals*. London: Friedmann; reprint, Chicago and London: University of Chicago Press, 1965.

Datel, W. and Legters, L. (1971). The psychology of the army recruit. *Journal of Biological Psychology, 12(2)*, 34–40.

Davis, K. (1968). Attitudes toward the legitimacy of management efforts to influence employees. *Academy of Management Journal, 11*, 153–162.

Dawson, J. L. M. (1971). Theory and research in cross-cultural psychology. *Bulletin of the British Psychological Society, 24*, 291–306.

DeParle, J. (1996, January 28). Newt's endgame. *New York Times Magazine, 6*, 35–66.

DeVries, D. L., Morrison, A. M., Shullman, S. L. and Gerlach, M. L. (1986). *Performance appraisal on the line*. Greensboro, NC: A Center for Creative Leadership.

Dicken, C. (1963). Good impression, social desirability, and acquiescence as suppressor variables. *Educational and Psychological Measurement, 23*, 699–720.

Dillon, S. (1994, January 20). Cortines says bad schools are facing takeovers. *New York Times*, p. B3.

Dinesen, I. (1938). *Out of Africa*. New York: Random House.

Dowell, B. E. and Wexley, K. N. (1978). Development of a work behavior taxonomy for first line supervisors. *Journal of Applied Psychology, 63*, 563–572.

Dubin, R. (1969). *Theory building*. New York: Free Press.

Dunnette, M. D. (1963). A note on the criterion. *Journal of Applied Psychology, 47*, 251–254.

Dyer, J. L. (1984). Team research and team training: A state-of-the-art review. In F. A. Muckler (Ed.), *Human factors review: 1984* (pp. 285–323). Santa Monica, CA: Human Factors Society.

Eichenwald, K. (1996, November 10). The two faces of Texaco. *New York Times*, pp. E2, F10–11.

Elizur, D. (1987). Effect of feedback on verbal and non-verbal courtesy in a bank setting. *Applied Psychology: An International Review, 36*, 147–156.

Erez, M. (1994). Toward a model of cross-cultural industrial and organizational psychology. In H. C. Triandis, M. D. Dunnette, and L. M. Hough (Eds.), *Handbook of industrial and organizational psychology, Vol. 4* (2nd edn, pp. 559–607). Palo Alto, CA: Consulting Psychologists Press.

Erikson, E. (1963). *Childhood and society* (2nd edn). New York: Norton.

Fairhurst, G. T., Graen, S. G., and Snavely, B. K. (1984). Face support in controlling peer performance. *Human Communication Research, 11*, 272–295.

Fairhurst, G. T., Rogers, L. E. and Sarr, R. A. (1987). Manager-subordinate control patterns and judgments about the relationship. In M. McLaughlin (Ed.), *Communication yearbook, 10* (pp. 395–415). Beverly Hills, CA: Sage.

Faraone, S. V. and Dorfman, D. D. (1987). Lag sequential analysis: Robust statistical methods. *Psychological Bulletin, 101*, 312–323.

Farkas, C. M. and Wetlaufer, S. (1996, May–June). The ways chief executive officers lead. *Harvard Business Review, 74*, 110–122.

Farson, R. E. (1987). Praise reappraised. In *People: Managing your most important asset* (pp. 103–108). Boston, MA: Harvard Business Review.

Feingold, M. (1996, June 11). Other people's plays. *Village Voice*, p. 77.

Ferster, C. B. and Culbertson, S. A. (1982). *Behavior principles*. Englewood Cliffs, NJ: Prentice Hall.

Festinger, L. (1954). A theory of social comparison processes. *Human relations, 7*, 117–140.

Fiedler, F. E. (1967). *A theory of leader effectiveness*. New York: McGraw-Hill.

Finn, C. D. (1996, February 6). Will "efficacy" help New York's schools? *New York Times*, pp. A23.

Firestone, D. (1996, April 30). Two child welfare employees are suspended in abuse death. *New York Times*, pp. 1, B5.

Fisher, C. D. (1979). Transmission of positive and negative feedback to subordinates: A laboratory investigation. *Journal of Applied Psychology, 64*, 533–540.

Fisher, B. M. and Edwards, J. E. (1988). Consideration and initiating structure and their relationships with leader effectiveness: A meta-analysis. *Proceedings of the Academy of Management*, 201–205.

Fleishman, E. A. (1953). The description of supervisory behavior. *Personnel Psychology, 37*, 1–6.

Fleishman, E. A. (1973). Twenty years of consideration and structure. In E. A. Fleishman and J. G. Hunt (Eds.), *Current developments in the study of leadership* (pp. 1–37). Carbondale: Southern Illinois University Press.

Fleishman, E. A., Harris, E. F. and Burtt, H. E. (1955). *Leadership and supervision in industry*. Columbus, OH: Bureau of Educational Research, Ohio State University.

Fleishman, E. A. and Hunt, J. G. (Eds.). (1973). *Current developments in the study of leadership*. Carbondale: Southern Illinois University Press.

Fleishman, E. A. and Quaintance, M. K. (1984). *Taxonomies of human performance: The description of human tasks*. New York: Academic Press.

Folger, R. and Greenberg, J. (1985). Procedural justice: An interpretive analysis of personnel systems. In K. Rowland and Ferris (Eds.), *Research in personnel and human resources management*. Greenwich, CT: JAI Press.

Foushee, H. C. (1984). Dyads and triads at 35,000 feet: Factors affecting group process and aircrew performance. *American Psychologist, 39*, 885–893.

Foushee, H. C. and Manos, K. L. (1981, September). Information transfer within the cockpit: Problems in intracockpit communications. In C. E. Bilings and E. S. Cheaney (Eds.), *Information transfer problems in the aviation system* (NASA Report No. TP–1875). Moffett Field, CA: NASA–Ames Research Center. (NTIS No. N81–31162)

Fox, D. K., Hopkins, B. L. and Anger, W. K. (1987). The long-term effects of a token economy on safety performance in open-pit mining. *Journal of Applied Behavior Analysis, 20*, 215–224.

Frederikson, L. W. (1982). *Handbook of organizational behavior management*. New York: Wiley.

Freud, S. (1960). *The ego and the id* (J. Strachey, trans.). New York: W. W. Norton. (Original work published 1927).

Gabarro, J.J. (1987). The development of working relationships. In J. W. Lorsch (Ed.), *Handbook of Organizational Behavior* (pp. 172–189). Englewood Cliffs, NJ: Prentice Hall.

Gali, J. (1992). How well does the IS-LM model fit postwar US data? *The Quarterly Journal of Economics, 107*, 710–738.

Gardner, J. W. (1990). *On leadership*. New York: Free Press.

Gargan, E. A. (1996, February 18). The Chinese are coming. Wait. They are already here. *New York Times*, pp. 41, 45, 46.

Gates, G. S. (1926). An observational study of anger. *Journal of Experimental Psychology, 9*, 325–336.

Gellerman, S. W. (1976, March-April). Supervision: Substance and style. *Harvard Business Review, 54*, 89–99.

Gevgilili, A., Komaki, J. and Chu, S. (1996, March). Research in innovation. In D. A. Hantula (Chair), *Advances in organizational behavior analysis*. Symposium conducted at the meeting of the Eastern Psychological Association, Philadelphia, PA.

Gibson, E. J. (1984). Perceptual development from the ecological approach. In M. E. Lamb, A. L. Brown and B. Rogoff (Eds.), *Advances in developmental psychology*, (Vol. 3, pp. 243–285). Hillsdale, NJ: Erlbaum.

Gilbert, T. F. (1978). *Human competence; engineering worthy performance*. New York: McGraw-Hill.

Gladwell, M. (1996, November 10). The science of shopping. *New Yorker*, 65–75.

Goldstein, I. L. (1980). Training in work organizations. *Annual Review of Psychology, 31*, 229–270.

Goltz, S. M. (1993). Dynamic of leaders' and subordinates' performance-related discussions following monitoring by leaders in group meetings. *Leadership Quarterly, 4* (2), 173–187.

Goodman, P. S., Raulin, E. C., and Argote, L. (1986). Current thinking chout group: Setting the stage for new ideas. In P. S. Goodman & Associates, *Designing effective work groups* (pp. 120–167). San Francisco, CA: Jossey-Bass.

Gottman, J. M. (1979). *Marital interactions*. New York: Academic Press.

Gottman, J. M. and Bakeman, R. (1979). The sequential analysis of observational data. In M. E. Lamb, S. J. Suomi and G. R. Stephenson (Eds.), *Social interaction analysis: Methodological issues* (pp. 185–206). Madison: University of Wisconsin.

Graen, G. B. and Schiemann, W. (1978). Leader–member agreement: A vertical dyad linkage approach, *Journal of Applied Psychology, 63*, 206–212.

Graen, G. B. and Uhl-Bien, M. (1995). Relationship-based approach to leadership: Development of leader–member exchange (LMX) theory of leadership over 25 years: Applying a multi-level multi-domain perspective. *Leadership Quarterly, 6* (2), 219–247.

Grinde, O. (1982). Rolf Jacobsen: Poet of silence and light. *Scandinavian Review, 70*, 50–51.

Guzzo, R. A. and Shea G. P. (1992). Group performance and intergroup relations in organizations. In M. D. Dunnette and L. M. Hough (Eds.), *Handbook of industrial and organizational psychology, Vol. 3* (2nd edn, pp. 269–313). Palo Alto, CA: Consulting Psychologists Press.

Hackman, J. R. (1987). The design of work teams. In J. W. Lorsch (Ed.), *Handbook of organizational behavior* (pp. 315–342). Englewood Cliffs, NJ: Prentice-Hall.

Hackman, J. R. and Morris, C. G. (1975). Group tasks, group interaction process, and group performance effectiveness: A review and proposed integration. In L. Berkowitz (Ed.), *Advances in experimental psychology*. New York: Academic Press.

Hackman, J. R. and Morris, C. G. (1978). Group process and group effectiveness: A reappraisal. In L. Berkowitz (Ed.), *Group processes* (pp. 57–66). New York: Academic Press.

Hackman, J. R. and Oldham, G. R. (1980). *Work redesign*. Reading, MA: Addison-Wesley.

Hackman, J. R. and Walton, R. E. (1986). Leading groups in organizations. In P. S. Goodman and Associates (Eds.), *Designing effective work groups* (pp. 72–119). San Francisco, CA: Jossey-Bass.

Halpin, A. W. (1957). The leader behavior and effectiveness of aircraft commanders. In R. M. Stogdill and A. E. Coons (Eds.), *Leader behavior: Its description and measurement*. Columbus, OH: Bureau of Business Research, Ohio State University.

Halpin, A. W. and Winer, B. J. (1957). A factorial study of the leader behavior descriptions. In R. M. Stogdill and A. E. Coons (Eds.), *Leader behavior: Its description and measurement* (pp. 39–51). Columbus, OH: Bureau of Business Research, Ohio State University.

Hammer, M. (1985). Implications of behavioral and cognitive reciprocity in social network data. *Social Networks, 7*, 189–201.

Hammer, T. H. and Currall, S. C. (1989, April). From fieldnotes to numbers: The analysis of management and labor power strategies in the board room. In *Joining qualitative data collection with quantitative analysis*. Symposium conducted at the conference of the Society for Industrial and Organizational Psychology, Boston, MA.

Harrison, K. (1996, November 10). Death at an early age. *New York Times Book Review*, p. 15.

Hartmann, D. P. (1977). Considerations in the choice of interobserver reliability estimates. *Journal of Applied Behavior Analysis, 10*, 103–116.

Haussknecht, T. and Kuenzer, P. (1990). An experimental study of the building behavior sequence of a shell-breeding Cichlid-fish from Lake Tanganyika (Lamprologus Ocellatus). *Behavior, 116*, 127–142.

Hebb, D. O. (1955). Drives and the CNS (Conceptual Nervous System). *Psychological Review, 62*, 243–254.

Hempel, C. G. (1966). *Philosophy of natural science*. Englewood Cliffs, NJ: Prentice Hall.

Hemphill, J. K. (1959, September-October). Job descriptions for executives. *Harvard Business Review, 37*, 55–67.

Hemphill, J. K. and Coons, A. E. (1957). Development of the leader behavior description questionnaire. In R. M. Stogdill and A. E. Coons (Eds.), *Leader behavior: Its description and measurement* (pp. 6–38). Columbus, OH: Bureau of Business Research, Ohio State University.

Herbert, R. (1994, December 18). Can so many be wrong? *New York Times*, p. E15.

Hermann, J. A., de Montes, A. I., Dominguez, B., Montes, F. and Hopkins, B. L. (1973). Effects of bonuses for punctuality on the tardiness of industrial workers. *Journal of Applied Behavior Analysis, 6*, 563–570.

Herold, D. M. and Parsons, C. K. (1985). Assessing the feedback environment in work organizations: Development of the job feedback survey. *Journal of Applied Psychology, 70*, 290–305.

Herring, H. B. (1996, October 31). A whole planet for a patient. *New York Times*, pp. C1, C10.

Herzberg, F. (1968). One more time: How do you motivate employees? *Harvard Business Review, 46*, 53–62.

Hinrichs, J. R. (1976). Communications activity of industrial research personnel. *Personnel Psychology, 17*, 193–204.

Hofstede, G. (1984). The cultural relativity of the quality of life concept. *Academy of Management Review, 9*, 389–398.

Hollander, E. P. and Offerman, L. R. (1990). Power and leadership in organizations. Relationships in transition. *American Psychologist, 45*, 179–189.

Honey, P. (1978). *Face to face*. Englewood Cliffs, NJ: Prentice Hall.

Honig, W. K. (1966). *Operant behavior: Areas of research and application*. New York: Appleton-Century-Crofts.

Hopkins, B. L. and Sears, J. (1982). Managing behavior for productivity. In L. W. Frederiksen (Ed.), *Handbook of organizational behavior management*. New York: Wiley.

Horne, J. H. and Lupton, T. (1965). The work activities of "middle" managers: An exploratory study. *Journal of Management Studies, 2*, 14–33.

Horst, P. (1941). *The prediction of personal adjustment*. New York: Social Science Research Council.

Horst, P. (1966). *Psychological measurement and prediction*. Belmont, CA: Wadsworth.

House, R. J. (1977). A 1976 theory of charismatic leadership. In J. G. Hunt and L. L. Larson (Eds.), *Leadership: The cutting edge* (pp. 189–207). Carbondale Southern Illinois University Press.

House, R. J. and Mitchell, T. R. (1974, Fall). Path-goal theory of leadership. *Contemporary Business*, 81–98.

House, R. J., Spangler, W. D. and Woycke J. (1991). Personality and charisma in the US presidency: A psychological theory of leadership effectiveness. *Administrative Science Quarterly, 36*, 364–396.

Howard, A., Shudo, K. and Umeshima, M. (1983). Motivation and values among Japanese and American managers. *Personnel Psychology, 36*, 883–898.

Hundal, P. S. (1969). Knowledge of performance as an incentive in repetitive industrial work. *Journal of Applied Psychology, 53*, 224–226.

Hutchinson, R. R. (1977). By-products of aversive control. In W. K. Honig and J. E. R. Staddon (Eds.), *Handbook of operant behavior* (pp. 415–431). Englewood Cliffs, NJ: Prentice-Hall.

Ilgen, D. E., Fisher, C. D. and Taylor, M. S. (1979). Consequences of individual feedback on behavior in organizations. *Journal of Applied Psychology, 64*, 349–371.

Ilgen, D. R. and Knowlton, W. A., Jr. (1980). Performance attributional effects on feedback from superiors. *Organizational Behavior and Human Performance, 25*, 441–456.

Ivancevich, J. M., Donnelly, J. H. and Lyon, H. L. (1970). A study of the impact of management by objectives on perceived need satisfaction. *Personnel Psychology, 23*, 139–151.

Ives, D. (1995, February 26). The ancient Greeks did it; why can't we? *New York Times*, p. H13.

Jahoda, G. (1980). Theoretical and systematic approaches in cross-cultural psychology. In H. C. Triandis and W. W. Lambert (Eds.), *Handbook of cross-cultural psychology* (Vol. 1, Perspectives: pp. 69–141). Boston: Allyn and Bacon.

James, L. R. (1973). Criterion models and construct validity for criteria. *Psychological Bulletin, 80*, 75–83.

James, L. R. and Brett, J. M. (1984). Mediators, moderators, and tests for mediation. *Journal of Applied Psychology, 69*, 307–321.

Janis, I. L. and Mann, L. (1977). *Decision making: A psychological analysis of conflict, choice, and commitment*. New York: Macmillan.

Jensen, M. and Komaki, J. L. (1993, May). Beware of too many directives: Spotting a suppressor variable in the operant model of effective supervision. In J. Cannon-Bowers (Chair), *Optimizing team performance through team leader behavior*. Symposium conducted at the conference of the Society of Industrial and Organizational Psychology, San Francisco, CA.

Jordan, P. (1995, December 10). Belittled big men. *New York Times Magazine*, pp. 68–75.

Jorgenson, D. O., Dunnette, M. D. and Pritchard, R. D. (1973). Effects of the manipulation of a performance-reward contingency on behavior in a simulated work setting. *Journal of Applied Psychology, 57*, 271–280.

Kane, J. S. and Lawler, E. E. (1979). Performance appraisal effectiveness: Its assessment and determinants. *Research in Organizational Behavior, 1*, 425–478.

Kang, K. and Pearce, W. B. (1983). Reticence: a transcultural analysis. *Communication, 8*, 79–106.

Kanki, B. G., Lozito, S. and Foushee, H. C. (1989). Communication indices of crew coordination. *Aviation, Space, and Environmental Medicine, 60*, 56–60.

Kanter, R. M. (1982, July-August). The middle manager as innovator. *Harvard Business Review, 60*, 95–105.

Kanter, R. M. (1988). When a thousand flowers bloom: Structural, collective, and social conditions for innovation in organization. *Research in Organizational Behavior, 10*, 169–211.

Kanter, R. M. (1991, May-June). Transcending business boundaries: 12,000 world managers view change. *Harvard Business Review, 69*, 151–164.

Karau, S. J. and Williams, K. D. (1993). Social loafing: A meta-analytic review and theoretical integration. *Journal of Personality and Social Psychology, 65*, 781–791.

Katz, D. and Kahn, R. L. (1978). *Social psychology of organizations*. New York: Wiley.

Kazdin, A. E. (1989). *Behavior modification in applied settings* (4th edn). Pacific Grove, CA: Brooks/Cole.

Keller, F. S. and Schoenfeld, W. M. (1950). *Principles of psychology: A systematic text in the science of behavior*. New York: Appleton-Century-Crofts.

Kelly, J. R. and McGrath, J. E. (1988). *On time and method*. Newbury Park, CA: Sage Publications, Inc.

Kerr, S. and Schriesheim, S. (1974). Consideration, initiating structure, and organizational criteria: An update of Korman's 1966 review. *Personnel Psychology, 27*, 555–568.

Kim, K. I., Park, H. and Suzuki, N. (1990). Reward allocations in the United States, Japan and Korea: A comparison of individualistic and collectivistic cultures. *Academy of Management Journal, 33*, 188–198.

Klemp, G. O., Munger, M. T. and Spencer, L. M. (1977, August). *Analysis of leadership and management competencies of commissioned and noncommissioned Naval officers in the Pacific and Atlantic fleets* (final report). Boston, MA: McBer & Co.

Knutas, J. (Speaker). (1993, February 7). *60 Minutes*. New York: CBS News. (Obtained from Burrelle's Information Services, Box 7, Livingston, NJ 07039).

Kolata, G. (1995, January 15) . A new way to think about AIDS. *New York Times*, p. 2E.

Komaki, J. L. (1981). A behavioral view of paradigm debates: Let the data speak. *Journal of Applied Psychology, 66*, 111–112.

Komaki, J. L. (1986). Toward effective supervision: An operant analysis and comparison of managers at work. *Journal of Applied Psychology, 71*, 270–279.

Komaki, J. L. (1994). Emergence of the operant model of effective supervision or how an operant conditioner got hooked on leadership. *Leadership & Organization Development Journal, 15*, 27–32.

Komaki, J. L. (1997). Behind the scenes: Field-testing a measure of effectiveness for theater teams. In M. T. Brannick, E. Salas, and C. Prince (Eds.), *Team performance assessment and measurement: Theory, methods and applications*. New York: Springer.

Komaki, J. L. (in press). When performance improvement is the goal: A new set of criteria for criteria. *Journal of Applied Behavior Analysis*.

Komaki, J. L., Barwick, K. D. and Scott, L. R. (1978). A behavioral approach to occupational safety: Pinpointing and reinforcing safety performance in a food manufacturing plant. *Journal of Applied Psychology, 63*, 434–445.

Komaki, J. L. and Citera, M. (1990). Beyond effective supervision: Identifying key interactions between superior and subordinate. *Leadership Quarterly, 1*, 91–105.

Komaki, J. L. and Collins, R. L. (1982). Motivation of preventive maintenance performance. In R. M. O'Brien, A. M. Dickinson, and M. Rosow (Eds.), *Industrial behavior modification: A learning-based approach to business management* (pp. 243–265). New York: Pergamon.

Komaki, J. L., Collins, R. L. and Penn, P. (1982). Role of performance antecedents and consequences in work motivation. *Journal of Applied Psychology, 67*, 334–340.

Komaki, J. L., Coombs, T. and Schepman, S. (1991). Motivational implications of reinforcement theory. In R. M. Steers and L. W. Porter (Eds.), *Motivation and work behavior* (5th edn, pp. 87–105). New York: McGraw-Hill.

Komaki, J. L., Desselles, M. L. and Bowman, E. (1989). Definitely not a breeze: Extending an operant model of effective supervision to teams. *Journal of Applied Psychology, 74*, 522–529.

Komaki, J. L., Desselles, M. L. and Schepman, S. (1988, October). *Testing critical linkages in the operant model of effective supervision: Assessing subordinate performance and attitudes.* Paper presented at the conference of the Society of Organizational Behavior, Worthington, OH.

Komaki, J. L., Hyttinen, M. and Immonen, S. (1991, August). Cross-cultural research in work and leader behavior. In K. R. Thompson (Chair), *Managing across cultures from a behavioral perspective: Theory and research.* Symposium conducted at the meeting of the Academy of Management, Atlanta, GA.

Komaki, J. L. and Newlin, M. H. (1990, April). Walking on the wild side: Criterion-related validation of an in-basket exercise of supervisory behaviors. In M. H. Newlin (Chair), *Simulated performance assessment: Fact or fantasy?* Symposium presented at the conference of the Society for Industrial and Organizational Psychology, Miami, FL.

Komaki, J. L. and Reynard, M. (1995, July). *Cross-currents at sea: A time-series analysis of leaders in action.* Poster session presented at the conference of the American Psychological Society, New York.

Komaki, J. L. and Reynard, M. (in press). Developing performance appraisals: Criteria for what and how performance is measured. In C. M. Johnson, W. K. Redmon, and T. C. Mawhinney (Eds.), *Organizational performance: Behavior analysis and management.* New York: Springer.

Komaki, J. L., Reynard, M., Lee, C. and Wallace, J. (1995, October). *Apples and oranges at sea: Skippers' leadership styles make a difference.* Paper presented at the meeting of the Society of Organizational Behavior, Madison, WI.

Komaki, J. L., Urschel, J., Lee, C., Reynard, M., Julien, T. and Fass, S. (1993, August). The language of supervision. In E. R. Schnell and H. P. Sims, Jr. (Chairs), *Language in context: Observational studies of organizational verbal behavior.* Symposium presented at the conference of the Academy of Management, Atlanta, GA.

Komaki, J. L., Waddell, W. M. and Pearce, M. G. (1977). The applied behavior analysis approach and individual employees: Improving performance in two small businesses. *Organizational Behavior and Human Performance, 19*, 337–352.

Komaki, J. and Zlotnick, S. (1985). Toward effective supervision in business and industry. In L. L'Abate and M. Milan (Eds.), *Handbook of social skills training and research* (pp. 539–554). New York: Wiley.

Komaki, J. L., Zlotnick, S. and Jensen, M. (1986). Development of an operant-based taxonomy and observational index of supervisory behavior. *Journal of Applied Psychology, 71*, 260–269.

Korman, A. K. (1966). "Consideration," "initiating structure," and organizational criteria. *Personnel Psychology, 18*, 349–360.

Kotter, J. P. (1982). *The general managers.* New York: Free Press.

Kotter, J. P. and Lawrence, P. R. (1974). *Mayors in action: Five studies in urban governance.* New York: Wiley.

Krause, T. R. (1994). *Employee-driven systems for safe behavior.* New York: Van Nostran Reinhold.

Laming, D. (1973). *Mathematical psychology.* London: Academic Press.

Landy, F. J., Barnes, J. L. and Murphy, K. R. (1978). Correlates of perceived fairness and accuracy of performance evaluation. *Journal of Applied Psychology, 63*, 751–754.

Landy, F. J. and Farr, J. L. (1983). *The measurement of work performance*. New York: Academic Press.

Lanzetta, J. T. and Roby, T. B. (1960). The relationship between certain group process variables and group problem-solving efficiency. *Journal of Social Psychology, 52*, 135–148.

Larson, J. R., Jr. (1986). Supervisors' performance feedback to subordinates: The impact of subordinate performance valence and outcome dependence. *Organizational Behavior and Human Decision Processes, 37*, 391–408.

Larson, J. R., Jr. and Callahan, C. (1990). Performance monitoring: How it affects work productivity. *Journal of Applied Psychology, 75*, 530–538.

Latham, G. P. (1988). Human resource training and development. *Annual Review of Psychology, 39*, 545–582.

Lee, R. J. (1996, October 16). *Leading questions: Things we ask about leadership and careers, and a few personal answers*. Colloquium at Baruch College, New York.

Lehtonen, J. and Sajavaara, K. (1985). The silent Finn. In D. Tannen and M. S. Troike (Eds.), *Perspective on silence*. Norwood, NJ: Ablex Publishing Corporation.

Levine, J. M. and Moreland, R. L. (1990). Progress in small group research. *Annual Review of Psychology, 41*, 585–634.

Lewis, D. R. and Dahl, T. (1976). Time management in higher education administration: A case study. *Higher Education, 5*, 49–66.

Lewis, R. and Stewart, R. (1958). *The boss*. London: Phoenix House.

Liebert, R. M. and Liebert, L. L. (1995). *Science and behavior: An introduction to methods of psychological research*. Upper Saddle River, NJ: Prentice Hall.

Likert, R. (1967). *New patterns of management*. New York: McGraw-Hill.

Lincoln, J. R. (1989). Employee work attitudes and management practice in the US and Japan: Evidence from a large comparative survey. *California Management Review, 32*, 89–106.

Lindwall, B. and Olsen. (1983). The art of privacy: Two turn-of-the-century Nordic painters. *Scandinavian Review, 71*, 63.

Locke, E. A. and Latham, G.P. (1990). *A theory of goal setting and task performance*. Englewood Cliffs, NJ: Prentice Hall.

Lofland, J. (1971). *Analyzing social settings: A guide to qualitative observation and analysis*. Belmont, CA: Wadsworth.

Logan, F. A. and Wagner, A. R. (1965). *Reward and punishment*. Boston: Allyn & Bacon.

Lombardo, M. M. and McCall, M. W. Jr. (1978). Leadership. In M. W. McCall Jr. and M. M. Lombardo (Eds.), *Leadership: Where else can we go?* (pp. 1–12). Durham, NC: Duke University Press.

Longenecker, C. O., Sims, H. P., Jr. and Gioia, D. A. (1987). Behind the mask: The politics of employee appraisal. *The Academy of Management Executive, 1*, 183–193.

Lord, R. G. (1985). Accuracy in behavioral measurement: An alternative definition based on raters' cognitive schema and signal detection theory. *Journal of Applied Psychology, 70*, 66–71.

Lovaas, O. I. (1966). A program for the establishment of speech in psychotic children. In J. K. Wing (Ed.), *Early childhood autism*. London: Pergamon.

Lufthansa German Airlines (1987, May 4). "Going above and beyond what's expected." *Newsweek*, p. 65.

Luthans, F. (1979). Leadership: A proposal for a social learning theory base and observational and functional analysis techniques to measure leader behavior. In J. G. Hunt and L. L. Larson (Eds.), *Crosscurrents in leadership* (pp. 201–208). Carbondale Southern Illinois University Press.

Luthans, F., Hodgetts, R. M. and Rosenkrantz, S. A. (1988). *Real managers*. Cambridge, MA: Ballinger.

Luthans, F. and Lockwood, D. L. (1984). Toward an observation system for measuring leader behavior in natural settings. In J. G. Hunt, D. Hosking, C. A. Schriesheim and R. Stewart (Eds.), *Leaders and managers: International perspectives on managerial behavior and leadership* (pp. 117–141). New York: Pergamon Press.

Luthans, F., Rosenkrantz, S. A. and Hennessey, H. W. (1985). What do successful managers really do: An observation study of managerial activities. *The Journal of Applied Behavioral Science, 21*, 255–270.

McCall, M. W., Jr and Lombardo, M. M. (1983). *Off the track: why and how successful executives get derailed*. Greensboro, NC: Center for Creative Leadership.

McCall, M. W., Jr., Morrison, A. M. and Hannan, R. L. (1978). *Studies of managerial work: Results and methods* (Technical Report no. 9). Greensboro, NC: Center for Creative Leadership.

McCann, J. E. and Ferry, D. L. (1979). An approach for assessing and managing inter-unit interdependence. *Academy of Management Review, 4*, 113–119.

McClelland, D. C., Atkinson, J. W., Clark, R. A. and Lowell, E. L. (1953). *The achievement motive*. New York: Appleton-Century-Crofts.

McElvey, W. W. (1970). *Toward a holistic morphology of organisation*. Santa Monica, CA: Rand Corporation.

McFadden, R. D. (1997, May 12). Inscrutable conqueror. *New York Times*, pp. A1, B4.

McGrath, J. E. (1984). *Groups: Interaction and performance*. Englewood Cliffs, NJ: Prentice-Hall.

McGregor, D. M. (1957, November). The human side of the enterprise. *Management Review, 46*, 22–28.

McMichael, J. S. and Corey, J. R. (1969). Contingency management in an introductory psychology course produces better learning. *Journal of Applied Behavior Analysis, 2*, 79–84.

Mager, R. F. (1982). *Troubleshooting the troubleshooting course: Or debug d'bugs*. Belmont, CA: Pitman Learning.

Mager, R. F. and Pipe, P. (1984). *Analyzing performance problems* (2nd edn). Belmont, CA: Lake.

Magnusson, D. (1988). *Individual development from an interactional perspective: A longitudinal study*. Hillsdale, NJ: Erlbaum.

Manz, C. C. and Sims, H. P. (1989). *Super-leadership*. New York: Berkley.

Manz, C. C. and Sims, H.P. (1991). Superleadership: Beyond the myth of heroic leadership. *Organizational Dynamics, 19*, 18–35.

March, J. G. and Simon, H. (1958). *Organizations*. New York: Wiley.

Markle, S. M. and Tiemann, P. W. (1970). Problem of conceptual learning. *Journal of Educational Technology, 1*, 52–62.

Martinko, M. J. and Gardner, W. L. (1985). Beyond structured observation: Methodological issues and new directions. *Academy of Management Review, 10*(4), 676–695.

Masson, J. M. and McCarthy, S. (1995). *When elephants weep; the emotional lives of animals*. New York: Delacorte Press.

Mattila, M., Hyttinen, M. and Rantanen, E. (1994). Effective supervisory behaviour and safety at the building site. *International Journal of Industrial Ergonomics, 13*, 85–93.

Meredith, J. R. and Mantel, S. J., Jr. (1985). *Project management: A managerial approach*. New York: Wiley.

Merwin, G. A., Jr., Thomason, J. A. and Sanford, E. E. (1989). A methodology and content review of organizational behavior management in the private sector: 1978–1986. *Journal of Organizational Behavior Management, 10*(1), 39–57.

Meyers, J. (1972). *Fundamentals of experimental design*. Boston: Allyn & Bacon.

Millenson, J. R. (1967). *Principles of behavioral analysis*. New York: Macmillan.

Miller, L. K. (1997). *Principles of everyday behavior analysis* (3rd edn). Belmont, CA: Wadsworth.

Mintzberg, H. (1973). *The nature of managerial work*. New York: Harper & Row.

Mintzberg, H. (1975, July-August). The manager's job: Folklore and fact. *Harvard Business Review, 53*, 49–61.

Misumi, J. and Peterson, M. F. (1985). The performance-maintenance (PM) theory of leadership: Review of a Japanese research program. *Administrative Science Quarterly, 30*, 198–223.

Mitchell, T. R. (1982). Motivation: New directions for theory, research, and practice. *Academy of Management Review, 7*, 80–88.

Mitchell, S. K. and Gray, C. A. (1981). Developmental generalizability of the HOME inventory. *Educational and Psychological Measurement, 41*, 1001–1010.

Mobil Oil. Caught in the web. (1995, December 7). *New York Times*, p. A31.

Moos, R. (1973). Conceptualizations of human environments. *American Psychologist, 28*, 652–665.

Mueller, L. (1989). *Waving from shore*. Baton Rouge, LA and London: Louisiana State University Press.

Myers, S. L. (1996, January 12). Advocate with a heart. *New York Times*, p. B4.

Nasanen, M. and Saari, J. (1987). The effects of positive feedback on housekeeping and accidents at a shipyard. *Journal of Occupational Accidents, 8*, 237–250.

Nasar, S. (1994, July 26). Jett's supervisor at Kidder breaks silence. *New York Times*, p. D1.

Naylor, J. C., Pritchard, R. D. and Ilgen, D. R. (1980). *A theory of behavior in organizations*. San Diego, CA: Academic Press.

Newman, H. M. (1982). The sounds of silence in communicative encounters, *Communication Quarterly, 30*, 142–149.

Niehoff, B. P. and Moorman, R. H. (1993). Justice as a mediator of the relationship between methods of monitoring and organizational citizenship behavior. *Academy of Management Journal, 63*, 527–556.

Nitsch J. R. (1976). *Zur Theorie der sportlichen Beanspruchung [The theory of strain in sport]*. In J. R. Nitsch and I. Udris (Eds.), *Beanspruchung im Sport* (pp. 15–41). Bad Homburg: Limpert.

Nowak, M. A. and McMichael, A. J. (1995, August). How HIV defeats the immune system: A plausible hypothesis suggests the immune devastation that underlies AIDS stems from continuous – and dangerous – evolution of the human immunodeficiency virus in the body. *Scientific American, 273*, 58–65.

O'Hara, K., Johnson, C. M. and Beehr, T. A. (1985). Organizational behavior management in the private sector: A review of empirical research and recommendations for further investigation. *Academy of Management Review, 10*, 848–864.

Oldham, G. R. (1976). The motivational strategies used by supervisors: Relationships to effective indicators. *Organizational Behavior and Human Performance, 15*, 66–86.

O'Reilly, C. A. and Weitz, B. A. (1980). Managing marginal employees: The use of warnings and dismissals. *Administrative Science Quarterly, 25*, 467–484.

Orpen, C. (1974). The effect of reward contingencies on the job satisfaction–task performance relationship: An industrial experiment. *Psychology, 11*, 10–13.

Patterson, G. R. (1982). *A social learning approach: Coercive family process* (Vol. 3). Eugene, OR: Castalia.

Patton, M. Q. (1980). *Qualitative evaluation methods*. Beverly Hills, CA: Sage.

Peters, T. J. and Austin, N. (1985). *A passion for excellence: The leadership difference*. New York: Random House.

Peters, T. J. and Waterman, R. H. (1982). *In search of excellence: Lessons from America's best-run companies.* New York: Harper & Row.

Pfeffer, J. (1977). The ambiguity of leadership. *Academy of Management Review, 2,* 104–112.

Pfeffer, J. (1980). A partial test of the social information processing model of job attitudes. *Human Relations, 33,* 457–476.

Piaget, J. (1977). *The development of thought: Equilibrium of cognitive structures.* New York: Viking Press.

Pierce, C. H. and Risley, T. R. (1974). Improving job performance of Neighborhood Youth Corps aides in an urban recreation program. *Journal of Applied Behavior Analysis, 7,* 207–215.

Pinder, C. C. (1984). *Work motivation.* Glenview, IL: Scott, Foresman.

Plutchik, R. (1962). *The emotions: Facts, theories, and a new model.* New York: Random House.

Podsakoff, P. M. and Schriesheim, C. A. (1985). Leader reward and punishment behavior: A methodological and substantive review. Unpublished manuscript. Cited in B. M. Bass (Ed.), *Bass and Stogdill's handbook of leadership.* New York: Free Press.

Podsakoff, P. M., Todor, W. D. and Skov, R. (1982). Effects of leader contingent and non-contingent reward and punishment behaviors on subordinate performance and satisfaction. *Academy of Management Journal, 25,* 810–821.

Porter, L. W. and Lawler, E. E., III. (1968). *Managerial attitudes and performance.* Homewood, IL: Irwin-Dorsey.

Prien, E. P. (1963). Development of a supervisor position description questionnaire. *Journal of Applied Psychology, 47,* 10–14.

Rackman, J. and Woodward, J. (1970). The measurement of technical variables. In J. Woodward (ed.), *Industrial organization: Behavior and control* (pp. 19–36). London: Oxford University Press.

Raiffa, H. (1968). *Decision analysis: Introductory lectures on choices under uncertainty.* Reading, MA: Addison-Wesley.

Reichl, R. (1996, February 23). Paying attention to what New Yorkers want in dining spots. *New York Times,* p. C26.

Reynard, M. and Komaki, J. L. (1995, May). *The music of management: Rhythms of effective leaders.* Poster session presented at the conference of the Society of Industrial/Organizational Psychology, Orlando, FL.

Rifkin, G. (1994, February 27). It's not IBM and it's not big, but he's got big ideas. *New York Times,* p. 8.

Rock, A. (1987). Strategy versus tactics from a venture capitalist. *Harvard Business Review, 6 (65),* 63–67.

Ross, W. R. with Chapman, C. (1989). *Sail power: The complete guide to sails and sail handling.* New York: Alfred A. Knopf.

Runkel, P. J. and McGrath, J. E. (1972). *Research on human behavior.* New York: Holt, Rinehart.

Rush, M. C., Thomas, J. C. and Lord, R. G. (1977). *Organizational Behavior and Human Performance, 20,* 93–110.

Saarinen, E. (1987). Contemporary intellectual life in Finland. *Scandinavian Review, 75,* 141–147.

Sackett, G. P. (1977). The lag sequential analysis of contingency and cyclicity in behavioral interaction research. In J. Osofsky (Ed.), *Handbook of Infant Development.* New York: Wiley.

Sackett, G. P. (1978). Measurement in observational research. In G.P. Sackett (Ed.), *Observing behavior: Data collection and analysis methods* (Vol. 2, pp. 25–44). Baltimore, MD: University Park.

Salancik, G. R., Calder, B. J., Rowland, K. M., Leblebici, H., and Conway, M. (1975). Leadership as an outcome of social structure and process: A multi-dimensional analysis. In J. C. Hunt and L. L. Larson (Eds.), *Leadership frontiers* (pp. 81–101). Kent, OH: Kent State University Press.

Salancik, G. R. and Pfeffer, J. (1977). An examination of need-satisfaction models of job attitude. *Administrative Science Quarterly, 22*, 427–456.

Salancik, G. R. and Pfeffer, J. (1978). A social information processing approach to job attitudes and task design. *Administrative Science Quarterly, 23*, 224–253.

Sallinen-Kuparinen, A. S. (1986). *Finnish communication reticence: Perceptions and self-reported behavior.* Doctoral dissertation, *Studia Philologica Jyvaskylaensia, 19*, University of Jyvaskyla, Jyvaskyla.

Sasser, W. E., Jr. and Leonard, F. S. (1980). Let first-level supervisors do their job. *Harvard Business Review, 58*, 113–121.

Sayles, L. (1979). *Leadership: What effective managers really do ... and how they do it.* New York: McGraw-Hill.

Schmitt, N. W. and Klimoski, R. J. (1991). *Research methods in human resources management.* Cincinnati, OH: South-Western.

Schnake, M. E. (1986). Vicarious punishment in a work setting. *Journal of Applied Psychology, 71*, 343–344.

Schneier, E. C. (1974). Behavior modification in management: A review and a critique. *Academy of Management Journal, 17*, 528–548.

Schneier, C. E. and Beatty, R. W. (1978). The influence of role prescriptions on the performance appraisal process. *Academy of Management Journal, 21*, 129–135.

Scott, W. E., Jr. and Podsakoff, P. M. (1985). *Behavioral principles in the practice of management.* New York: Wiley.

Seabrook, J. (1994, January 10). E-mail from Bill. *New Yorker*, pp. 48–61.

Shaw, M. E. (1973). Scaling group tasks: A method for dimensional analysis. *Journal Supplement Abstract Service Catalog of Selected Documents in Psychology, 3*, 8.

Shirley, M. M. (1931). *The first two years.* Minneapolis: University of Minnesota Press.

Sims, H. P., Jr. and Manz, C. C. (1984). Observing leader behavior: Toward reciprocal determinism in leadership theory. *Journal of Applied Psychology, 69*, 222–232.

Skinner, B. F. (1948). *Walden two.* New York: Macmillan.

Skinner, B. F. (1974). *About behaviorism.* New York: Vintage.

Smith, P. C. (1976). Behaviors, results, and organizational effectiveness: The problem of criteria. In M. D. Dunnette (Ed.), *Handbook of industrial and organizational psychology* (pp. 745–776). Chicago, IL: Rand McNally.

Smith, R. H. P. (1979, January). *A simulator study of the interaction of pilot workload with errors, vigilance, and decisions* (NASA Report no. TM–78482). Moffett Field, CA: NASA-Ames Research Center. (NTIS no. N79–14769).

Smith, C. A., Organ, D. W. and Near, J. P. (1983). Organizational citizenship behavior: Its nature and antecedents. *Journal of Applied Psychology, 68*, 653–663.

Sommer, S. M., Bae, S. H. and Luthans, F. (1996). Organizational commitment across cultures: The impact of antecedents on Korean employees. *Human Relations, 49*, 977–993.

Stedje, A. (1983). "Brechen Sie dies ratselhafte Schweigen"-Uber Kulterbedingtes, Kommunikatives und strategisches Schweigen. In I. Rosengren (Ed.), *Sprache und Pragmatik*. Lunder Symposium 1982, 7–35. Stockholm: Almqvist & Wiksell International.

Steers, R. M. and Porter, L. W. (Eds.) (1990). *Motivation and work behavior.* New York: McGraw-Hill.

Stewart, R. (1976). *Contrasts in management.* London: McGraw-Hill.

Stewart, R. (1982). *Choice for the manager: A guide to understanding managerial work*. Englewood Cliffs, NJ: Prentice-Hall.

Stogdill, R. M. (1974). *Handbook of leadership*. New York: Free Press.

Stolz, S. B., Wienckowski, L. A. and Brown, B. S. (1975). Behavior modification: A perspective on critical issues. *American Psychologist, 30*, 1027–1048.

Stone, E. F. (1978). *Research methods in organizational behavior*. Santa Monica, CA: Goodyear Publishing.

Sulzer-Azaroff, B. and Mayer, G. R. (1991). *Behavioral analysis for lasting change*. Fort Worth: Holt Rinehart & Winston.

Tainio, R. and Santalainen, T. (1984). Some evidence for the cultural relativity of organizational development programs. *Journal of Applied Behavioral Science, 20*, 93–111.

Tannen, D. and Saville-Troike, M. (Eds.) (1985). *Perspectives on silence*. Norwood, NJ: Ablex Publishing.

Tannenbaum, S. I. and Yukl, G. (1992). Training and development in work organizations. *Annual Review of Psychology, 43*, 399–441.

Terkel, S. (1975). *Working: People talking about what they do all day and how they feel about what they do*. New York: Avon.

Terpstra, D. E. (1981). Relationship between methodological rigor and reported outcomes in organizational development evaluation research. *Journal of Applied Psychology, 66*, 541–543.

Tesser, A. and Rosen, S. (1975). *The reluctance to transmit bad news(1)*. Athens: University of Georgia, Department of Psychology.

Thomas, E. A. C. and Malone, T. W. (1979). On the dynamics of two-person interactions. *Psychological Review, 86*, 331–360.

Thompson, D. E. and DiTomaso, N. (1988). *Ensuring minority success in corporate management*. New York: Plenum.

Thompson, J. D. (1967). *Organizations in action*. New York: McGraw-Hill.

Thorndike, E. L. (1898). Animal intelligence. *Psychological Review Monograph Supplement, 8*.

Thorndike, R. L. (1949). *Personnel selection*. New York: Wiley.

Tichy, N. M. and Ulrich, D. O. (1984). The leadership challenge – a call for the transformational leader. *Sloan Management Review, 26(1)*, 59–68.

Tornow, W. W. and Pinto, P. R. (1976). The development of a managerial job taxonomy: A system for describing, classifying, and evaluating executive positions. *Journal of Applied Psychology, 61*, 410–418.

Triandis, H. C. and Berry, J. W. (Eds.). (1980). *Handbook of cross-cultural psychology: Vol 2. Methodology*. Boston: Allyn & Bacon.

Triandis, H. C., Kurowski, L. L. and Gelfand, M. J. (1994). Workplace diversity. In H. C. Triandis, M. D. Dunnette and L. M. Hough (Eds.), *Handbook of industrial and organizational psychology, Vol. 4* (2nd edn, pp. 769–827). Palo Alto, CA: Consulting Psychologists Press.

Trice, H. M. and Beyer, J. M. (1991). Cultural leadership in organizations. *Organization Science, 2*, 149–169.

Tzelgov, J. and Henik, A. (1991). Suppression situations in psychological research: Definitions, implications, and applications. *Psychological Bulletin, 109(3)*, 524–536.

Tziner, A. and Eden, D. (1985). Effects of crew composition on crew performance: Does the whole equal the sum of the parts? *Journal of Applied Psychology, 70*, 85–93.

Uchitelle, L. and Kleinfield, N. R. (1996, March 3). On the battlefields of business, millions of casualties. *New York Times*, pp. 1, 26, 28, 29.

Ulrich, R., Stachnik, T. and Mabry, J. (Eds.). (1966–1974). *Control of human behavior* (Vols 1–3). Glenview, IL: Scott, Foresman.

United States Yacht Racing Union. (1985). *1985–1988 international yacht racing rules* . Newport, RI: United States Yacht Racing Union.

Van Maanen, J. and Kunda, G. (1989). "Real feelings": Emotional expression and organizational culture. *Research in Organizational Behavior, 11*, 43–103.

Victor, B. and Blackburn, R. S. (1987). Interdependence: An alternative conceptualization. *Academy of Management Review, 12*, 486–497.

Vroom, V. H. (1964). *Work and motivation*. New York: Wiley.

Vroom, V. H. (1976). Can leaders learn to lead? *Organizational Dynamics*, 17–28.

Vroom, V. H. and Jago, A. G. (1978). On the validity of the Vroom-Yetton model. *Journal of Applied Psychology, 63*, 151–162.

Vroom, V. H. and Yetton, P. W. (1973). *Leadership and decision making*. Pittsburgh, PA: University of Pittsburgh Press.

Wakabayashi, M. and Graen, G. B. (1984). The Japanese career progress study: A seven-year follow-up. *Journal of Applied Psychology, 69*, 603–614.

Wald, L. M. (1994, April 15). L. I. inquiry finds errors, not snow, stopped railroad. *New York Times*, pp. A1, B4.

Warner, R. M., Kenny, D. A. and Stoto, M. (1979). A new round-robin analysis of variance for social interaction data. *Journal of Personality and social psychology, 37*, 1742–1757.

Watson, K. M. (1982). An analysis of communication patterns: A method for discriminating leader and subordinate roles. *Academy of Management Journal, 25*, 107–120.

Watson, D. L. and Tharp, R. G. (1996). *Self-directed behavior: Self-modification for personal adjustment* (7th edn). Pacific Grove, CA: Brooks/Cole.

Weber, B. (1996, March 24). Sculpturing a play into existence. *New York Times*, pp. H7, H11.

Weiss, H. M. (1990). Learning theory and industrial and organizational psychology. In M. D. Dunnette and L. M. Hough, (Eds.), *Handbook of industrial and organizational psychology*, *Vol. 1* (2nd edn, pp. 171–221). Palo Alto, CA: Consulting Psychologists Press.

Welsh, D. H. B, Luthans, F., and Sommer, S. M. (1993). Organizational behavior modification goes to Russia: Replicating an experimental analysis across cultures and tasks. *Journal of Organizational Behavior Management, 13*, 15–35.

Wexley, K. N. (1984). Personnel training. *Annual Review of Psychology, 35*, 519–551.

Whaley, D. L. and Malott, R. W. (1971). *Elementary principles of behavior*. New York: Appleton-Century-Crofts.

Witchel, A. (1992, June 2). On stage, and off. *New York Times*, p. C2.

Wolf, M. M. (1978). Social validity: The case for subjective measurement or how applied behavior analysis is finding its heart. *Journal of Applied Behavior Analysis, 11*, 203–214.

Wolf, M. M., Kirigin, K. A., Fixsen, D. L., Blause, K. A. and Braukmann, C. J. (1996). The teaching-family model: A case study in data-based program development and refinement (and dragon wrestling). *Journal of Organizational Behavior Management, 15 (1/2)*, 11–68.

Yukl, G. A. (1994). *Leadership in organizations* (3rd edn). Englewood Cliffs, NJ: Prentice-Hall.

Yukl, G. A. and Vanfleet, D. D. (1992). Theory and research on leadership in oranizations. In M. D. Dunnette and L. M. Hough (eds), *Handbook of industrial and organizational psychology*, *Vol. 3* (2nd edn, pp. 147–198). Palo Alto, CA: Consulting Psychologists Press.

Zedeck, S., Imparato, N., Krausz, M. and Oleno, T. (1974). Development of behaviorally anchored rating scales as a function of organizational level. *Journal of Applied Psychology, 59*, 249–252.

Zimmerman, W. (1976). *Desert plants: Conversations with 23 American musicians*. Vancouver, Canada: A.R.C. Publications.

Name index

Subject index

Operant Supervisory In-Basket
Assessment (OSIBA) 74, 78, 81–4, 97,
130, 212, 232; validity study 81–2
Operant Supervisory Taxonomy and
Index (OSTI) 31, 38–41, 63–72, 74,
81, 97–8, 106–8, 129–30, 149, 156,
169, 178, 181, 232; and
effectiveness 102, 103; properties
of 81; reliability of 81
Operant Supervisory Team Taxonomy
and Index (OSTTI) 72–3, 174;-by
Sequence (OSTTI-S) 118, 123
orders *see* antecedents
organizational: citizenship 223;
development (OD) 6; resources 28,
152, 154, 180
outcome expectancies 132
own performance 64, 65, 66, 67, 77,
108, 194, 205, 225–6

pacing hypothesis 118, 119, 125, 130,
189, 193; as predictor 232, 234–5; *see
also* AMC sequence, timing
passive leadership 186
path-goal theory 157
performance 7, 8, 9, 10, 11; and
antecedents 13, 20, 26–7, 29, 39, 63–7,
102, 118, 121–5, 156, 184, 190, 193,
205; and consequences 12–14, 22, 38,
44–52, 64, 113–14, 117, 130, 146, 150,
163, 216; group 105, 107–8, 172;
inflation 17; and interaction 12, 14,
28, 29, 51, 102, 108, 125, 130, 133–6,
138, 140, 195, 206, 209, 225–6,
230–31, 236; maintenance 2, 9, 10–11,
12, 13, 156, 177, 180; optimal 107–8;
own 64, 65, 66, 67, 77, 108, 194, 205,
225–6; ratings 85–6, 93; and SLAW
profiles 206; *see also* evaluation *and*
monitors
personality traits, and effective
leadership 7–9, 210–11
placement hypothesis 123, 124, 125,
130, 191, 193; as predictors 235; *see
also* AMC sequence
police, evaluation 86, 104, 132–3, 168
positive reinforcement *see* consequences
praise *see* consequences
precursor hypothesis 149
prediction, of effectiveness 112, 170,
205, 232–5; of model 178, 184, 232;
pacing as 232, 234–5; placement
as 235; selection 231–2; SLAW
behaviors as 232

Presidents, US 2, 8
preventive maintenance (PM) 208
problem-solving 9, 154
process-oriented hypothesis 136
product sampling 38
productivity 11
prototypicality 3
punishment 13, 20, 45; *see also*
consequences, negative

quality decision-making model 177
questionaires *see* self-reporting
quick AMC profile *see* AMC profile

recognition, in house 101
reinforcement *see* consequences
reinforcement theory *see* operant
conditioning
reliability (R), interrater 84, 86, 91, 93;
see also accuracy *and* CRU
reserve *see* silence
resources, organizational 28, 152, 154,
180
responsibility 42, 52, 65
results, leadership by 4, 5, 208; *see also*
performance
reticence *see* silence
reward *see* consequences

safety, occupational 20, 21
sailing: effectiveness measure
(SEM) 86–7, 97, 107, 173–4;
managing 49, 54–8, 119, 158, 168–9,
217, 238; strategy measure (SSM) 89,
94–5, 97, 159; teamwork effectiveness
measure (STEM) 87–90, 97, 108, 119,
159, 175, 233
sampling, work *see* work sampling; *see
also* monitoring
satisfaction, workforce 92–3, 106, 152;
see also attitude *and* morale
selection: criterion 231; of leaders
231–5; of personnel 229;
predictors 231–2; validation
process 231
self-confidence *see* attitude *and* morale
self-reporting (by managers) 30–34;
accuracy 31–2; monitoring via 35–7,
49, 65, 101, 104–5, 127, 140, 163, 184,
214–15; by subordinates 150; value
of 215
silence, value of 177–9
SLAW profile 193–4, 200–201, 204–6,
231–3, 235–6; and monitors 205–6;